WASHINGTON'S PACIFIC COAST

A GUIDE TO HIKING, CAMPING, FISHING & OTHER ADVENTURES

GREG JOHNSTON

MOUNTAINEERS BOOKS

TO MY PARENTS, WHO INTRODUCED ME TO THE MAGIC OF THE OCEAN AND SHOWED ME THE WAY, EVEN IF I DIDN'T ALWAYS FOLLOW: WILLIAM MARCELLUS JOHNSTON AND PATRICIA JOAN (SOCKWELL) JOHNSTON

Mountaineers Books is the nonprofit publishing division of The Mountaineers, an organization founded in 1906 and dedicated to the exploration, preservation, and enjoyment of outdoor and wilderness areas.

1001 SW Klicktat Way, Suite 201 • Seattle, WA 981034
800.553.4453 • www.mountaineersbooks.org

Printed in China
Distributed in the United Kingdom by Cordee, www.cordee.co.uk
First edition, 2015

Copy Editor: Julie Van Pelt
Design and Layout: Heidi Smets Graphic Design
Cartographer: Pease Press Cartography
Front cover photographs: (clockwise from top) *Giant's Graveyard, Olympic National Park; Makah Marina at Neah Bay; Shipwreck Point Natural Area; Razor clams*
Back cover photographs: (left to right) *sea lion; Ericsons Bay on Lake Ozette*
All photographs by the author unless otherwise credited.

Library of Congress Cataloging-in-Publication Data
Johnston, Greg.
Washington's Pacific Coast : a guide to hiking, camping, fishing, and other adventures / by Greg Johnston. — First edition.
pages cm
Includes bibliographical references.
ISBN 978-1-59485-939-7 (pbk : alk. paper) — ISBN (invalid) 978-1-59485-940-3 (ebook)
1. Outdoor recreation—Washington (State)—Pacific Coast—Guidebooks. 2. Hiking—Washington (State)—Pacific Coast—Guidebooks. 3. Camping—Washington (State)—Pacific Coast—Guidebooks. 4. Fishing—Washington (State)—Pacific Coast—Guidebooks. 5. Washington (State)—Guidebooks. I. Title.
GV191.42.W2J65 2015
796.509797—dc23

ISBN (paperback): 978-1-59485-939-7
ISBN (ebook): 978-1-59485-940-3

CONTENTS

MAP LEGEND

5	Interstate Highway		Trailhead		Park
101	US Highway		Point of Interest		National Forest
105	State Highway		Ranger Station		Indian Reservation
813	Forest Road		Campground		Private Land
	Local Road		City or Town		Detail Map Boundary
	Featured Trail or Route		Small Town		
	Other Trail		Bridge		
	International Boundary				
	State Boundary				
	County Line				

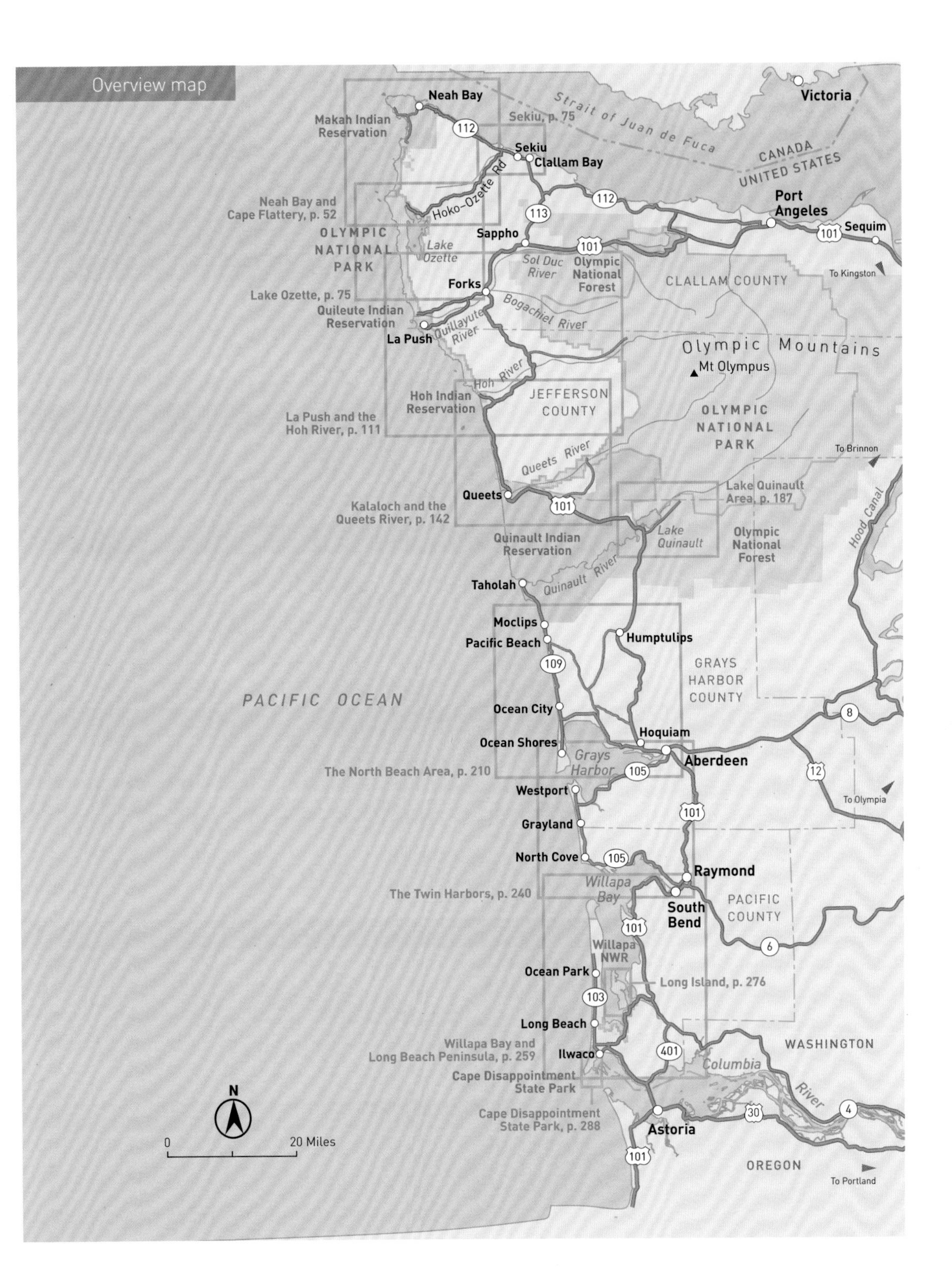

Overview map
Neah Bay
Makah Indian Reservation
Sekiu, p. 75
Strait of Juan de Fuca
Victoria
CANADA
UNITED STATES
112
Sekiu
Clallam Bay
Hoko-Ozette Rd
Neah Bay and Cape Flattery, p. 52
113
112
Port Angeles
101
Sequim
OLYMPIC NATIONAL PARK
Lake Ozette
Sappho
101
Sol Duc River
Olympic National Forest
CLALLAM COUNTY
To Kingston
Lake Ozette, p. 75
Forks
Quileute Indian Reservation
Bogachiel River
La Push
Quillayute River
Olympic Mountains
Mt Olympus
Hoh River
Hoh Indian Reservation
JEFFERSON COUNTY
La Push and the Hoh River, p. 111
OLYMPIC NATIONAL PARK
To Brinnon
Queets River
Queets
101
Kalaloch and the Queets River, p. 142
Lake Quinault Area, p. 187
Hood Canal
Quinault Indian Reservation
Lake Quinault
Olympic National Forest
Taholah
Quinault River
Moclips
Pacific Beach
Humptulips
109
GRAYS HARBOR COUNTY
PACIFIC OCEAN
Ocean City
8
Hoquiam
Ocean Shores
Grays Harbor
Aberdeen
The North Beach Area, p. 210
105
12
Westport
To Olympia
101
Grayland
North Cove
105
Raymond
Willapa Bay
The Twin Harbors, p. 240
South Bend
PACIFIC COUNTY
101
Willapa NWR
6
Ocean Park
Long Island, p. 276
103
Long Beach
Willapa Bay and Long Beach Peninsula, p. 259
Ilwaco
401
WASHINGTON
Columbia River
Cape Disappointment State Park
N
Cape Disappointment State Park, p. 288
30
4
0
20 Miles
Astoria
101
OREGON
To Portland

AT A GLANCE: HIKES, CAMPGROUNDS, PADDLE ROUTES

HIKE	Distance (round-trip)	Difficulty	Kid-Friendly	Dog-Friendly	Wildlife	Beachcombing	Geology	History	Big Trees	Fishing	Backpacking
Neah Bay and Cape Flattery											
Shipwreck Point	1.6 miles	1–4	•	•	•		•				
Cape Flattery	1.5 miles	2	•		•		•	•			
Shi Shi Beach to Point of Arches	9 miles	3	•		•	•	•	•			
Shi Shi to Ozette Through-Hike	15.8 miles one-way	5			•	•	•	•	•	•	•
Lake Ozette and Sekiu											
Clallam Bay/Slip Point	1.5 miles	2–3	•	•	•	•	•	•			
Ozette Loop	9.4 miles	3–4			•	•	•	•	•		•
Ozette to Rialto Beach Through-Hike	20+ miles one-way	4			•	•	•		•		•
La Push and the Hoh River											
Rialto Beach/Hole in the Wall	3 miles	2	•		•	•	•	•			•
James Pond and Slough Trails	2.2 miles	1–2	•		•				•		
Second Beach	4 miles	2	•		•	•	•		•		•
Third Beach to Hoh River Through-Hike	17.1 miles one-way	4			•	•	•		•	•	•
Spruce Nature Trail and Hall of Mosses	2 miles	2	•		•				•		
Kalaloch											
Ruby Beach to Hoh River	6 miles	2–3		•	•	•	•	•		•	
Beach 4 to Ruby Beach	9.4 miles	3+		•	•	•	•		•	•	
Kalaloch to Beach 4	6.2 miles	2–3	•	•	•	•	•			•	
Kalaloch to Queets River	7.5 miles	2	•		•	•			•	•	
Kalaloch Creek Nature Trail	0.8 miles	1–2	•	•					•		
Sams River Loop	3 miles	2			•				•		
Lake Quinault Area											
Quinault Giant Red Cedar Trail	0.4 miles	2	•						•		
Kestner Homestead and Maple Glade Trails	1.8 miles	2	•		•			•	•		
Quinault National Recreation Area Trail Loops	4.4 miles	3	•	•					•		
World's Largest Sitka Spruce	0.5 miles	1	•	•					•		
Mount Colonel Bob	8.4 miles	5		•	•				•		•
Moclips to Ocean Shores: North Beach Area											
Copalis Spit and Griffith-Priday State Park	2.5–3 miles	2	•	•	•	•	•			•	
Weatherwax Forest	1 miles	1	•	•	•						
Damon Point	4 miles	2–3	•	•	•	•	•	•		•	

HIKE	Distance (round-trip)	Difficulty	Kid-Friendly	Dog-Friendly	Wildlife	Beachcombing	Geology	History	Big Trees	Fishing	Backpacking
Grays Harbor National Wildlife Refuge	0.5 miles	1	•		•						
Westport–Tokeland: The Twin Harbors											
Essential Westport Loop	5.5 miles	2	•	•	•	•	•			•	
Johns River Wildlife Area	2 miles	1	•	•	•					•	
Bottle Beach State Park	1.4 miles	1	•		•						
Washaway Beach	4.8 miles	2–3	•	•	•	•	•	•			
Graveyard Spit	Less than 2 miles	1	•	•	•	•	•	•			
Willapa Bay and Long Beach Peninsula											
Willapa River Trail	7 miles	2	•	•	•	•					
Leadbetter Point	4 miles	2–3	•		•	•					
Discovery Trail	6.2 miles one-way	1–3	•	•	•			•			
Willapa National Wildlife Refuge: Long Island											
South Long Island Loop	4.8 miles	3	•		•				•	•	•
Teal Slough Cedar Trail	0.9 miles	2		•					•		
Cape Disappointment State Park											
Westwind Trail	1.6 miles	2	•	•					•		
Bells View Trail	0.4 miles	1	•	•				•	•		
North Head Trail and Lighthouse	4.1 miles	3	•	•	•		•	•	•		
McKenzie Head Trail	0.5 miles	1–2	•	•	•		•	•			
Coastal Forest Loop	1.5 miles	2	•	•					•		
Cape Disappointment Trail	2.4 miles	2–3	•	•	•			•			

CAMPGROUND	Open	Sites	Water	Hookups	Restrooms	Showers	RVs	Reservations	Wildlife	Beachcombing	Big Trees	Fishing
Neah Bay and Cape Flattery												
Lake Ozette	Year-round	15	Summer only		•		To 21 feet		•			
Bear Creek	Year-round	11			•		To 25 feet		•		•	•
Lake Ozette and Sekiu												
Mora	Year-round	94	•		•		To 35 feet		•		•	•
Bogachiel State Park	Year-round	26	•	6 sites	•	•	To 40 feet		•			•

CAMPGROUND	Open	Sites	Water	Hookups	Restrooms	Showers	RVs	Reservations	Wildlife	Beachcombing	Big Trees	Fishing
Hoh River	Year-round	88	•		•		To 21 feet		•		•	•
Hoh Oxbow	Year-round	7			Vault toilet		Small ones					•
Willoughby Creek	Year-round	3			Vault toilet		Small ones		•			•
Minnie Peterson	Year-round	8			Vault toilet		Small ones		•			•
Cottonwood	Year-round	9			Vault toilet		•					•
Kalaloch												
Kalaloch	Year-round	170	•		•		To 35 feet	June 18–Sept 6	•	•	•	•
South Beach	Memorial Day weekend–mid-Sept	55	•		•		To 35 feet		•	•		•
Queets	Year-round	20			Vault toilet				•		•	•
Lake Quinault Area												
Willaby	Year-round	31	•		•		To 16 feet				•	•
Falls Creek	Memorial Day weekend–Labor Day weekend	31	•		•		To 16 feet		•		•	•
Gatton Creek	Memorial Day weekend–Labor Day weekend	15			•		To 24 feet		•			•
Moclips to Ocean Shores: North Beach Area												
Pacific Beach State Park	Year-round	64, plus 2 yurts	•	•	•	•	•	•	•	•		•
Ocean City State Park	Year-round	178	•	•	•	•	To 50 feet	•	•	•		•
Quinault Marina and RV Park	Year-round	46	•	•	•	•	To 35 feet		•	•		•
Westport–Tokeland: The Twin Harbors												
Twin Harbors State Park	Year-round	265, plus 2 yurts	•	•	•	•	To 35 feet	•	•	•		•

CAMPGROUND	Open	Sites	Water	Hookups	Restrooms	Showers	RVs	Reservations	Wildlife	Beachcombing	Big Trees	Fishing
Grayland Beach State Park	Year-round	104, plus 16 yurts	•	•	•	•	To 60 feet	•	•	•		•
Willapa Bay and Long Beach Peninsula												
Bruceport County Park	Mid-May–Labor Day	40	•	•	•	•	To 30 feet		•		•	
Bush Pioneer County Park	Mid-May–Labor Day	10	•		•	•	Small ones		•		•	
Willapa National Wildlife Refuge: Long Island												
Lewis (boat-in)	Year-round	2			Vault toilet				•		•	
Sawlog (boat-in)	Year-round	6			Vault toilet				•		•	
Sandspit (boat-in)	Year-round	3			Vault toilet				•		•	•
Smoky Hollow (boat-in)	Year-round	4			Vault toilet				•		•	
Pinnacle Rock (boat-in)	Year-round	5			Vault toilet				•		•	•
Cape Disappointment State Park												
Cape Disappointment State Park	Year-round	137, plus 14 yurts, 3 cabins	•	•	•	•	To 45 feet	•	•		•	•

PADDLE ROUTE	Distance (round-trip)	Difficulty	Wildlife	Beachcombing	History	Big Trees	Fishing	Overnight
Lake Ozette	8 miles	2	•	•	•	•		•
Willapa Bay Tidewaters	3–4 miles	2–3	•		•	•	•	
Long Island	Various options	3	•		•	•	•	•

INTRODUCTION

THE MAGIC OF WASHINGTON'S OCEAN SHORELINE first captivated me years ago, when each summer my parents took the family for a week's vacation to Kalaloch. At the time I didn't know what intrigued me, but it was unlike any other place I'd been. Perhaps it was the endless procession of waves crashing powerfully and insistently along miles of broad, sandy beach, the regular morning mists that blew over bluffs of wildly wind-shaped spruce trees, or the way the surf each day slowly crept up toward massive piles of sea-stacked driftwood and then just as certainly withdrew back out toward the immense fetch of the Pacific.

I only knew the coast was enchanting in an almost mystical way. And nothing was quite as fun as kicking off my shoes and chasing the receding waves toward the sea and then pivoting to be chased back up the beach by the next wave. But my fascination wasn't inspired only by the sea and sand and bluffs and trees; my mother and father also gathered intriguing things from these environments. On morning minus tides, dad would lead us onto the beach with clam gun in hand to dig the mysterious and delectable razor clam.

Dad was a fishing wizard, and he never returned from a flood tide without five or six red-tailed surf perch or a bucket of surf smelt caught by dip net at Beach 4. Mother was a biologist by education, and our hikes up Kalaloch Creek were as exasperating as they were enjoyable, since she could never resist stopping to discuss matters such as the semipermeable membrane of the inner bark of *Thuja plicata* (red cedar), or some other tree or shrub—I can't remember. She knew the genus and species of all plants in the forest, which didn't matter to me back then, but ultimately her enthusiasm rubbed off. Sometimes we returned from those hikes with handfuls of huckleberries, or some herbal vegetation from the forest floor to steep into tea. The cabin we rented at Kalaloch was regularly scented with the bouquet of razor clam fritters, fried perch or smelt, and once, ever so memorably, fresh-baked red huckleberry pie.

Later, after I grew up—or reached adulthood, since some say I'm still in the process—a four-year stint as a reporter/copy editor for Aberdeen's *Daily World* allowed me to approach the Washington Coast and the people who lived there

Hanging moss drapes a big-leaf maple along the Maple Glade Trail in the Quinault Rain Forest.

as a journalist. Grays Harbor and the entire coast teemed with stories: of loggers, fishermen, Indians, salmon and steelhead, elk, clams, giant conifers, and civic grand schemes that often threatened those other things. For several years around this time, dad co-owned a salmon charter fishing business at Westport, which introduced me to even more colorful coastal characters. I left the *World* and Grays Harbor all the more intrigued, knowing I would return to the coast time and again. The next twenty-four years as outdoors reporter for the sadly extinguished beacon of journalism, the *Seattle Post-Intelligencer*, indeed afforded repeated ventures to the coast to fish, day hike and backpack, beachcomb, dig razor clams, kayak, or simply knock about and explore.

To this day I love the coast of Washington more than any other place on this planet. The ocean stimulates so many senses. How can you not stare at a crimson sun setting into the seemingly boundless sea without thinking about time, space, and the endless cycles of nature and life? It makes you think. But it also offers more practical benefits, as I learned one day from a fellow surf perch angler. He was a soldier stationed at Fort Lewis near Tacoma and had just returned from Iraq, at the height of the turmoil. He loved surf perch fishing, he said, got out every chance he could, and I thought I knew why. Being out there on the ocean, with the continual wash of the sea and its Zen-like ambience, I told him, it's therapeutic, it's healing. "Yeah," he replied, "plus it clears up my sinuses."

The ocean is good for the heart and soul—and respiration. It's just a fun place to be, on the edge of earth and sea and sky. And when you visit the Washington Coast over time, you get to know it better—you start finding beach agates; you see otters, seals, and dolphins in the surf; maybe you find a glass fishing float washed ashore—and it piques your curiosity. You find yourself wondering things like, how did two 90-foot sea stacks end up side by side like giant geologic teeth on an otherwise sandy beach?

The coast casts a spell. You can't get enough of it. You want to know Washington's Pacific Ocean shoreline. For me at least, now that I do know it, I feel compelled to tell others about its singularity, its beauty, its history both natural and cultural, its fragility, and its exquisite importance. This is a place humanity must love, nurture, protect, and enjoy forever and ever.

The hollow core of the giant red cedar tree at Lake Quinault supports a host of other species, quite typical of old-growth cedars.

PART 1

THE WASHINGTON COAST
AN OVERVIEW

THE FIRST PEOPLE, THE LAND, AND THE SEA

CHAPTER 1

IT CAN FEEL LIKE YOU'RE TOUCHING the pulse of the earth when you walk the Washington Coast, perceiving its rhythms all the while mesmerized by a beauty as extraordinary as anywhere on the planet. You hear the coast, smell it, see it, feel it, taste it; here nature is insistent and must be met on its own terms. The unimaginable vastness of the Pacific Ocean rushes in; the tides come and go. In many places, the result of two plates in the earth's crust colliding head-on thrusts upward before you in the form of time-weathered volcanic rockscapes.

The land here is in constant, sometimes violent motion. Cliffs and headlands slide and slough and fall in on themselves. Wind and waves push sand into

The weathered skull of a gray whale north of Beach 4 near Kalaloch, Olympic National Park dunes and islands, lakes, and bogs. Earthquakes lift and lower the coast irregularly over time, but measurably and with certainty. Tsunamis have killed in the past and likely will again. The forests encroach on the ocean but—met by gales, near-constant salt mists, and the sea—recoil at the edge in wild gargoyle-like forms. Through all this landscape, incredibly diverse species of birds, beasts, and creatures of the sea earn their niches.

The sheer beauty of the coast is what grips people first; it has for centuries. Sailing off the Long Beach Peninsula on April 27, 1792, Captain George Vancouver wrote, "The country before us presented a most luxuriant landscape. The whole had the appearance of a continued forest extending as far north as the eye could reach."

The next day Vancouver named Point Grenville to the north, a headland that marks a distinct change in coastal character, as he noted: "From hence, as we proceeded to the north the coast began to increase regularly in height, and the inland country, behind the low land bordering the sea shore, acquired a considerable degree of elevation. The shores we passed this morning differed in some respects from those we had hitherto seen. They were composed of low cliffs rising perpendicularly from a beach of sand or small stones; had many detached rocks of various romantic forms lying at a distance of about a mile."

What makes the Washington Coast even more compelling is its fascinating cultural and natural history, its rich fish and wildlife and profuse flora, and along much of it, its exquisite isolation and wildness.

ANCIENT CULTURES OF THE COAST

Some of the most complex ancient cultures of the Americas sprang up here sometime after the great Cordilleran ice sheet began retreating between 20,000 and 9000 years ago. Exactly when and how the people who developed these cultures arrived remains uncertain. Archaeologically, the Washington Coast is understudied. Furthermore, because sea and land levels have changed dramatically due to climate changes and the ice age, not to mention tectonic effects, the places where people first arrived may be deep under the sea. Curiously, when Europeans arrived some 240 years ago, the Native people spoke four mutually unintelligible languages: from the Wakashan (Makah), Chimakuan (Quileute and Hoh), Salishan (Queets, Quinault, Chehalis), and Chinookan (Chinook) families. The count reaches five if you include the Athapaskan tongue of the Kwalhioqua, bands of which lived on the lower Willapa River.

This remarkable diversity of languages, along a coast of less than 200 miles, suggests first, a diversity of heritage, and second, a desirable living environment rich in resources. When each of these peoples arrived is not known with certainty. But evidence of humans hunting with bone projectile points has been dated at about 13,000 years ago, less than 70 miles east of this coast—a three-day walk or a two-day paddle—at the Manis mastodon site near Sequim. Many of the Native people of the coast today would say they have been here forever. A friend once mentioned to a Makah elder at Neah Bay that Cape Flattery "sure is at the end of the earth!" He smiled and replied, "To us it's the beginning."

This petroglyph of a whale was left by the Ozette band of Makah Indians, who for centuries maintained a whaling village nearby.

It is known for sure that people have been on the Washington Coast for at least 4000 years, and they were from cultures of multiple linguistic origins who developed fairly complex societies. They lived in permanent towns with sturdy wooden houses, were socially stratified, developed ingenious yet primitive technologies for resource exploitation and living needs, engaged in warfare, traded across a large regional network, and practiced a rich tradition of art, song, and dance.

Visitors to the Washington Coast today will find these people's ancestors on the Makah Indian Reservation to the north, the Quileute and Hoh reservations just south, the Quinault Indian Reservation on the central coast, and the Shoalwater Bay Reservation on the south coast. The Chinook Indian Nation, once large

The artifacts of plate tectonics and erosion, sea stacks rise up from the ocean near Hole in the Wall, north of Rialto Beach.

and powerful and spread from the south coast well up the Columbia River, maintains its struggle for federal recognition from a small office at Bay Center on Willapa Bay.

It is difficult to visit, say, Point Grenville or Cape Alava, and not feel a profound sense of those who came before. Whenever and however they arrived—I believe time will show most came from the north in boats—they lived in an incredibly rich environment, one that was and is tempestuous climatically and turbulent geologically. These are the same forces that make this coast so special.

SHAPE CHANGERS: WIND, RAIN, AND WAVES

Winter storms are more frequent along the Northwest Coast and the Gulf of Alaska than anywhere else on Earth. I am regularly amused when natural historians and ethnographers describe the climate of the Northwest Coast as mild. They must not have spent many nights on this coast.

I know they were nowhere near Norwegian Memorial on Olympic National Park's wilderness beach strip on a February night I spent shivering inside my tent and 35-degree sleeping bag. After I returned from this trip, I checked the weather data for that night recorded at Quillayute Airport, about 15 miles away—22 degrees Fahrenheit. On another day in March, my family and I checked into our cabin at Kalaloch in 40-knot winds and nearly sideways rain. At dawn the storm had broken, so I pulled on my boots and backpack, hit the beach, and found a basketball-sized glass fishing float washed ashore.

Those scholars must not have ever spent a day steelhead fishing on the Bogachiel River during a Quillayute-class downpour, or driven from Queets to Hoquiam with rain falling so hard it hit the pavement and bounced 1.5 feet high. While the weather on the Washington Coast can be sunny and warm, to describe it overall as mild is like saying the Hoh River is a gentle stream that always stays in its channel, or that the Quinault Rain Forest gets a little wet sometimes.

The weather on the Washington Coast is regularly brutal midfall through midspring. I will allow that the range of temperatures is mild relative to other areas of the planet; subzero temperatures (Fahrenheit) almost never occur, if they ever have. But in winter, the black ice on US 101 between Forks and Port Angeles is often slipperier than a storm-tossed pile of bull kelp. And there is nothing mild about the rest of this maritime climate, which shapes the very form and character of the coast and indeed is a primary source of its richness.

Wind on the Washington Coast doesn't just howl, it screams. The Coast Guard crews who staffed the Destruction Island Lighthouse before it was automated in the 1960s routinely described waves blowing clear across the barren rock of 60 acres, with spray sometimes hitting the top of the 94-foot beacon. A weather station at North Head on the south Washington Coast in January of 1921 recorded winds of 126 miles per hour—before the instrument allegedly blew away.

Rain on this coast doesn't just fall, it plummets, plunges, pummels, and pounds. Rainfall averages 80 inches per year—more than 6.5 feet—on the Washington Coast proper. But just miles inland, that climbs to more than 100 inches annually; near Mount Olympus about 30 miles inland, the average is 250 inches, the highest in the continental United States.

Storms blow in from the Pacific to release their bluster, and the result is a host of beautiful rivers that send it right back. These include the Quillayute and its legendary tributaries, the Sol Duc, Calawah, and Bogachiel; the great misty rain-forest rivers, the Hoh, Queets, and Quinault; the Humptulips and the associated Chehalis and its fine tributaries, the Wishkah, Wynoochee, and Satsop; the several smaller streams that flow into Willapa Bay, the most significant being the Willapa and Naselle; and of course, the mighty Columbia, which drains a huge portion of the continent and in so doing supplies the silty raw material that forms the south coast. Every one of these rivers once produced thousands of salmon and steelhead every year, before humans altered and polluted the watersheds in numerous ignorant ways, and many still do produce viable fish runs and fisheries. The northern coastal streams together are considered the last, best bastion of wild, native steelhead in the contiguous forty-eight states.

The most obvious way I see what all this weather does is by hiking the 70-some miles of protected wilderness beaches in Olympic National Park. Every year, campsites disappear and rugged routes over headlands change. The first time I camped at stunning Toleak Point was on a bench above the surf, where a seasonal Indian village once stood. The bones of whales and seals were scattered about. That must have been in 1979. When I returned several years later, the sea had washed most of the bench away and there were no bones, nothing but a shrub-covered hillside. A lovely campsite on a low bluff just north of Mosquito Creek, where the Coast Guard maintained dog kennels during World War II, disappeared between visits five years apart. On a backpack from Sand Point near Lake Ozette south to Rialto Beach at the mouth of the Quillayute, I noted a cozy campsite on the point just south of Chilean Memorial. When I returned about four years later, the sea had swallowed it up.

Storm-driven seas and winds so relentlessly pound the coast that it regularly falls in on itself; it erodes and recedes, on the one hand, and accretes into islands and spits, on the other. This process is hastened perhaps by the fact that much of the coast is a convoluted jumble of ancient volcanic rock mixed with cemented sediments from the ocean floor, often topped by thick layers of sand, gravel, and clay delivered by large rivers that formed as glacial lobes during the Pleistocene some 12,000 years ago.

The exquisite sea stacks that line the shore—from Cape Flattery and the Tatoosh Rocks, south past a curious crescendo at the Giants Graveyard and Quillayute Needles, to Point Grenville—are all remnants of this eroding coast. Most of the Washington Coast is geologically unstable. But there is an upside: this is what makes the coast so scenically compelling.

SHAKES AND QUAKES: THE CASCADIA SUBDUCTION ZONE

Most of the coastal spires, pinnacles, blocky ramparts, and flat-topped islands are what I like to think of as tectonic teeth. They are composed largely of volcanic rock that issued miles offshore as lava between 20 and 50 million years ago, sometimes mixed with long-since consolidated sediments from the ocean floor. The Washington Coast represents the very edge of two giant colliding plates in the earth's crust. The seaward Juan de Fuca Plate is moving ever so gradually but most certainly east, where it meets and dives beneath the lighter rocks of the North American Plate. Washington is basically in the center of a larger zone where this occurs, known as the Cascadia Subduction Zone, stretching from northern California past Canada's Vancouver Island.

Some of the material not thrust under the continent (subducted) skims off, piles up, crumples, folds, tilts, and accretes atop the edge of the North American Plate. The Olympic Mountains represent the top of this pile. The rocky headlands and sea stacks along the coast, weathered and eroded by wind, rain, currents, and the surging sea, are also tangible manifestations of this mind-boggling incremental process.

Although it has taken millions and millions of years for the coast to attain its present state, changes can happen pretty fast, geologically speaking. Arches photographed along the Quinault Indian Reservation shore in 1902 were eroded away by 1970.

The coastal landscape can change dramatically even faster than that: in minutes, in fact. The collision of the tectonic plates here over the millennia has caused repeated subduction earthquakes and tsunamis of catastrophic magnitude—at least six times over the last 7000 years. United States Geological Survey scientist Brian Atwater has uncovered convincing evidence that in the year 1700, a magnitude-9 quake dropped parts of the Washington Coast 6 to 9 feet. Remnants of this subduction quake stand weathered and gray in the form of a red cedar ghost forest in the tidal areas of the Copalis River. Apparently this event exists in the lore of coastal tribes, and archaeologists speculate that this same quake might have triggered a landslide that buried several cedar-plank houses at the Makah village of Ozette on the north coast. Excavations led by Washington State University professor Richard Daugherty in the 1960s and 1970s uncovered thousands of wood, bone, shell, and stone artifacts—a remarkably complete inventory of pre-European-contact tools and living implements, many of which are now displayed at the fascinating Makah Museum at Neah Bay.

Atwater and other scientists estimate that these earthquakes and tsunamis occur at an average of every 300 to 600 years. Thus, the possibility of another geologic catastrophe on the Washington Coast within the next 100 years is high. Even though it might not happen for another 100 or 1000 years, I think about the possibility frequently while on the coast—which lends a definite sense of adventure. An earthquake is a sudden thing; about all you can do is seek cover and hold on. But tsunamis are usually preceded by distinct signs, the first of which could well be an earthquake, all of which means you need to get your butt moving inland for high ground posthaste.

In any event, please don't be afraid to visit the beach. Most of how the earth's physical properties affect this coast are absolutely beneficial. For example, the

The author while backpacking amidst the scenic Quillayute Needles (Photo by Bryn Beorse)

prevailing storm track and currents of the North Pacific set the stage for the incredible abundance of fish and wildlife here. The flow of wind and waves draws up nutrient-rich, high-salinity cold waters from deep off the continental shelf—upwelling, it's called—causing phytoplankton blooms that set the foundation for the food chain.

BIRDS AND BEASTS, FORESTS AND TREES

I am continually amazed by the abundance of wildlife—absolutely terrific wildlife watching—particularly along the protected beaches of Olympic National Park on the north coast. A lot of casual visitors stop in briefly at the more accessible spots and enjoy the ocean, but they never see its richness. If you stop and look, especially if you bring binoculars—an essential tool for coastal observers—you will regularly see gray whales, seals, sea lions, porpoises, otters (usually river otters but sometimes sea otters too), raccoons, bald eagles, pelicans, oystercatchers, harlequin ducks, wrens, hummingbirds, and deer.

Four times in the last six years, we have come upon seals or sea lions—a couple of them massive beasts—hauled out on wilderness beaches. If this happens to you, don't get too close; leave them alone. They are not necessarily in distress; they just like to come ashore sometimes, and mother seals often leave pups on the beach while they fish. Less often you'll see elk, bear, cougar, and bobcat, but you can regularly spot their tracks and scat. I also avidly fish for surf perch and dipnet for surf smelt, straight out of the ocean, and I seek salmon and steelhead that still run abundantly up many coastal rivers. On minus tides, the rocks of the north coast present a dazzling maze of diversity, each pool a complex world of its own, a niche for sculpins, blennies, sea stars, snails, anemones, urchins, mussels, limpets, crabs, copepods, squirts, and on and on.

The copious weather here also benefits inland species, generating magnificent cathedral forests of towering, gargoyle-like Sitka spruce and western red cedar, with trunks as thick as transit buses, as well as spooky, moss-draped big-leaf maples, giant western hemlock, and Douglas fir.

Along much of the coast these old forests have long since been logged and replaced by tree farms and timber production. But Olympic National Park preserves and protects large tracts of these old and magical temperate rain forests, primarily along the Bogachiel, Hoh, Queets, and Quinault rivers. Here live large herds of Olympic, or Roosevelt, elk, and fairly dense populations of black bear, cougar, and bobcat, all of which can find their way to the ocean beaches

MOUNT OLYMPUS

A lot of people wonder how the most grand of all mountains near the Washington Coast got its name, which later was applied to the entire peninsula it crowns. The name at first seems inappropriate, having nothing at all to do with the original Olympus in Greece. Our Mount Olympus, a complicated spiral of rocky ridges and glacial ice that tops out at 7976 feet (West Peak), was first recorded by Spanish explorer Juan Perez in 1774—of course the Native tribes knew it and hunted along its flanks long before. Perez called the mountain Cerro de Santa Rosalia.

Fourteen years later, the name that stuck was given to it by the English ship captain John Meares, an explorer and fur trader who applied an undeniable logic upon witnessing the mountain's presence: "If that not be the home where dwell the gods, it is certainly beautiful enough to be, and I therefore will call it Mt. Olympus."

Indeed, if you've been fortunate to see it from near or far, you know that this mountain is absolutely heavenly.

at times. Gray wolf populations were once strong and healthy here too, but the animals were hunted to local extinction by early in the twentieth century.

ROCK VS. SAND, NORTH COAST VS. SOUTH COAST

If you look at the Washington Coast in its entirety, it is the north part that appears so striking geologically. There is a distinct change in character between north and south, marked by the headlands of Point Grenville on the Quinault Indian Reservation, just about halfway between Cape Flattery and the Columbia River. The scenic northern half of the coast is marked, in a word, by rock; and the southern half, in another word, by sand.

The north coast is a chaotically marvelous complexity of rocky headlands and coves, pocket beaches, sea caves, arches, small islands, stone pinnacles, and multishaped sea stacks. Archibald Menzies, a doctor and naturalist during Captain Vancouver's exploration of the Northwest Coast, put it most appropriately on April 29, 1792: "The whole shore we saild along this forenoon is steep and rocky and entirely lind with a vast number of elevated rocks and islets of different forms and sizes, but the land itself is of a very moderate height coverd with

Brown pelicans, with their big bucket bills, are common sights along the central and south coast of Washington.

Pines stretching back with a very gradual acclivity to form an inland ridge of high mountains, in which Mount Olympus claimd a just preeminence."

That mountain crowns a northern coast we are most fortunate to have largely protected and preserved, such that it appears basically as it did when Bruno de Hezeta, commanding the Spanish ships *Santiago* and *Sonora*, made the first landing of Europeans on the Northwest Coast in 1775. Olympic National Park, its ecosystems so diverse and remarkable that it's recognized as a UN World

Wood tannins stain the waters of many Olympic Peninsula streams, such as this tributary of the Queets River.

Heritage Site, embraces not only the Olympic Mountains but also some 70 miles of rugged headlands, otherworldly sea stacks, and sandy beaches on the north coast. Just south, the Quinault Indian Nation maintains stewardship of another 23 miles in a similar untrammeled state. After almost forty years of closure to nontribal members, most of these beaches, some of them spectacular indeed, were opened to the general public, for a small permit fee. Sadly, in 2013, they were closed once again, an action I hope is soon reversed.

In addition to Olympic National Park, various other designations define and protect the north coast. In 1994 Congress designated more than 3188 square miles, including 162 miles of shoreline, as the Olympic Coast National Marine Sanctuary. Within it are three national wildlife refuges—the Flattery Rocks, Quillayute Needles, and Copalis Rocks—all of which are also afforded protection under the Wilderness Act as the Washington Islands Wilderness.

The coast noticeably changes character south of Point Grenville. South of Grenville there are only two major outcroppings of stone, the Copalis Rocks and the lithic ramparts on the north side of the Columbia River mouth, Cape

Disappointment and North Head. The rest is a series of long, sandy beaches, accreted islands and spits (often enclosing bays, lagoons, lakes, and bogs), typically topped by dunes and a thick carpet of beach grasses, scrubby shore pines, and short spruce, along with shrubs such as kinnikinnick and evergreen huckleberry. The sand has been delivered daily over the ages by the Columbia River and rivers just north, to be molded into its present shape by the persistent, often storm-driven winds and waves. When you hike, say, Copalis Spit or Damon Point near Ocean Shores, you really get a sense for this process.

While the southern part of the Washington Coast is not as scenic as the northern half, it offers its own peculiar attractions, not least a huge population of razor clams, the popular and tasty quarry for thousands of beachgoers. The southern environments, along with the bounty of the adjacent marine environment, attract a huge variety of birds, so bird-watching is usually superb, and waterfowl hunting is excellent in the enclosed bays and inland tidewaters. Beachcombing can be very good. The sandy shores tend not to break the much sought-after glass fishing floats that still wash up after storms. Most importantly, just as to the north the waves roll in here relentlessly, the sun sets often brilliantly, and the lack of visual stimuli allows a visitor to take in and contemplate the vast sweep of the Pacific.

The south coast—long since inhabited, much less rocky than the north, and offering substantially less offshore wildlife habitat—is afforded relatively little protection. But twelve state parks dot its shores from Pacific Beach south to the Columbia River, including the incomparable Cape Disappointment at the mouth of that mighty waterway, one of the finest state parks in all of Washington. State wildlife and conservation lands protect numerous patches here and there, such as the sandspit Damon Point at the north entrance of Grays Harbor. Federal designations also protect some critical habitats, such as the shorebird-rich Bowerman Basin inside Grays Harbor and the surprisingly wild 15,000 acres of rich tidelands of the Willapa National Wildlife Refuge.

In occasional glimpses of vision and foresight, humankind hereabouts have taken actions that help keep much of the Washington Coast the way it has always been. But threats remain. Our never-ending need for energy is one. We have already seen the potential of devastating oil spills on this coast (in 1972, 1988, and 1991). For the love of all the gods of every religion and culture ever, I pray that oil drilling never be allowed off the Washington Coast. It is too precious and priceless, and far too much is at stake.

PLANNING YOUR TRIP

CHAPTER 2

ONE OF THE MOST WONDERFUL ASPECTS of the Washington Coast is its year-round recreation opportunities. If you're primarily a mountain backpacker, sometime in October or November you must hang up your boots until the following June. You can snowshoe, ski, snowboard, or climb on a snowmobile, for sure. But you're not going to hike the Pacific Crest Trail for any distance. On the coast, though, if you're properly prepared, you can hike from Lake Ozette to Rialto Beach anytime of year. The only possible exception is during winter's fierce storms, and they do occur with regularity.

In fact, in winter the coast offers much more solitude and feels more wild and more primal. You can even dig razor clams in the dead of winter—some years, when tides and clam populations allow, even on Christmas or New Year's Eve. On coastal rivers, you can catch a hard-charging, chrome-bright winter steelhead from November through April. The nastiest off-season weather often results in

Cedar Creek spills into the ocean at Ruby Beach north of Kalaloch, Olympic National Park.

the best beachcombing of the year, and those storms and swells rolling in also improve agate hunting.

At the same time, the margin for survival is considerably thinner during the stormy months, making it even more imperative that you be completely prepared, not only physically but also mentally. If you're backpacking along Olympic National Park's wilderness beach strip, you should be prepared to spend an extra unplanned night out—in winter, make that two extra nights, because help could be a long way off. On this wilderness coast, anytime of year, you really need to be ready.

RECOMMENDED GEAR

Everyone has heard about the so-called Ten Essentials for hikers, and while the exact list can be debated, particularly in this era of ultralight backpacking, the concept is valid. Just ask any National Park Service ranger. Unfortunately, they are often called on to rescue ill-prepared hikers.

The three critical elements of survival you need to consider are food, water, and most importantly, shelter. Sure, you can live for several days without food, but you'll be more comfortable in a dire situation if you can eat and maintain your energy. I carry at least one day's extra on each overnight trip. Water is not usually a problem on our very wet coast. This is not the desert. But I always start a hike with 2 liters, and when backpacking I bring a filter or iodine tablets to protect myself against giardia, the parasitic cysts that are known to occur all along the coast.

THE TEN ESSENTIALS: A SYSTEMS APPROACH

1. Navigation (map and compass)
2. Sun protection (sunglasses and sunscreen)
3. Insulation (extra clothing)
4. Illumination (headlamp or flashlight)
5. First-aid supplies
6. Fire (firestarter and matches/lighter)
7. Repair kit and tools (including knife)
8. Nutrition (extra food)
9. Hydration (extra water)
10. Emergency shelter

—The Mountaineers

When weather and tides allow, the beach makes a fine campsite.

Shelter is the category I never skimp on, and by shelter I don't just mean a tent. I like to carry enough apparel to survive any weather event short of a hurricane or tornado, which fortunately almost never happen here. I don't wear cotton on overnight trips, because it won't keep you warm when wet, and lord knows if you spend time here you will get wet. Good wool or synthetic hiking socks are mandatory, along with good waterproof boots. I prefer Gore-Tex-lined boots, but well-oiled and sealed leather boots are fine. For coastal backpack trips, I almost always wear gaiters, to keep the mud and water out of my boots; gaiters also provide an extra layer of protection for ankles and feet against reefs, loose rocks, barnacles, mussels, slivery driftwood, piles of slimy seaweed—you think I'm kidding? Just wait.

For outer garments, nylon pants with zip-off lower legs are my preference, but other synthetic pants are fine. Typically I'll wear a polypropylene T-shirt under a fleece jacket, and when it's cold I'll add a long-sleeved fleece undershirt. For cold nights I also carry polypropylene long underwear, a down jacket, a fleece stocking cap, and lined synthetic gloves.

And that brings us to the most important apparel for coastal hikers—raingear. Don't hike here with cheap raingear—just don't. This is not stinkin' Arizona; it's the damned rain forest. I use that language to impress upon you the urgency of

Hiking to the ocean across Ahlstroms Prairie near Lake Ozette

this necessity. Of all places on this entire sun-circling, spinning orb, the Washington Coast is where you want to have the best raingear you can afford, both jacket with hood and pants. Gore-Tex or another highly breathable fabric is preferable. Just make sure the fabric is rainproof enough to keep you mostly dry if you're forced to bivouac in a howling gale.

In short: Carry enough warm, synthetic or wool clothing and raingear so that if you get caught in a sudden storm or suffer some injury, you can put everything on and curl up under a drift log or downed spruce, or climb into a hollow cedar stump, and not have to worry about hypothermia while waiting for help or the storm to break.

Map, compass, headlamp, knife, fire-starter, whistle—they all find a place in my pack, even on day hikes. GPS device? I don't need one on land and don't use one. Some of my tech-savvy friends asked if I would include GPS coordinates in this book. Hell no! A goal of this book is to tell people where they can go to get their heads screwed on naturally straight, where to escape this crazy, harried, hurry-up world we live in. GPS is counterproductive to that pursuit. The last thing I want when out on a wilderness beach is to be consulting a computerized gadget. I want to watch the waves and the otters. Besides, the shoreline will show you the way; you don't need a GPS receiver here.

I carry a detailed topographical map to plan my itinerary, to know how far I've gone and how far I've got to go, to learn all the place names, and to note obstacles like headlands that can be rounded only at lower tides. I don't recall ever taking the compass out of my pack while hiking the coast, except out of curiosity to identify islands, named sea stacks, and other offshore landmarks. Cell phones and pistols, y'all can debate that on your own. At times I've carried one or both, but I've never needed either.

STAYING SAFE: CAUTIONS AND CONCERNS

Just as important as what to pack is how to prepare mentally. On the north coast, lined with rocky headlands, sea stacks, rivers, streams, reefs, slides, and massive piles of drift logs, you really must follow the rhythms of nature to hike. It can be extremely dangerous to hike the beach at high tide. When the surf is up in the driftwood, it can roll 2-ton logs like a big-legged lumberjack in a millpond. You don't want to be there then. When the tide is up, a knee-deep stream can become nipple-high. You won't be crossing. Let's say you have to round a half-mile headland that is awash at any tide higher than 3 feet, and as you approach it the tide is at 2 feet and rising. That's risky business. This comes from someone who has pushed his luck, listening to his hiking buddy say things like "This is not prudent!" as the waves washed in. We made it. But he was right.

You need to know the tides and write them down before you go, research your route and the obstacles you face, and then hike accordingly. You also must be aware that hiking the north coast wilderness can be slow, tedious, and tough. For most of the way there is no trail per se, just shoreline, which can involve rough terrain that requires traversing slippery reefs, picking your way through jumbles of boulders ranging in size from bowling balls to hippos to houses, wading streams, climbing steep, muddy headlands, and walking on loose gravel that provides little purchase. It can be mentally draining.

Before any trip to the coast, carefully watch the National Weather Service forecasts, both marine and land. The marine forecast will provide the prevailing direction of approaching fronts and, more importantly, predictions of swell heights. If you've got 10-foot swells rolling in, the surf is going to be snarling and tides will be higher than tide charts estimate. If you're going razor clam digging, swells greater than 8 or 9 feet are going to make it difficult, since the clams will remain deep and be reluctant to show. The same is true with surf perch fishing. In my opinion, it's just not worth it if swells are bigger than 5 or 6 feet, since the perch will remain outside the breakers and won't come in to feed.

Don't attempt hiking the coast during howling gales. That's when slides happen, the surf climbs way up the beach over the driftwood at high tides, and gusts can knock you down. (A cabin on the beach during a strong storm, however, is a fantastic place to watch and wait it out.) That said, immediately after a howling gale is a great time to comb the beach for floats, agates, and other booty. The forecast will give you a good idea of when a storm will break.

Of course, it does rain hard here regularly, and that will have a direct impact on your coastal recreation. If an inch of rain or more is forecast for the town of Forks, the rivers will rise and become dirty brown, and you won't be catching any steelhead. Or if you're hiking from Third Beach to Oil City, fording Goodman and Mosquito creeks will be a tough go. Plus, it will be plain miserable for hiking.

OH BEHAVE! RULES TO RECREATE BY

It surprises me how many people seem to think that rules are meant for others. We all chafe at certain regulations. But there are good reasons for almost all of them, and before you head out, you need to familiarize yourself with all the rules and requirements for hiking the shore. If you're visiting the national park, you must follow park guidelines (all posted on the Olympic National Park website). But no matter where you go, you should consider the following.

Food storage: You must carry all your food in a bear-proof container while backpacking Olympic National Park's wilderness coast—and not just for bears. Raccoons on this coast are almost savvy enough to solve a Rubik's Cube, so hanging your food won't always work. Bears will wander through camp at times, as will the occasional Pepé Le Pew (if you're too young to recall the cartoon, that's a skunk). Raccoons, bears, skunks, and ravens are all coastal culprits—keep a clean camp and store your food. Check with the park for where you can borrow a bear canister if you don't have one of your own.

Pets: By and large, you can't take Rover into any wilderness area of Olympic National Park. On the park's coastal strip, pets are allowed on-leash on all Kalaloch-area beaches (from Ruby Beach south to South Beach) and from Rialto Beach north to Ellen Creek (0.8 mile). Other than that, leave 'em home. In most other jurisdictions, such as state parks, they must be kept on-leash.

Campfires: You may build small fires on ocean beaches of Olympic National Park, except for the area from the Wedding Rocks headland south to Yellow Banks on the north wilderness coast. Burn only driftwood—don't you dare cut any part of a tree—and remember that fires right on the beach have the least impact. At upland campsites, the park asks that you use existing fire rings.

Party size: The maximum group size in Olympic National Park is twelve people.

Litter and a clean camp: Leaving anything outdoors is unacceptable anywhere, most especially in the park. Wherever you camp, front or backcountry, you're asking for critter trouble if you leave food scraps laying around or out in the open. See more on both issues below.

Beachcombing etiquette: Beachcombing is a blast, but keep in mind that collecting regulations vary by jurisdiction. It's hard to envision authorities frowning upon the collection of simple rocks, such as agates. But national wildlife refuges, such as the Willapa, prohibit the collection of any stones. Coastal Indian nations prohibit the collection of anything on their reservations by non–tribal members, since Native peoples have been using what the sea sends for centuries, and

FISHING RULES AND REGULATIONS

Seasons, limits, and regulations are tightly controlled and managed by three primary entities. Foremost among them is the Washington Department of Fish and Wildlife. Waters within Olympic National Park are managed by the National Park Service, usually in conjunction with the state, with the park tending to be more conservative. Non-Indians can fish under tribal regulations on two reservations, the Quinault and Makah. The Quinault Nation manages often excellent sport fisheries for steelhead and salmon on the Quinault and Salmon rivers; non-Indians must hire a guide. The tribe also usually opens Lake Quinault to non-Indians, which produces an excellent cutthroat trout fishery. A tribal license is required. The small Sooes River, supported by a federal salmon and steelhead hatchery, is open to non-Indians with a permit from the Makah tribe. For full contact information, see "Contacts and Resources."

Looking for agates like this shiny beauty is a fun way to pass the time as you hike, but remember that visitors are not allowed to keep them in certain jurisdictions.

still do. Olympic National Park allows the collection of small amounts of stones for personal use.

The collection of cultural objects of any sort on public lands is prohibited by state and federal law. If you find a cultural object, such as an arrowhead or other stone tool, and especially anything you suspect might be human remains, contact local authorities immediately.

This is a contentious issue. Some argue that searching for arrowheads and other artifacts is a legitimate recreational pursuit and adds value to cultural knowledge, since those things might not otherwise be found. I strongly disagree. Cultural diversity is the essence of humanity and little can be learned about cultures that have vanished without rigorous scientific inquiry. Leave it to the experts. If you find something, report it and feel good about yourself.

Swimming: Not a good idea on the Washington Coast, due to regular stiff currents and riptides. During June and July of 2014 alone, four people lost their lives after being swept to sea by rip currents at Ocean Shores and Long Beach in Washington and Seaside and Garibaldi in northern Oregon. That prompted this warning from Commander Bill Gibbons of the Coast Guard's Columbia River sector: "The only way to avoid the risk is to avoid going in the water. At a minimum, people should never enter the water alone, children should never be allowed near the water unattended, and people who are near the edge of the surf line must be prepared for what many refer to as 'sneaker waves'—disproportionately large and powerful coastal waves that can appear without warning."

Air mattresses and dime-store rafts—they're death craft on this ocean. As a reporter, I've written about people who did not heed this advice and died. Wading is OK up to your knees on an incoming tide, but be careful, and never take your eyes off the waves.

TSUNAMI ESCAPE ROUTES/AWARENESS

"Tidal waves," as we know now, are an ever-present concern on the coast, even though they are rare. I think about them a lot whenever I'm on the coast, and especially while backpacking and away from any quick road escape. As inevitable as a tsunami is—tomorrow or in a hundred years—there are ways to prepare, signs to watch for, and actions to take should either a quake or indications of a monster wave occur. I urge you to thoroughly read the tsunami information from the Washington Department of Ecology (www.ecy.wa.gov/programs/sea/coast/waves/tsunami.html).

The main message is that if you see any sign of a potential tsunami—an earthquake or a sudden lowering of the sea, for example—you need to flee toward the highest ground available. Fifty feet high might not be enough. The 2011 tsunami in Japan sent waves of about 30 feet, but other recorded tsunamis have been higher. If you're hiking the coast, it's a good idea to frequently scan your surroundings for escape routes. If you're backpacking the wilderness beaches of the north coast, try to find a campsite with high ground nearby, and plan your route to it.

CHEW ON THIS: CRITTER CONCERNS

On the coast, the actual danger to humans from wild creatures is minimal; the occasional scary incidents I've heard of have all occurred inland. Several years ago one or more black bears began boldly taking hikers' food along the Elwha River Trail, about 50 miles from the coast. Parts of the trail were closed to camping, and hikers were required to keep their food in bear-proof containers. That solved the problem. Also several years ago, a mountain-bike rider was chased by a cougar on the Spruce Railroad Trail along Lake Crescent, just to the west, and as I recall the pair tussled over a daypack before the cat ran off. Cougars are indeed spotted, if infrequently, along the north coast: Several years ago, National Park Service authorities were forced to kill a cat near Kalaloch Campground that had

Olympic or "Roosevelt" elk are common sights in the rain forest valleys of the Hoh, Queets, and Quinault rivers.

become accustomed to human food. Apparently, misinformed employees at the nearby lodge had been throwing out food scraps for the cougar.

In the very unlikely event you are approached aggressively by either cougar or bear on this coast, it is usually not a good idea to play dead. There are no grizzly bears here. If you spook a mother bear with cubs, she may well bluff-charge you, and in that event dropping to the ground might be a good idea. But in any other situation, you should act aggressively yourself. If a cougar or bear is coming at you, make yourself look as large as possible, and yell at it. If you have kids with you, gather them up and get them behind you. Do not run, which might trigger a predatory response in the animal. If necessary, pick up a stick and defend yourself. Throw rocks. Now, I'm not talking about if you simply see a cat or bear. If the animal is not acting in a threatening way, leave it be, or at the most talk gently to let it know you're there. The friendly folks at the Washington Department of Fish and Wildlife website have prepared a lot of information about dealing with bears, cougars, and other wildlife, and it's worth reading.

Far more confounding are the less fearsome creatures on the coast. Bees and wasps can pose severe danger, especially to people who are allergic—if you are allergic, always carry an anaphylactic shock kit, available with a doctor's prescription. As mentioned, raccoons are as persistent and pesky as a bad habit, from the Strait of Juan de Fuca all the way south to the Columbia River. While you're not looking, they'll jump on the picnic table and steal any food they can. If you leave a cooler out during the night, say, at Kalaloch Campground, they'll open it and take whatever is inside. This happened to my best friend; worst part is they got the beer. Put the cooler in your vehicle at night. If you don't stow your food properly where required to do so, you also risk a big fat ticket from Mr. Ranger.

So, stow your food, keep a clean camp, and be aware of your surroundings. By and large the wildlife on the coast are not to be feared. They are to be celebrated, protected, nurtured, and perpetuated.

SHOW SOME R-E-S-P-E-C-T

Another concern is the behavior of two-legged critters: people. I don't want to pontificate or preach. However, having hiked virtually every inch of the north coast and visited almost every area on the south, I see people doing downright disgusting things, or see the results. The more accessible areas are the most problematic. At the wilderness camping area on Lake Ozette's Ericsons Bay, for example, I spent two spring days completely alone after paddling in. But previous boaters had left a cheap compressed-gas barbecue, cans in the fire pits, and a plastic tarp they tried to hide in the bushes. Olympic National Park officials have considered banning motorboats on Lake Ozette—this is one tangible reason why (presumably it's motorboats that carry in bulky things like the barbecue). Don't force the park's hand.

Our campsite at Norwegian Memorial one winter night, along the park's wilderness coast, was next to a ragged structure of plastic sheeting tied on a frame of poles cut from live trees. That spot is more than 10 miles from the Lake Ozette trailhead. But if you know the network of logging roads east of the park's far too narrow wilderness beach strip—and obviously a certain number of nitwits do—you can short-cut it to a mile. I appreciate the need for accessibility, but scenes like this one prompt me to wonder whether the Park Service ought to urge timberland owners to strategically gate certain roads.

On the bay just north of stunning Hole in the Wall near Rialto Beach, my hiking buddies and I passed a party camping with a German shepherd, off-leash and barking, despite the national park's rule specifically prohibiting pets on wilderness beaches. On a previous visit I'd seen a sea lion hauled out on that very beach. Crude graffiti has been scratched on sandstone rocks within feet of prehistoric petroglyphs left by the Ozette people south of Cape Alava. I've seen plastic foam bait containers and beer cans left by anglers on the park beaches north of Kalaloch, and all kinds of crap left by hunters and others on Long Island in the Willapa National Wildlife Refuge, which allows hunting in season. I've seen people keep Dungeness crabs quite obviously under the minimum size limit (6 inches across the back in ocean waters, and males only), more than a few times.

I could go on, but you get the point. Short of a bona fide emergency, not one damned thing other than footprints should be left by anyone, anytime, anywhere on this coast—not any sign of your visit, not one thing! If you pack it in, then pack it out. There is no excuse for cutting live trees in a national park, for leaving tarps and other garbage anywhere outdoors, for desecrating images left by people who lived on this coast for perhaps nine thousand years. If you can't approach the Washington Coast as a rule-abiding, conscientious visitor who leaves it as it is, then read no further, please return this book.

Other issues in the behavior category to keep in mind revolve around the one little word that Aretha and Otis sang so soulfully about: respect. You need to demonstrate a little of it at all times, not only toward other visitors, but to coastal residents as well. The owner of that dog on the national park beach showed no respect to other hikers. Dogs and wildlife do not mix and mingle. The dog's presence very likely limited what wildlife other visitors could see. Where they are allowed, I am completely OK with hounds. I had a beautiful yellow Lab named Maddy who was a faithful hiking companion—rest her sweet soul! But there should be a few places managed and reserved specifically for wildness and wildlife: the wilder areas of national parks.

Visitors to the coast, especially along the national park's beach strip, should respect others' expectations for peace, quiet, and some sense of solitude. That doesn't mean you shouldn't get together for a beach fire and a favorite beverage while strumming your guitar or dancing with your bikini-clad babycakes—say, at accessible beaches like Ocean Shores or even Kalaloch. But if I'm hiking several miles to Chilean Memorial or Toleak Point, I'd rather listen to the wind and waves than someone playing their tin whistle—as much as I love Celtic music. It's just not the place for it. The wilderness beaches can get pretty busy May through September, and you might have to camp close to other parties. Do the best you can to be neighborly and to tuck your camp away from others.

The coast of Washington State is truly an amazing, awe-inspiring place, and I encourage you to get to know it well, because there is so much more to learn and discover than you'll find at first blush. But please approach it safely, sensibly, and with the sensitivity that it deserves.

JAPANESE TSUNAMI DEBRIS?

The Great East Japan Earthquake of 2011, and the devastating tsunami and Fukushima nuclear plant disaster that resulted, vividly and tragically illustrated the potential impact of such events. Another tangible manifestation of that tsunami is the potential for marine debris washing ashore here on the Washington Coast and throughout the North Pacific.

Such debris poses little danger, and in my opinion the issue has been overblown and mischaracterized. First, let's clear up a few misconceptions:

- Human remains coming ashore as the result of the tsunami are unlikely. Bodies do wash ashore from time to time. But the likelihood of human remains making it across 7000 miles of Pacific Ocean is small.
- There is no massive patch of tsunami debris floating around the Pacific.
- Most stuff that washes up with Japanese or other Asian writing on it is not tsunami debris. Beachcombers have eagerly sought Japanese glass fishing floats for decades, and for years literally hundreds and hundreds of Asian plastic fishing floats, bottles, lightbulbs, and other flotsam have come ashore.

That being said, debris from the tsunami has washed up in Washington and is likely to do so for years. A 65-foot dock came ashore in Olympic National Park near Mosquito Creek in 2012; it was cut apart and removed. Two 20-foot boats washed up on the Long Beach Peninsula in 2012 and 2013. More boats came ashore in 2014.

There is some minimal danger from hazardous materials, for example, inside of drums, fuel tanks, cylinders, gas cans, and the like. Don't touch that stuff. Leave it in place and call local authorities. Take a photo if you can and note the precise location. The Washington Department of Ecology has recommendations for what to do should you encounter flotsam that seems tsunami related (http://marinedebris.wa.gov). If you find personal effects with identification, contact NOAA (DisasterDebris@noaa.gov) and/or the Japanese consulate in Seattle (206-682-9107). In the unlikely event you do find what appears to be human remains, do not hesitate: call 9-1-1 as soon as possible.

HOW TO USE THIS BOOK

CHAPTER 3

THIS BOOK IS PRETTY STRAIGHTFORWARD: to use it, simply read it! At the same time, many readers might find it useful to have some explanation of what to expect in this guide and how to navigate it.

After the coast overview chapters in part 1, the book is organized in regional chapters north to south. Chapter 4 starts at the northernmost tip of the Washington Coast, and the final chapter ends at the Columbia River, across from Oregon. In each chapter, all activities—camping, hiking, paddling, and so on—are also listed generally north to south.

Each regional chapter begins with an introduction describing the area and its highlights, followed by general information under the headings "Getting There/Staying There" and "Fees and Permits." Descriptions of area activities follow—camping, hiking, paddling, and the like. Specific hikes and paddles begin with a synopsis that characterizes the outing: what makes it special, or not, what you'll find of interest, any relevant history and associated activities—for example, a

Weirdly tilted strata at Browns Point in the Kalaloch area vividly illustrate the tectonic pressures in the coastal zone where the Juan de Fuca and continental plates collide.

great hike with good agate hunting. Each hike/paddle then lists **distance**, **elevation gain** (hikes only), level of **difficulty**, appropriate **maps** (USGS or Custom Correct topo maps, park brochures, and/or online maps), the **contact** agency (with specific contact information in "Contacts and Resources"), and any additional **notes** (such as required permits, whether dogs are allowed, and unusual conditions or special precautions).

A few words about elevation gain and distance: First, this is the coast, so in many cases there is little to no gain. Second, coastal hiking to a great extent is not on a trail at all. You follow the beach, often over boulders, across reefs, and often at the whim of the tide. Conditions and the path of least resistance determine the way; when the tide is up, you often must climb headlands. Actual gain and distance will vary, sometimes significantly. So don't be mad at me when your GPS device says you hiked 17.8 miles on a route I say is 17.4.

The sand and gravel bluffs south and north of Ruby Beach are likely composed of sediments deposited by glaciers during the Pleistocene Epoch.

The difficulty of each route is also subjective. A twenty-eight-year-old ultra-marathon runner will probably not find any hike in this book overly difficult. But the following **difficulty scale of 1 to 5** is based on the average hiker or paddler:

1. An easy walk or paddle for anyone without mobility issues, like granny and the kids. In the case of paddling, I'm assuming you have basic paddling skills.
2. An easy walk/paddle but perhaps longer and/or with some elevation. You might have to carry the toddler.
3. Healthy adults and strong kids can handle these hikes, but you're going to sweat a bit; maybe there are some headlands to climb and rocky stretches, and the length might be 3 or more miles. Paddlers might expect afternoon winds and some long fetches.
4. Casual hikers and paddlers will not want to take these trips. There will be some gain, rough footing and/or length, or in the case of paddling, potential winds and currents and open water.
5. Prepare for distances of more than 7 miles, a lot of up and down or total elevation gain, rugged footing, reef and boulder-field navigation, or steep headland climbs. There are only a few hikes in this book that fit this category, no paddles. You need to be a fit, fairly strong hiker for these adventures.

Finally, the following **icons** provide a quick glimpse of what an outing or area has to offer:

Wildlife: Potential sightings of marine and terrestrial mammals, birds, and tide-pool creatures.

Beachcombing: Certain stretches of the coast collect neat stuff like glass fishing floats, cool-shaped driftwood, and agates, petrified wood, and other pretty stones.

Geology: Areas with sea stacks, tectonically tilted strata, accreted sand dunes and spits, and so on.

History: Knowing pivotal events makes a place feel tangible and poignant for me. This icon alerts like-minded readers to noteworthy occurrences across the winds of time.

Giant trees: Look for this if monster trees make you go "Wow!" There are plenty of bigguns along the coast.

Fishing: Potential for actual rod and reel fishing or clam digging, oyster shucking, smelt dipping.

Readers will also get a definite sense of my opinions. I don't want to tout something that ain't all that, so to speak. Tourist brochures tend to embellish local attractions, often with superlatives like the best, the longest, or the biggest. But I want you to get an honest sense of the overall quality of an activity or, say, a campground. I list activities you must do to best experience an area versus those to put on your optional list. For example, in the Kalaloch area, if you don't hike Ruby Beach you'll miss the best scenery. But if you skip the Kalaloch Creek nature trail you won't miss a lot—even though Kalaloch Creek is nice enough. Ultimately you might disagree. I'm OK with that—go generate your own perspective!

I also want to apologize if this fairly comprehensive guidebook fails to satisfy a particular perspective. I don't cover all the kayak or canoe paddles available on this coast, and my descriptions of those I do are less defined than the hike descriptions. I also wish I could have been more definitive on fishing opportunities. But the book is already long. There are so many adventures available on the Washington Coast! Each activity could have a book of its own. I hope you use the information to stimulate your own explorations.

Finally, a word about rates. Camping, permit fees, and the like are as up to date as possible. But prices change over time. Other things change too. Slides occur on the coastal routes, campgrounds close, trails are rerouted, access is often restricted. Before your trip, please contact the various agencies and businesses mentioned so you won't be in for a surprise.

Sitka spruce trees on bluffs along the seashore often exhibit strange nodules, such as these on the Spruce Burl Trail near Kalaloch's Beach 1.

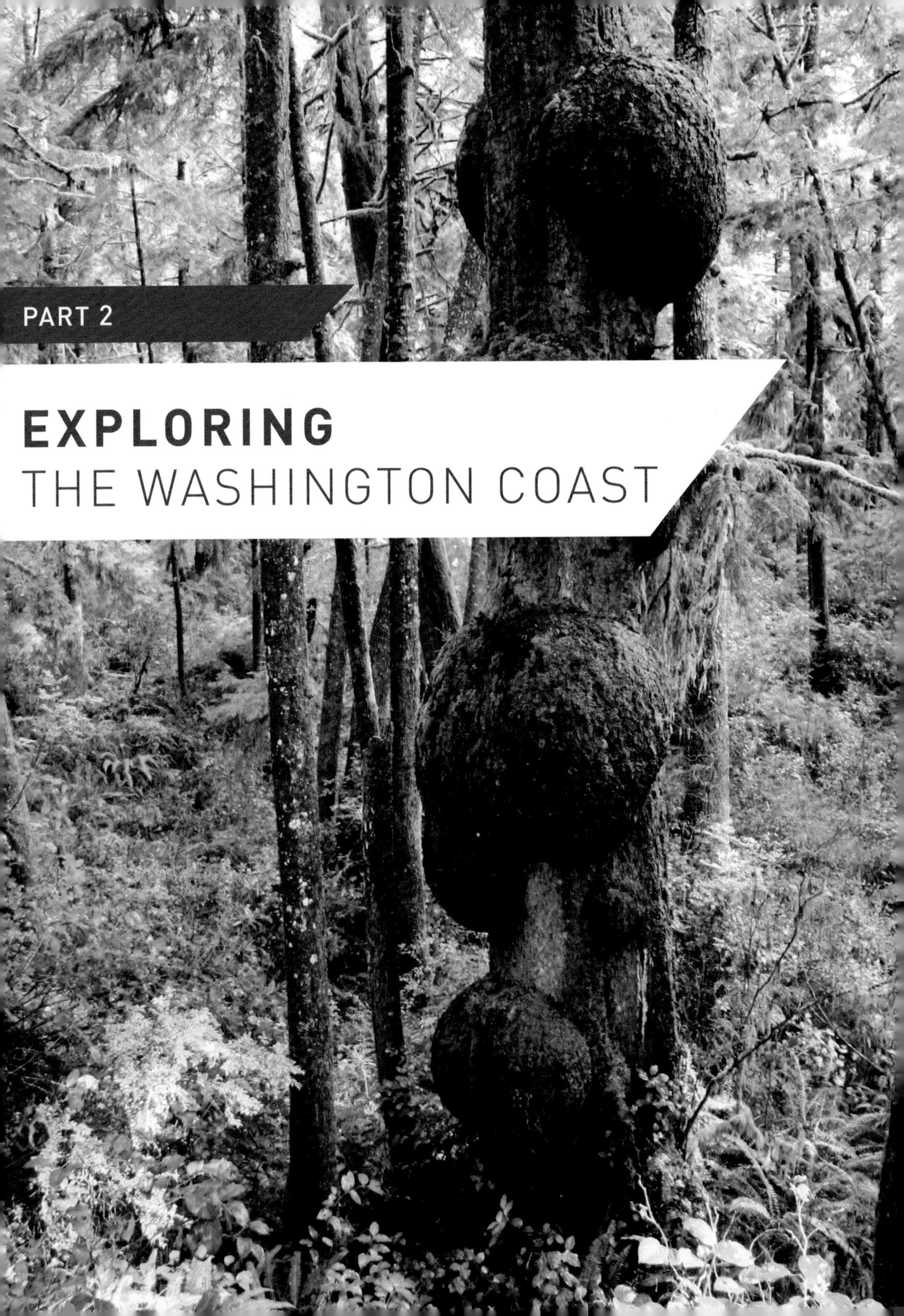

PART 2

EXPLORING THE WASHINGTON COAST

THE NORTHWEST CORNER

CHAPTER 4

THE NORTHERN TIP OF THE WASHINGTON COAST is one of the most geologically spectacular spots of the entire Pacific Rim, essential in the early history of what became Washington State and a sublime place for hiking, fishing, paddling, and exploring. This stunning shoreline is one of those rare places that can make you feel fully in the here and now but with a distinct sense of forever. You can feel wistful and wishful at once.

Crowned by the tide-washed sea stacks of Cape Flattery and Point of Arches, this area is the rugged manifestation of ancient volcanic flows combined with tectonic activity in the earth's crust. The resulting rocky seascape provides habitat for an enormous variety of marine life, from tiny flitting crustaceans and purple urchins in the tide pools to massive gray and humpback whales just offshore.

Bounded by the Pacific Ocean on the west and the Strait of Juan de Fuca on the north, the region has a lot going on and always has. It was pivotal for early European seafarers and home to one of the most powerful Native nations on the

A sea arch along the overland route south of Shi Shi Beach, Olympic National Park

A warren of sea caves as seen from the magnificent Cape Flattery Trail on the very northwest tip of the contiguous forty-eight states

West Coast, the Makah. Tribal legend tells of a catastrophic rise of the sea, and it is quite possibly a true story—several hundred years ago a tsunami was indeed propelled by a mega quake offshore.

Geographically, this region is the top left corner in the puzzle of the forty-eight contiguous states of America. Cape Flattery, the very northwest tip of the continental United States, was named by none other than Captain James Cook, who sighted land here in March of 1778 after discovering and sailing from the Hawaiian Islands.

In stormy, foggy weather Cook's crew spotted what they thought was "a small opening in the land which flattered us with the hopes of finding a good harbor." They found no harbor, however, arriving within sight of the cape but a bit south, just missing the entrance to the Strait of Juan de Fuca. Finding no anchorage, Cook was forced by the bad weather to stand back out to sea, and he then sailed north.

The hiking is superb at this northernmost latitude of the Washington Coast, the fishing great, the surfing decent in a few locations. The kayaking ranges from the challenge of open ocean to flatwater paddling on a large inland lake. Plus, there is rich history to explore—possibly beginning with some of the earliest unrecorded wanderings of humans in the New World. A few miles south of Cape Flattery is the northern boundary of Olympic National Park's marvelous wilderness ocean strip, 70 unrivaled miles of pristine beaches, mind-boggling geology, marine diversity, and mesmerizing adventures.

TRIBAL LEGEND SUGGESTS TSUNAMI

The Makah legend of a sudden, devastating rise in the sea is stunningly prescient, given our relatively new understanding of the cataclysmic potential of the tectonic plates that meet and mash here in the northwest corner of the state, and the lithic manifestations of that fact dotting the coast. This shore is a seismic hot spot where the Continental and Juan de Fuca plates bump and grind, rise and slump. We know now that massive offshore subduction quakes have occurred and will occur along this coast, and they do cause significant tsunamis.

Early coastal resident James Swan, the first school teacher at Neah Bay, in 1864 related a story by Makah tribal member Billy Balch about an event in the not too distant past, when the sea rose and flooded across Waatch Prairie from the Pacific Ocean to the Strait of Juan de Fuca:

> He says that "ankarty" but not "Irias ankarty" that is at not a very remote period, the water flowed from Neah Bay through the Waatch prairie, and Cape Flattery was an Island. That the water receded and left Neah Bay dry for four days and became very warm. It then rose again without any swell or waves and submerged the whole of the cape and in fact the whole country except the mountains back of Clyoquot. As the water rose those who had canoes put their effects into them and floated off with the current which set strong to the north. Many canoes came down in the trees and were destroyed and numerous lives were lost.
>
> There is no doubt in my mind of the truth of this tradition. The Waatch prairie shows conclusively that the waters of the ocean once flowed through it. And as this whole country shows marked evidence of volcanic influences, there is every reason to believe that there was a gradual depressing and subsequent upheaval of the earth's crust which made the waters to rise and recede as the Indian stated.

Researchers have found unmistakable evidence along the Washington Coast of a major subduction quake in the early 1700s. It created ghost forests of dead trees and possibly buried in a landslide the Makah village of Ozette at Cape Alava.

NEAH BAY AND CAPE FLATTERY

IF YOU NEVER REACH THIS REMOTE corner of the planet, you'll miss some of the very best ocean shoreline scenery and hiking on the Washington Coast—on any coast. There are four primary reasons to put this region on your must-see list.

The first and most spectacular is Shi Shi Beach and Point of Arches, the geologically stunning northern end of Olympic National Park's 70-mile wilderness beach strip. Shi Shi itself makes for a superb day hike and easy backpack, but it is also the northern end of the most punishing and demanding of the four major wilderness beach backpacks in the park, the 15 miles from the Shi Shi trailhead south to Lake Ozette.

Second is the short and easy Cape Flattery Trail, beautifully built by the Makah tribe, which leads to the most northwesterly spot in the Lower 48, and a scenic and historic one at that.

Fishing boats moored at the Makah Marina in Neah Bay. The one at the boat ramp is a small "bowpicker," its gill net tended from the bow.

Third is the superb salmon, halibut, and other bottomfish angling off of Neah Bay, the small port village and tribal headquarters on the Strait of Juan de Fuca, just a few miles "inside" and east of the ocean. Boat launches, moorage, and charters are available in the small harbor here.

Finally, the Makah Museum and Cultural Center in Neah Bay is the single best place to see and learn how the Native tribes on this coast industriously exploited their rich environment and created complex, socially stratified cultures with individual specialization—using nothing more than Stone Age technologies.

Neah Bay is also notable historically as the site of the first settlement built by white men in what is now Washington State. As part of their effort to establish primacy in the northern part of the New World, the Spanish in 1792 built Fort Nuñez Gaona. They were not well received by the Makah, who demonstrated their displeasure by killing a Spaniard. The Spanish retaliated disproportionately, firing on the village and killing at least several Makah. In less than a year the Spanish

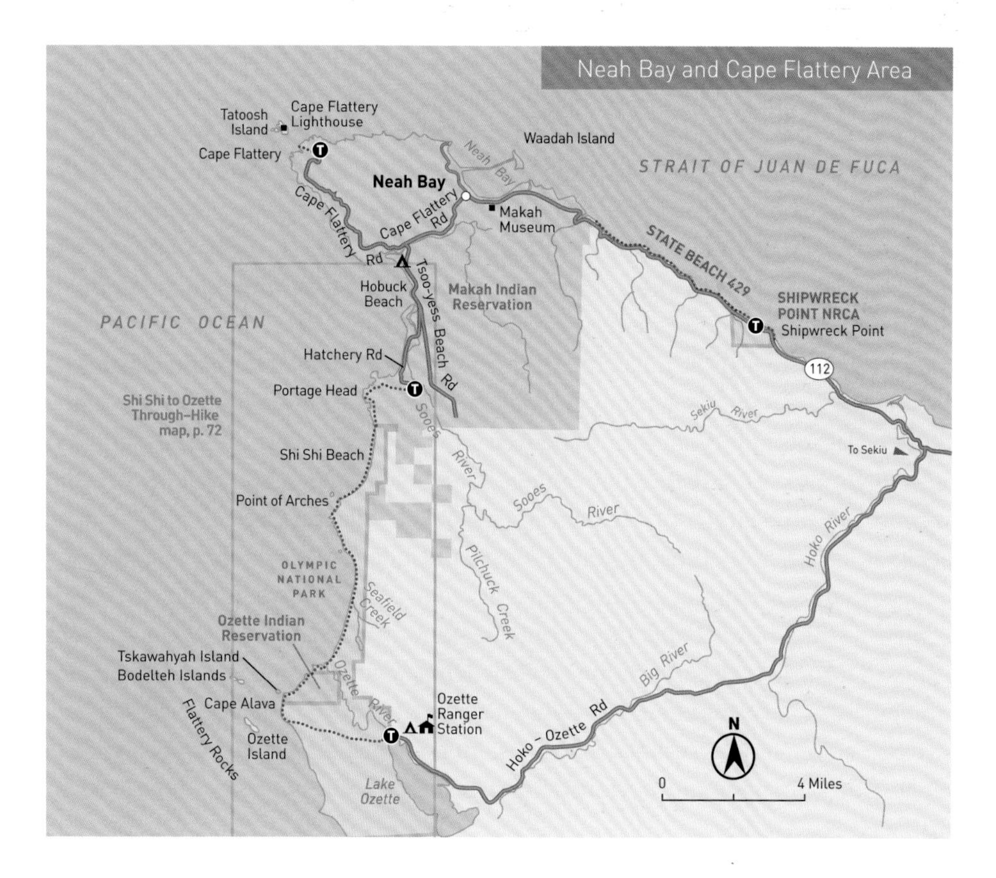

MAKAH MUSEUM AND CULTURAL CENTER

Open:	Daily year-round, 10:00 AM–5:00 PM; but closed New Year's Day, Thanksgiving, Christmas
Admission:	$5 general admission; $4 seniors, military in uniform, students
Location and contact:	1880 Bayview Avenue, Neah Bay, makahmuseum.com, 360-645-2711
Notable:	Cameras are not allowed in exhibit areas.

departed for their larger settlement at Nootka Sound on Vancouver Island, across the strait. Today, Diah Veterans Park on Bayview Avenue marks the site and memorializes the almost three hundred Makah veterans of the US military.

The Makah were and are people of the sea, originally fishing from dugout canoes for halibut as far as 20 miles out and closer in catching chinook, coho, sockeye, and pink salmon, which in bygone days migrated through here in unbelievable numbers. The Makah hunted marine mammals as well, with some specializing in catching seals and sea otters on and near offshore rocks and islands, and others devoting themselves to the spirit power to chase down humpback and gray whales on the big waters of the ocean. Today many people are dismayed by Makah efforts to return to their whale-hunting practices. But it is who they were and, for many, who they want to be.

You can see that at the museum, the repository for many of the artifacts uncovered in the 1970s during famous archaeological excavations at Cape Alava on the outer coast south of Neah Bay. Cape Alava is the very westernmost point on the Washington Coast, a distinct advantage for whale hunters, and the site of what was probably the largest of five permanent Makah villages: Ozette, or as the tribe spells it, Osett. Sometime around 1700 a landslide, quite possibly triggered by a magnitude-9 earthquake, buried several cedar-plank houses in mud and clay.

Because the houses and their contents were covered by wet layers and not exposed to oxygen, the excavations revealed intact wood, bone, and fiber tools and implements rarely found on other digs, along with stone artifacts. Baskets, ropes, netting, boxes, bowls, combs, fishhooks, mussel-shell whale harpoons, paddles, clubs, bows, arrows, and curiously, iron blades were among the thousands of artifacts recovered.

What made this dig so important, drawing the attention of archaeologists worldwide, is that the landslide preserved Pompeii-like a moment in time, before aboriginal contact with Europeans. A nearly complete record and inventory of Makah precontact life was unearthed. The dig has long since ended, but you can still hike to Cape Alava and the old village site. Virtually nothing remains of the dig, but here and there you can find signs the Ozette people left, most notably a series of petroglyphs that provide a palpable sense of their presence.

Probably the most fascinating aspect of the Makah museum is its display of whaling and fishing articles, including four replicated cedar dugout canoes. Bent-cedar boxes, basketry, fishing hooks and spears, and other tools are on display as well, along with an interesting collection of historical photos.

Makah Days, the tribe's annual powwow—with dancing, singing, traditional games, canoe races, and fireworks—is celebrated in late August.

GETTING THERE/ STAYING THERE

Neah Bay is literally on the edge of the continent, about four hours' drive from Seattle by any route and about two hours and 71 road miles west of Port Angeles, the largest town on the north Olympic Peninsula. From Port Angeles, or PA in local parlance, head west on US 101 and in about 44 miles turn right on State Route 113. Head north 10 miles to Clallam Bay, where SR 113 becomes SR 112. Follow SR 112 west; you'll pass the fishing village of Sekiu in 1 mile and reach Neah Bay in 17 miles. For a more scenic but winding route, turn right on SR 112 about 6 miles west of PA and follow signs west to Clallam Bay and Neah Bay.

LET IT BE

Beachcombing is not allowed on reservation beaches. For centuries the sea has been sending the Makah wood, whales, and just maybe iron on wrecked Asian junks that washed up centuries ago, and tribal members still use what various items wash ashore.

Don't expect a resort mecca when you arrive. There are a couple stores, gas, some lodging, cafés, and the Big Salmon Fishing Resort (see "Contacts and Resources" for all contact information). But this is a small reservation town. You won't find the Ritz, and there aren't any restaurants with a sous chef. If you want upscale, Port Angeles has what approximates that. There are also comfortable accommodations at Sekiu, just west of Clallam Bay along state SR 112.

Camping is available, along with cabins, at Hobuck Beach Resort, on the ocean side of Neah Bay. This spot is extremely popular among surfers and surf kayakers, who find decent breaks especially from late fall into spring, when storms generate big ocean swells at Hobuck Beach itself and just south at Tsoo-Yess Beach. The resort is also popular among anglers during the spring/summer halibut and salmon seasons. It offers an expansive, grassy camping area, with access to the ocean and room for several hundred tents ($20 each/night), plus 10 RV sites with full hookups ($30/night) and 26 cabins in several styles and prices. You can reserve the cabins, but campsites are first come, first served. A day pass for surfing and kayaking costs an additional $15.

FEES AND PERMITS

Any overnight visit in the Olympic National Park backcountry—Shi Shi Beach, for example—requires a wilderness fee of $5 for the party, plus $2 per person per night. You can get a permit at the Olympic National Park Wilderness Information Center in Port Angeles (see "Contacts and Resources" for all contact information). Hours are variable and iffy in the off-season, but you can pick up a fee envelope at park trailheads and mail the money in after your hike.

To visit Makah beaches, the marina, and trails, non–tribal members must purchase the Makah Recreation Pass, which is $10 per vehicle and good for one year. The permit is available at the museum, tribal headquarters, the marina, and stores in town. The money is put into maintaining recreational facilities.

Elsewhere in the region, on the way to Neah Bay, are trailheads that require the Washington State Discover Pass to park. The pass is $30 a year or $10 a day and is available online, from many hunting and fishing license vendors, and at various state park locations.

HIKING

SHIPWRECK POINT

LONESOME BEACH WITH BIG VIEWS

An often moody, lonesome stretch along the Strait of Juan de Fuca, Shipwreck Point anchors a state natural resource conservation area (NRCA) of the same name. The NRCA is 472 acres, with about 1 mile of shore along the strait, the point itself offering fine views that can include whales and other marine mammals. This trip is a great leg-stretcher after the long drive out to the so-called West End of Clallam County, or for a break from fishing. There are no actual trails here, just the beach and views across the strait to Vancouver Island. This is also a pleasant spot to just plunk your butt down and watch the watery world of the strait go by. The point and the conservation area are within the larger public lands of State Beach 429, which stretches ruggedly another 6 rocky miles west toward Neah Bay, if you're in the mood for a good workout.

Distance: 1.6 miles round-trip; up to 12 additional miles round-trip if you continue past the NRCA
Elevation gain: Almost none
Difficulty: 1–4, depending on the tide and how far you explore
Map: Google-map "Clallam County, WA" and zoom in on the west end along the strait; or Benchmark Maps' *Washington Road and Recreation Atlas*
Contact: Washington Department of Natural Resources
Notes: Discover Pass required to park. Rover must be on-leash inside the NRCA. Beware slippery footing on reefs and rocks.

Low tide is the best time to visit the Shipwreck Point area since you'll be able to explore tide pools and see the intertidal reefs along the shore.

DRIVING DIRECTIONS

From Sekiu, drive 8 miles west on State Route 112 and look for a pullout on the right (north) with interpretive signs. It's about 1 mile west of Chito Beach Resort and Ray's Grocery (friendly folks!). This is the main access to the conservation area. But from here west toward Neah Bay there are at least nine other obvious pullouts along SR 112 with easy access to the beach.

THE HIKE

Shipwreck Point offers a good illustration of how differing conditions can completely change the ambience of a stretch of shoreline. The first time I hiked here, the weather was misty-foggy, with sporadic drizzle but dead calm, and the tide was moderately low. The second time was cloudy and windy on a moderately high tide. The first time it felt like a mysterious and isolated shoreline ringed by rocks and reefs covered with algae that glowed green in the unusual light; an ordinary bald eagle flying overhead made it feel primordial. The second time it was just a nondescript gray shoreline landscape that lacked excitement, nothing stirring but seagulls.

So I'd say go on a morning low tide so you can poke around the rocks and tide pools. Sunny and clear weather will give you the best views of the strait and Vancouver Island. You could very well see marine mammals too, such as otters, seals, porpoise, even gray whales, although reefs keep most of them a bit offshore.

From the dirt pullout, walk the obvious short path north through the salmonberry bushes to the beach. You can only head east along the shore about 0.3 mile before reaching private land, so best head west, a more interesting direction anyway, with two rocky points ahead in the distance.

Here the shore is sandy, strewn with bull kelp and seaweed, the uplands heavily forested and deep green. If the tide is down, note the rocky, reefy nature just a short distance out. Continue west, looking out over the strait for ships, blows from whales, or the heads of seals. In about ⅛ mile, reach the first point, marked by horizontal rock slabs.

As you proceed west, the going gets more rocky and tough. About 0.5 mile from your rig, the mini sea stacks take on curious shapes. Here along the reefs scientists have found fossils of two extinct marine snails in sandstone strata and concretions (spherical compactions of sediments), one previously unknown and the other never before found on the Pacific Coast of North America.

At a bit more than 0.75 mile, you'll reach the end of the conservation area proper. But the public beach, State Beach 429, goes on. Turn around when you're so inclined.

KEEP EXPLORING

You can continue west for 6 more miles, though the going gets really rugged and difficult, except for sandy stretches around Jansen Creek (1.1 miles from the trailhead) and Rasmussen Creek (2.2 miles). The character of the shore becomes curious, with small, tree-topped sea stacks leaning precariously, resembling spots on the outer coast like Cape Flattery, but on a smaller scale.

CAPE FLATTERY

A HIKE TO THE EDGE OF THE EARTH

An easy but spectacular trail on the Makah Indian Nation leads to a historic spot at the very northwest corner of the contiguous forty-eight states, overlooking the entrance to the Strait of Juan de Fuca and a crazy labyrinth of sea stacks and sea caves. Just offshore is stunning Tatoosh Island, once the site of a Makah fishing camp and seasonal home to a feared chief, who gave the island its name. This is not a wilderness trail. It's short and easy, ideal for casual tourists. However, those with mobility issues will find it difficult. Put this hike on your must-do list.

Distance: 1.5 miles round-trip
Elevation gain: 200 feet
Difficulty: 2
Map: Custom Correct North Olympic Coast
Contact: Makah Indian Nation
Notes: Makah Recreation Pass required to park. Dogs prohibited.

DRIVING DIRECTIONS

From the town of Neah Bay, follow the main road (Bayview) west to Fort Street and turn south. Then shortly take a right on 3rd Street. Shortly again, go left on

One of the many coves of Cape Flattery

Cape Flattery Road, passing the tribal center in 2.5 more miles and reaching the marked trailhead at 4.5 miles, on the left.

THE HIKE

Skip downhill on this good trail through thick and pretty spruce, cedar, and salal shintangle—it's a little muddy in spots most of the time. Built commendably by the tribe, the trail is on a gravel surface, then boardwalk, reaching wooden viewing platforms above rocky coves at the cape's edge in 0.75 mile. These are exquisite spots, perched atop a rock spine above the sea. Offshore rocks and sea stacks are awash in the tide, the water a pretty aquamarine.

Amazingly, you can look on either side of this spine to the twin portals of the Makah version of Hole in the Wall (another version is farther south, just north of Rialto Beach). A sea cave cuts through the rock spine you're on. You can see both openings from platforms on either side. At the last split-cedar platform at the trail's end, you're looking out over Tatoosh Island. Bring binoculars to watch for seabirds and marine mammals, sometimes even gray whales, so I'm told.

This is one of the most historic points in the early annals of Washington State, searched for hundreds of years ago by numerous explorers in wooden ships seeking the fabled Northwest Passage. Geographically it's literally Land's End, the edge of the continent, the point at which the great inland Salish Sea (Puget Sound and associated waters) empties into the Pacific Ocean at the entrance of the Strait of Juan de Fuca. Geologically it's fascinating and scenically stunning, a tide-washed warren of sea coves and caves and rocky islets, marked by a historic lighthouse atop an island once used as a summer whaling and fishing village by the Makah.

British fur trader John Meares stopped at Tatoosh Island briefly while sailing south in the *Felice Adventurer* on June 29, 1788: "In a very short time we were surrounded by canoes filled with people of a much more savage appearance than we had hitherto seen," he wrote in his journal. This is quite a statement about the Makah, since Meares had just spent weeks on the west coast of Vancouver Island among related Nootka people, led by two feared and famous chiefs, Maquinna and Wickaninnish.

The large Makah canoes were each filled with twenty to thirty warriors dressed in sea otter skins. The warriors' faces were painted red and black, each in his own fashion, and they were armed with spears, bows, and arrows. Their chief was Tatoosh, his face painted entirely black and sprinkled with glitter—perhaps sand or crushed mica. It was an appearance that left a lasting impression. "So surly and forbidding a character we had not yet seen," Meares wrote. Tatoosh "informed us that the power of Wickananish ended here, and that we were now within the limits of his government."

The federal government built Washington Territory's third lighthouse on Tatoosh Island, the 64-foot Cape Flattery Light, which became operational in 1857. Bring your longest lens and a tripod if you want to capture photos of it. Today access is restricted on Tatoosh Island to researchers, most prominently from the University of Chicago marine biology program, and periodically to Coast Guard maintenance crews.

KEEP EXPLORING

A rough, boot-beaten path departs northerly from the main trail about ⅛ mile from the trailhead, dropping along two of the cape's other rocky spines. One spine reaches the strait at Mushroom Rock, which marks a fabled fishing spot for chinook salmon. DO NOT take Granny and the kids on this side path. It is used mostly by local fishermen and includes some serious exposure.

MUDDY SLOG ALONG BLUFF-TOP ROUTE

The northern access to Shi Shi begins on the Makah Reservation, and for several years it was officially closed due to liability issues with tribal landowners. The tribe acquired a state grant to reroute the trail away from private property and reopened the trail in the 1990s. The tribe did a great job with the reroute but apparently ran out of money short of the park boundary. The result is a 0.5-mile slog through deep mud most of the year on the final approach to the beach, a straight stretch atop the oceanside bluff that used to be a dirt road. I highly recommend waterproof boots—standard gear for any avid hiker—and gaiters.

SHI SHI BEACH TO POINT OF ARCHES

A BEACH SO SWEET IT HURTS TO LEAVE

Shi Shi Beach is stunningly beautiful and makes a great day hike or overnighter—it has made several "Best Beaches in America" lists. Shi Shi—pronounced "shy-shy"—is a phenomenal day hike, hands down one of the best on the coast. The mind-blowing configuration of primordial rock known as Point of Arches on Shi Shi's south end is why, a spot some consider the most beautiful on the entire coast. Because the approach is relatively easy, this is a great spot to take kids for a short backpack trip, if you hit the weather right. This is an extremely popular beach, jammed on sunny weekends spring through fall and busy anytime the weather isn't howling or spitting. So be forewarned if solitude is your goal.

Distance: 9 miles round-trip
Elevation gain: 200 feet
Difficulty: 3
Map: Custom Correct North Olympic Coast
Contact: Olympic National Park and Makah Indian Nation
Notes: Makah Recreation Pass required to park at Shi Shi trailhead. The tribe recommends against leaving your vehicle overnight due to occasional vandalism; nearby private homes offer protected parking for a small fee—add about 0.25 mile to your round-trip if you park there. Dogs prohibited. Fires allowed, but be courteous; don't build monster bonfires and make a racket late into the night. Pit toilets available.

As you approach Shi Shi Beach, you'll get glimpses of weirdly shaped sea rocks off Portage Head.

Be sure to check tide tables to plan exploration of Point of Arches (on the south end of the route) and Portage Head (on the north).

DRIVING DIRECTIONS

From the town of Neah Bay, follow the main road (Bayview) west to Fort Street and turn south. Then shortly take a right on 3rd Street. Shortly again, go left on Cape Flattery Road, following the signs for "Cape Flattery and Beaches" for a couple miles until you reach Hobuck Road. Go left, over the bridge across the Waatch River, and follow the signs for the fish hatchery for 4.3 miles to the marked trailhead.

THE HIKE

Shi Shi Beach has a storied history, once the target of developers and long a home to counterculture squatters. It was finally acquired by and incorporated into Olympic National Park in 1976, a damned good thing too, since it's such a treasure.

From the trailhead parking lot, the trail begins in second-growth forest, quickly dips through an old logging clear-cut, and then enters deep-green spruce and

The curious rock forms of Portage Head are worth exploring on a minus tide.

cedar forest, much of it on cedar puncheon boardwalk. In about 1.5 miles you intercept the old route atop the bluff and a muddy slog begins, ending at the park boundary and a descent to the beach, reached at 2.2 miles. Along the bluff-top route to the beach are at least two short boot trails leading west to the top of spectacular Portage Head, the site of World War II–era bunkers, now well overgrown.

The descent to the beach is steep, but short and easy. Shi Shi is a beach of gravel on the upland side and sand when the tide recedes, lined by a rocky reef at low tide. Probably because of its shape and aspect to the sea—a 2.3-mile crescent open to the northwest—Shi Shi is a nifty little beachcombing spot. Several years ago I found a softball-sized glass fishing float here. A couple weeks later a friend found two more about the same size.

Once you reach the beach and head south a few yards, look back north toward Portage Head. The rocks are shaped like none I've ever seen. If the tide is low, walk north and in less than 0.5 mile, find a sea cave with multiple openings and rusty remains of a shipwreck, the *General M. C. Meigs* (1972).

On the south end of Shi Shi Beach is magnificent Point of Arches, 4.5 miles from the trailhead, with several arches and more wild rock. It's also a rich ecosystem best explored on a minus tide: acres and acres of huge, blue-black California mussels, barnacles, purple and orange sea stars, deep-green anemones, hermit crabs, limpets, chitons, snails, and little flitting isopods (small crustaceans).

Several lovely camps line the beach, most near Petroleum Creek, 3.6 miles from the trailhead, tannin-stained brown but fine for drinking if filtered, treated,

If you don't time your hike to coincide with low tides in certain places like this spot south of the Ozette River, you'll find yourself clambering narrow ledges to keep your feet dry.

or boiled. Don't drink it straight from the flow; this area is known for rampant giardia, which produces the dreaded "beaver fever."

With all the cool rock, you can spend all day or two exploring here, and if you camp and skies are mostly blue, the sunset will knock your socks off.

FISHING THE NORTH COAST

The lore of the north Washington Coast is steeped in stories about fishing on the ocean and inside the Strait of Juan de Fuca, and most of them revolve around salmon—big salmon. These include three state records for sport-caught salmon, all taken off Sekiu, 17 miles inside the strait from the ocean: the biggest documented catch of any salmon by a sport fisherman in Washington, a 70.5-pound chinook caught in 1964; a 25.34-pound coho taken in 2001; and a 9.37-pound sockeye caught in 2004.

The north coast is also known for its superb bottomfish angling—arguably the best anywhere in the United States outside of Alaska—and it has produced a host of state records. The most notable was the 288-pound halibut caught at Swiftsure Bank in 1989—so big a backhoe was used to hoist it up for photos when it was landed at Neah Bay.

This part of the planet is just a fishy place: the waters surrounding this northwesternmost corner of the Lower 48 are incredibly rich and diverse, and there are a couple reasons why. All along the Washington Coast, a broad and relatively shallow continental shelf extends offshore some 6 miles before the ocean bottom drops off into the abyss of the Pacific. Prevailing winds and currents create an upwelling of nutrient-rich waters from these great depths, primarily in spring and summer, which generates an intense phytoplankton bloom along the shelf and lays a fertile foundation for the food chain—all the way from krill, herring, anchovies, bottomfish, shellfish, salmon, sharks, seabirds, marine mammals, right up to humans.

Throw into this mix a complex of interspersed rocky and sandy shores, extensive and hugely productive kelp forests, along with tides that swing back and forth twice each day, and the result is an incredible diversity of species. The geography of this part of the coast is also critical. Here the Strait of Juan de Fuca meets the Pacific and delivers the flow of many rivers from the great inland Salish Sea. So not only are these waters rich in forage for salmon, they are also a critical intersection on the homeward migrations of these fish.

Sunrises viewed while fishing at Sekiu along the Strait of Juan de Fuca can be breathtaking.

The open ocean is fished for salmon and halibut primarily by charter boats out of Neah Bay and by private anglers who have larger boats that can handle big seas. But Sekiu, 17 miles inside the strait, is known as an excellent small-boat fishery. Although seas can blow up here as well, and fog often obscures navigation, this area is safe for smaller boats, say 16 to 22 feet, most of the time from late spring well into fall. Rental boats are available at Sekiu as well.

Several small rivers that flow into the sea provide fair angling for winter steelhead, but none are among the biggest producers of these fish in Washington. These streams are definitely fun to explore but are fished mostly by local anglers, a few of whom also fish for sea-run cutthroat in summer and fall.

For regulatory purposes, the saltwaters here are divided at the Sekiu River, with those to the west part of the state's Marine Area 4 and those to the east part of Marine Area 5. Seasons and limits for Marine Area 4 are set as part of the ocean fisheries, while those for Marine Area 5 are set as part of the inland marine fisheries. The seasons do overlap in many cases, but when you check the regulations you need to check both areas. It's complicated for sure. Check with the Washington Department of Fish and Wildlife and relevant tribes (see "Contacts and Resources" under "Fishing Information and Regulations"), and be sure to pick up a copy of the Washington Sport Fishing Rules Pamphlet when you purchase your fishing license.

Here's a synopsis of the year-round fishing opportunities on the north coast:

January: Winter steelhead is the primary fishing activity, and the best river in this region is the pretty Hoko, where a native run is holding its own, supplemented by hatchery steelhead. January is prime time for hatchery steelhead, and other hatchery-augmented rivers include the Sooes on the Makah Indian Reservation (tribal license required) and the Sekiu. The Clallam and Pysht rivers are no longer planted but do have small wild runs and get a few hatchery strays.

February: Winter steelhead continues in the aforementioned rivers, and most years in mid-February fishing for "blackmouth," or feeding chinook, opens in Marine Area 5 off Sekiu. Blackmouth fishing can be very good here anytime of the year (when open), and some of these chinook push 20 pounds. Fishing is limited primarily by the weather, which can be stormy in winter. This season usually extends into April and is fished mostly by locals, but if you've got a boat and the time to wait for fair weather, this is a fishery to keep in mind.

March: Most local rivers are closed by March for winter steelhead, except the Hoko, which is open through March 15 and can be good. Blackmouth fishing also continues, weather allowing, and a few locals start heading out about now for rockfish in the waters of Marine Area 4, west of the Sekiu River.

April: Blackmouth fishing continues when open, and a few more anglers start heading out into Marine Area 4 off Neah Bay for rockfish and lingcod—the latter usually opens midmonth.

May: This is a bottomfish month throughout the region, with rockfish and lingcod the primary target and then halibut, which typically opens mid- or late month, with different seasons and regulations between Marine Areas 4 and 5. The Area 4 halibut season is tightly regulated and variable to the extent that many private-boat anglers now ignore it, although it can be extremely good both offshore and nearshore. Charter boats out of Neah Bay do fish halibut whenever it's open and do extremely well.

June: The salmon season usually opens late in the month off Neah Bay, but June remains primarily a bottomfish period, with halibut fishing in full swing off Sekiu. This is usually a deep-water fishery, with anglers using as much as 2 pounds of weight to hit the bottom anywhere from 140 to 300 feet down, dragging baits such as large "horse" herring or octopus. Anglers who obtain and study bathymetric charts and then use GPS to locate sandy shelves and ledges offshore where halibut feed can do very well. However, halibut are taken throughout the waters of the strait east and west of Sekiu, most of which are sandy bottom just offshore. Sea-run cutthroat begin to move into most rivers and creeks late in the month.

July: This is the month of the king salmon, the time when mature chinook head in from the ocean, feeding ravenously as they go, bound for their home rivers. Mid-July to the second week in August is the best time for kings anywhere from just inside the strait east past Sekiu. The same holds true for the ocean off Neah Bay, perhaps a week or so earlier at the peak. And anywhere in the Neah Bay region coho salmon will be snapping as well, beginning to gain respectable size by the end of the month. Chinook spots include Mukkaw Bay and the point known as Skagway south of Cape Flattery; Slant and Mushroom rocks inside the strait east of the cape; and Waadah Island right off Neah Bay. In the Sekiu area, great king spots include "the Caves" just west of Sekiu Point and the whole shore from there west for a few miles; the 20-fathom line on the outer edge of Clallam Bay; the bell buoy off Slip Point and numerous spots from there east, including Mussolini Rock, the Slides, Little Mussolini, and past "the Coal Mines" to Pillar Point. In odd-numbered years, pink salmon begin to appear in big numbers by the end of the month. Sea-run cutts can be found in the deeper pools of lower rivers as they move upstream out of tidewater.

August: During the first week or ten days of this month I'm still hunting big king salmon, but as the days pass the salmon runs transition to a preponderance of coho. By midmonth the bulk of the king run has moved inland, and the front end of the ocean coho run is nosing in, joining schools of smaller "resident" coho that spend most of their sea time foraging on herring and candlefish closer to home. In odd-numbered years, the main push of pink salmon is now moving on through this region, and in big years a bonus limit of sometimes six per day is allowed. "Humpies" are easy to catch and provide plenty of action, so they're fun for the kids. If you take proper care of them, bleeding them immediately and cleaning and icing them as soon as possible, they're very good on the barbie or in the smoker.

September: This is peak time for big ocean coho, some of which can be 16, 18, even more than 20 pounds, and in good years provide frenzied action here. They prefer surface waters well offshore, as opposed to chinook, which tend to stay near the bottom and near the shore most of the time. Usually I'll start at depths of about 250 feet and head out, with the lines set at 15 or 20 feet. I'll typically use a plug-cut herring behind a shiny dodger attractor on one line and a plastic "hootchie" squid with a herring strip on the hooks on the other, also behind a dodger.

October: The ocean salmon season is over by now, and things are getting quiet along the strait at Sekiu too. But the tail end of the coho run is still around, especially early in the month, and many years fishing for feeding chinook, or "blackmouth," is open in October in Marine Area 5 off Sekiu. In recent years, most of the local rivers have remained closed for salmon. But in strong coho years when rivers are open, anglers will fish them—a medium-sized spinner is your best lure.

November: This is the slowest month of the year for fishing in this region, with a few winter steelhead appearing in the rivers by around Thanksgiving.

December: It's all a winter steelhead show now, and by late in the month the bulk of the hatchery run has arrived. The Hoko and Sooes rivers are heavily fished by locals, who also hit the Sekiu, Clallam, and Pysht.

SHI SHI TO OZETTE THROUGH-HIKE

COASTAL BACKPACKING AT ITS FINEST

During his coastal explorations in the 1790s, Captain George Vancouver described the area thus: "Beetling cliffs, ragged reefs, and huge masses of rock cut by the waves abound on every side." You'll feel like an explorer too, or Robinson Crusoe, while scaling the steep, isolated headlands and navigating remote pocket coves as you hike your way past Point of Arches toward the Lake Ozette area. This is the single roughest stretch of shore within Olympic National Park's 70-mile wilderness strip, arguably the most rugged area of the entire Washington Coast. It's also one of Washington's—and America's—most adventurous ocean backpack trips, 15+ rocky, exquisite, wild miles. The hike from Point of Arches south is best done during the milder months, with minus tides. You must ford the Ozette River (or take a boring inland detour) and you can't cross that stream from midfall through midspring because of high flows,

LOOK FOR THE ORANGE AND BLACK

When approaching headlands that you must climb, look for the round signs with an orange and black cross. They mark the route, and you'll find the end of a rope for climbing nearby.

except during dry spells. The rugged up and down of the headlands south of Point of Arches culminates in a boulder-field scramble that is some serious business if you don't have a minus tide or close to it. You finally emerge, all sweaty I guarantee, on a crescent-shaped and open 3-mile sand/gravel beach that leads to the mouth of the Ozette River.

GLOVES HELP ON STEEP HEADLAND CLIMBS

Gloves are highly functional for hiking Shi Shi to Ozette, since you'll be grabbing lengths of rope to scale and descend steep headlands up to six times, depending on tide levels. Some headlands can be rounded at tides lower than 4–6 feet. I haven't measured them, but these are some of the highest headlands on the coast, the southernmost at least 250 feet. Park rangers have fixed ropes at several points to assist the journey, like elsewhere along the park's beach strip—but nowhere as intense as here.

Distance: About 15.8 miles one-way
Elevation gain: Up to 600 feet
Difficulty: 5
Map: Custom Correct North Olympic Coast
Contact: Olympic National Park and Makah Indian Nation
Notes: Makah Recreation Pass required to park at Shi Shi trailhead. The tribe recommends against leaving your vehicle overnight due to occasional vandalism; nearby private homes offer protected parking for a small fee. Olympic National Park wilderness permit required for overnight stays; reservations required May 1–September 30 to camp south of Point of Arches. Food must be kept in bear-proof container. Dogs prohibited. Fires allowed. Pit toilets available at Shi Shi Beach and Cape Alava. You'll need tide tables to know when you can round certain headlands.

DRIVING DIRECTIONS

From Neah Bay, follow the main road (Bayview) to Fort Street and turn south. Then shortly turn right on 3rd Street. Shortly again, go left on Cape Flattery Road, following the signs for "Cape Flattery and Beaches" for a couple miles until you reach Hobuck Road. Go left, over the bridge across the Waatch River, and follow the signs for the fish hatchery for 4.3 miles to the marked trailhead. To leave a

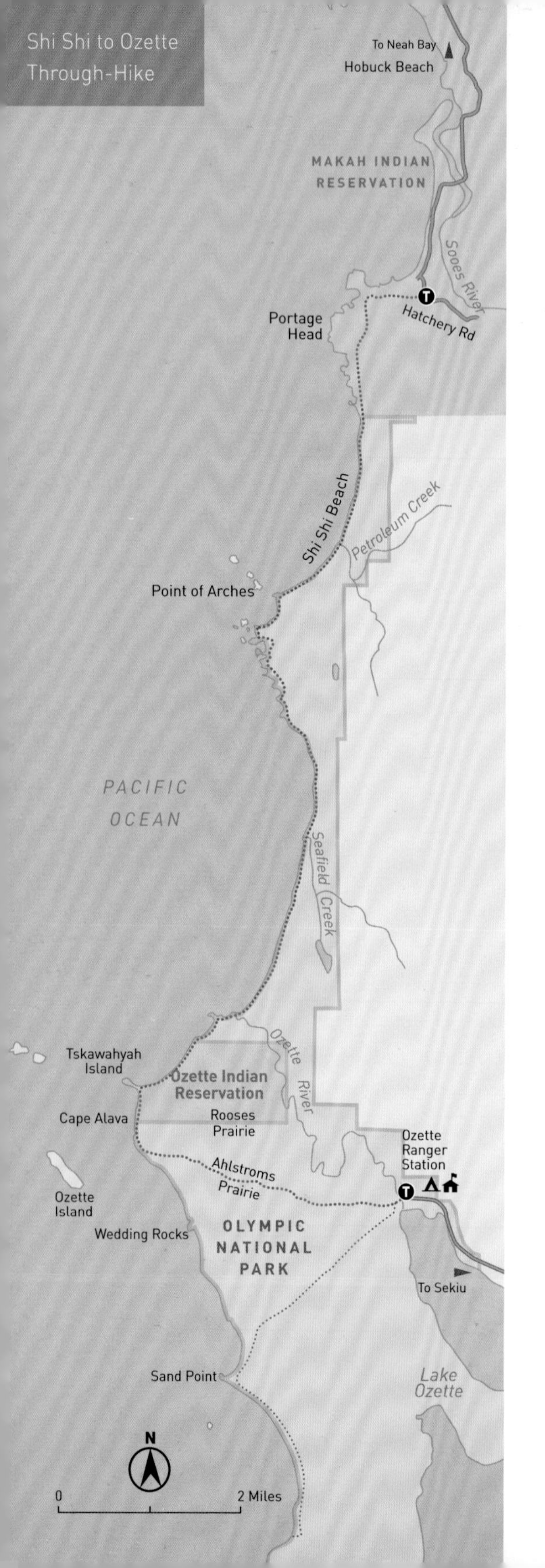

car at the south end of this hike, see "Getting There/Staying There" in this chapter's Lake Ozette and Sekiu region; the south trailhead is at the Ozette Ranger Station. If someone is picking you up, that's where they'll need to go.

THE HIKE

From the Shi Shi trailhead, hike along the muddy bluff and follow the wondrous beach to its south end at 4.5 miles, at a pyramid-shaped sea stack, the nearest to shore of a myriad that make up Point of Arches. Round a rocky corner to a cobble-littered cove and make your way south to a sort of keyhole-shaped arch—go directly through it! Look for birds like black oystercatchers and harlequin ducks here, feeding among the reefs and tide pools. At the end of the cove, 4.6 miles in, reach a steep bluff and crane your neck to find the rope and route to the top. Sit down, tighten your boot laces, and prepare yourself for the roughest section of the entire Washington Coast. Then climb, matey, and don't look down!

Reach the top of this shrub-carpeted headland and find an intersection. To the right there's a crazy narrow spine of a headland that can be climbed to its end—be careful, there is some exposure—where the sea breeze will whip through your hair and the ocean will be crashing on all sides below. Out there

Don't be surprised to find sea lions hauled out on wilderness beaches. Give them space; they can move on land faster than you might imagine.

it feels like you're perched in the crow's nest of Vancouver's twenty-gun HMS *Discovery.* As you scout the way, look down to the shore on the left; there's a large arch and the ocean is surging right through it. That's where you'll end up if you slip. Don't say I didn't warn you.

The way to the left is the main trail and enters forest and circles a cove below. In less than 0.5 mile, the route descends with rope assist to another cove, a tiny boulder-strewn pocket beach 5 miles from the Shi Shi trailhead. I call this Spray Cove, because the ocean bashes into the rock on either side, sending white spray flying when the tide is just so. Pick your way over the rocks to another headland and more rope.

At the top you've got an up-and-down forest walk of better than 0.5 mile. Toward the south end of this headland trail, look for mature Sitka spruce with impressive girth and huge burls low on the trunks, at least one of them hippo-sized. These round growths are common on bluff-top spruce along the northern Washington Coast. No one knows why, but you've got to suspect it's either the strong winds, salt spray, or both.

The route descends, reaching the beach at 5.7 miles. From here south it's more up and down for the next 0.5 mile. At low tide you can round the points. Otherwise, you can climb up and over. Ultimately, at about 6.4 miles, there's a field of boulders at the south end of this rugged complexity of up-and-down headlands. The boulders are daunting if the tide is not very low, requiring serious scrambling over and around house-sized rocks. On a minus tide you can skirt most of the boulders on an intertidal reef that nonetheless requires slow and careful hiking.

Reach the end of this difficult section and breathe a sigh of relief: it's 3+ relatively gentle miles all on the beach to the Ozette River. On your way, look out beyond the breakers to the cluster of offshore rocks in the vicinity of Seafield Creek. This area is known for its concentration of sea otters, which have rebounded after being hunted nearly to extinction all along the Washington Coast by early in the twentieth century. (See "Return of the Sea Otter" in this chapter.)

As for the Ozette River (at 10.4 miles), for much of the year it's not fordable. Even during the dry season, it can't be crossed when the tide is high. So wait until flows are low, typically late June through October, and always cross at low tide.

There is a bail-out route if you get stuck by sudden high flows, or if you simply must do this trip during the wetter months. About 2.2 miles north of the Ozette River, near Seafield Creek, you'll notice two cabins in the bluffs above the beach, both park in-holdings. You can find logging roads in this area that lead inland and south to the Ozette Ranger Station. As for the in-holdings, the wilderness character of this beach would certainly be enhanced if the cabins weren't there. But when I've been here, they were relatively unobtrusive.

Back on the main route, once you get across the Ozette River, it's about 5.4 miles south and then east to the Ozette Ranger Station. There are two small headlands south of the river that require moderately low tides to cross, but both can easily be climbed over. Cape Alava, the westernmost point on the Washington Coast, is now in sight 1 mile south, and you've also just entered the uninhabited Ozette Indian Reservation, site of a renowned archaeological excavation in the 1970s.

Rounding the cape, you'll pass several campsites, always busy in summer, and find a trail marker at the base of a grassy bluff. Here the route leads inland to the ranger station on a 3.1-mile trail, much of it cedar puncheon boardwalk that is slippery when wet. If you've got camp shoes, change into them, since lug-soled boots are especially slippery on the boards. This trail is part of the 9-mile Ozette Loop, one of the premier day hikes on the coast and a popular short backpack (fully described later in this chapter).

As you leave the beach, congratulate yourself: you have just traveled one of the wildest stretches of coast in America. One October night a few years ago, a massive bull sea lion hauled himself up on shore not 200 yards away from our beach camp near Seafield Creek. In the morning he was gone, but not more than 200 yards from our camp in the other direction, we found fresh black bear tracks.

You really feel like you're part of nature on this stretch of the coast. It truly engages your senses. You can taste the saltwater on your lips, smell it in the air, hear it in your ears. Your heart races a little at times. The challenge is to be part of it and not be part of it. Take home the emotional bonding that experiences like this can offer. But don't leave anything of yourself. Wander through and wonder, and then leave this place to the lions and bears.

LAKE OZETTE AND SEKIU

THE LITTLE VILLAGE AT THE NORTH end of Lake Ozette is really nothing more than an access point and campground, but this gateway leads to fascinating history, beautiful ocean beaches, superb hiking and backpacking, and a fine big sheet of freshwater for paddling and camping. The Ozette Ranger Station is the starting point for the wildly popular Ozette Loop, which can be done as a 9-mile day hike or overnighter. It also is the starting or ending point for two challenging through-hikes on Olympic National Park's priceless 70-mile wilderness beach strip: north leads to Shi Shi Beach, south to Rialto Beach at the mouth of the Quillayute River. The lake itself makes for an intriguing canoe or kayak paddle, and it is not heavily used.

Sekiu is a small fishing village on the Strait of Juan de Fuca, which virtually everyone passes through en route to Ozette and Neah Bay. It's a legendary salmon

A dead calm morning at Ericsons Bay on Lake Ozette

fishing locale among anglers (early July–September, mostly chinook and coho), with accommodations, some services, and along with the adjacent town of Clallam Bay, pleasant beaches. During the spring through fall fishing seasons, Sekiu is populated primarily by fishermen, but plenty of tourists stop here to spend the night or hit one of the few restaurants.

The proposed 835-acre Hoko River State Park a few miles west of Sekiu would greatly expand tourist appeal, with its dispersed collection of beaches, former farms and ranches, and the river's estuary, site of important archaeological

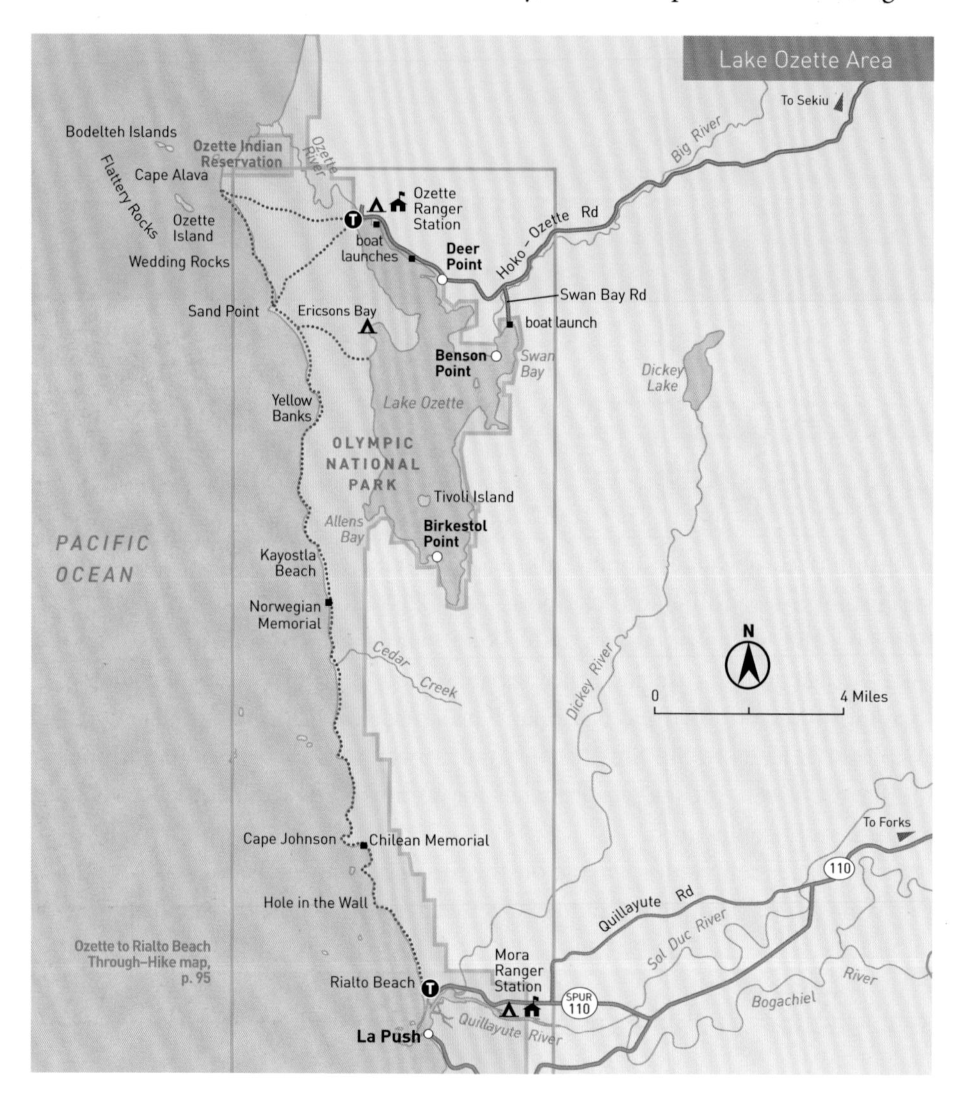

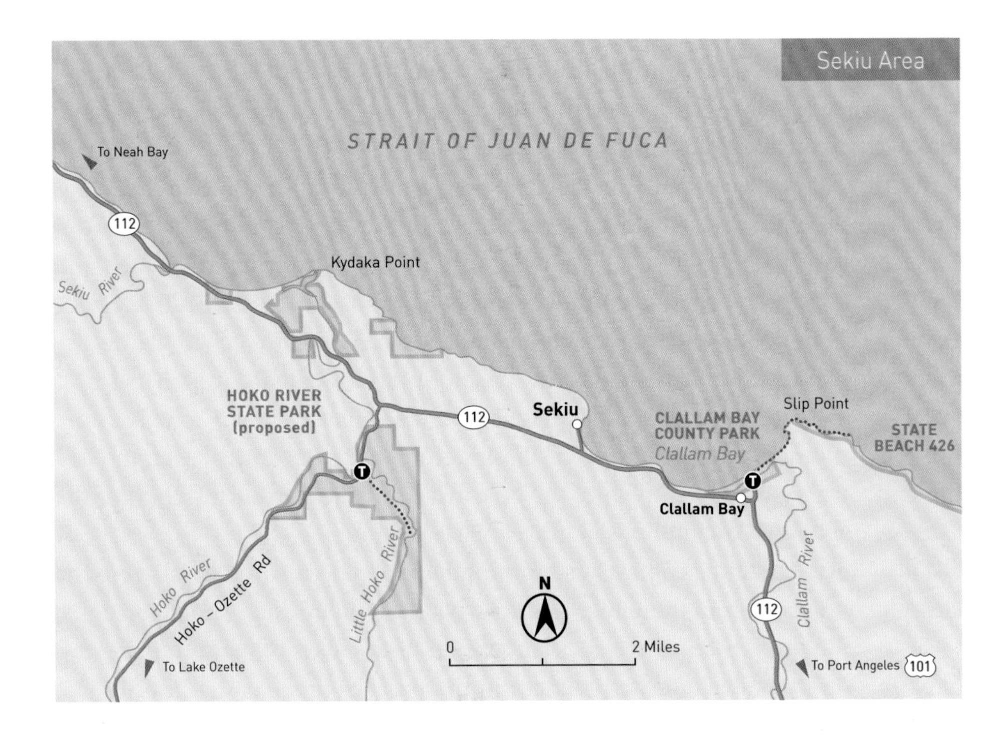

excavations in the 1970s and early 1980s. The park could become a culturally fascinating area masterpiece, with a sorely needed public campground.

You'll follow the course of the Hoko River en route to the Ozette area, which was once the domain of the Ozette, or Osett, people, a large and powerful band of the Makah tribe who lived at Cape Alava and hunted whales, sea lions, seals, dolphins, and sea otters. Seasonally, they followed salmon up the Ozette River to the lake, and every few summers they burned the prairies between to encourage the growth of ferns, roots, and berries (salal, salmonberry, huckleberry, cranberry). The burns also promoted the growth of shrubs, grasses, and sedges that attracted the deer, elk, and bear that the tribe hunted. Although a small reservation was established here and remains, most of the band was gone by the late nineteenth century, devastated by introduced smallpox and other diseases, the survivors all moving to Neah Bay by the 1920s. In the 1970s, archaeologists excavated several cedar-plank houses at Cape Alava that had been buried by a slide about three hundred years ago, revealing a fascinating record of life here before Europeans arrived.

The Lake Ozette area and prairies were also home to an active European community during the late nineteenth and early twentieth centuries, and signs of their farms and orchards remain on islands in the lake and on the prairies. There is still some private land on the lake, and just to the east are large tracts of private, intensively managed timberlands. But by and large this region is public land, managed by the National Park Service.

Culturally and recreationally the Ozette region is intriguing in itself and leads to some of the finest coastal hiking in America—no exaggeration! But all is not perfect here. The Park Service folks who work at Lake Ozette are dedicated and do a terrific job. But they need more resources. Some of the trails are in poor shape. For years the beaches west of Lake Ozette have been reached via decaying, often rickety, and usually slippery, unsafe split-cedar boardwalk. Miles of it need to be replaced by a better alternative, and it seems that finally a fix is under way. With a grant from the nonprofit Washington's National Parks Fund, in 2014 the Park Service replaced much of the boardwalk on the northern stretch of the Ozette Loop with a tread of raised gravel beds—yay!

I also worry about the cultural resources and habitats here, some at risk from the elements and some from thoughtless visitors. More could be done, should be done, to restore the threatened native sockeye salmon of the lake, brought to the brink of extinction by poor land-use practices in the past. Unique coastal prairies just inland from the sea are gradually being eliminated by encroaching forest. These boggy heaths were created by centuries of periodic burning by the Ozette people and now host rare species, including two butterflies, the Ozette skipper and Makah copper. The Park Service has suggested prescribed burns to restore the prairies, but the controversial plan has been put on the back burner, so to speak.

I realize that the Park Service is seriously short of funding and people power, chronically and perpetually. Salmon restoration is also the responsibility of the state, which lacks adequate funding for natural resources. But the park does charge overnight backcountry camping fees and an entrance fee at Ozette—I wish more of that revenue would go to the needed work here. The Ozette area is, after all, one of the most popular and important places in Olympic National Park. This fascinating and beautiful region is absolutely worth not just visiting, but spending some serious time exploring.

GETTING THERE/STAYING THERE

Ozette is about as far west as you can go in the United States, close to five driving hours from Seattle. Sekiu is on the way, about 45 minutes closer to the big city. From Port Angeles, head west on US 101 and in about 44 miles turn right on State Route 113. Head north 10 miles to Clallam Bay, where SR 113 veers west

A backpacker weaves her way through a typical rocky beach along the wilderness shore of Olympic National Park.

and becomes SR 112. Continue on west on SR 112 and reach Sekiu in about 1 mile. For Lake Ozette, drive about another 2.5 miles west and turn left at the Olympic National Park sign, heading south on the Hoko–Ozette Road. Follow it for 21 miles to the campground, ranger station, trailhead parking area, and restrooms.

Many who come to day hike the Ozette area stay at any of several motels in the Sekiu–Clallam Bay area. There is a food co-op and store with gas at Clallam Bay and two or three restaurants at Sekiu, plus several fishing resorts. I often stay at Bay Motel just off of SR 112. The rooms are basic but clean, comfortable, and affordable, and there's a restaurant next door. For all your options here, check the Clallam Bay–Sekiu Chamber of Commerce (see "Contacts and Resources" for all contact information).

At Lake Ozette, the private Lost Resort about 0.25 mile short of the ranger station (north side of road) offers 30 campsites ($20/night) spread over 10 acres, 3 cabins ($80/night), and a café—with beer on tap! Pets are not allowed at the campsites or cabins.

There are also private campgrounds along SR 112 from Clallam Bay to Neah Bay, mostly geared toward fishermen and none of them particularly appealing. Hobuck Beach Resort, all the way in Neah Bay, has camping and cabins too. The Ozette–Sekiu area desperately needs a great campground, so keep your fingers crossed that the Hoko River State Park becomes a reality.

A sea stack island off the bay at Chilean Memorial

FEES AND PERMITS

Olympic National Park charges an entrance fee at Lake Ozette. If you've already paid the wilderness overnight fee for backpacking, you're OK. Otherwise, you'll need an annual park pass (Federal Interagency Pass, $80; or the Olympic-specific pass, $30, available at the WIC and entrance stations), or you can pay a day-use fee ($15 per vehicle; $5 by foot, bike, or motorcycle; good for seven days). Find the pay box and envelopes at the signpost near the parking area and deposit your fee.

Any overnight visit in the park's backcountry requires a wilderness fee of $5 for the party, plus $2 per person per night. Obtain permits at the park's Wilderness Information Center (WIC) in Port Angeles (see "Contacts and Resources" for all contact information). Hours are variable and iffy in the off-season, but you can pick up a fee envelope at park trailheads and mail the money in after your hike. From May 1 through September 30, you must make a reservation through the WIC to camp anywhere between Yellow Banks and Point of Arches, a stretch of about 10 miles, including the entire Ozette Loop.

As for the Ozette Ranger Station, it keeps regular hours during the late spring and summer but is often closed in the off-season, which for me is the best time to visit. This area is heavily visited and super busy in summer.

CAMPING

LAKE OZETTE

The lake sports one of Olympic National Park's smallest campgrounds (and mediocre at that). It's open year-round but is a stark place in winter, the lake often flooding much of it, no leaves on the trees, and no privacy. Late spring through fall is more pleasant, with the shrubs and trees leafing out and lightening the ambience, plus adding a bit of privacy. The campground is right on the lake, with a few of the sites just back from the shore. In summer it's a busy place, very close to the ranger station, boat ramp, and trailhead parking area, but it's a decent base camp for exploring the nearby wildlands.

The campground has 15 sites, running water (in summer), and pit toilets. RV space is limited (longer than 21 feet not recommended), and there are no hookups. Sites are first come, first served, all $12 per night, and all with fire pits and picnic tables.

Contact: Olympic National Park. **Driving directions:** From State Route 112 in Sekiu, drive west about 2.5 miles to the Hoko–Ozette Road and turn left. Drive 21 miles to the end of the road and the campground.

BEAR CREEK

Located in a lovely forest of tall conifers along the pretty riffles and rapids of the Sol Duc River, this free Washington Department of Natural Resources campground is open year-round. The bummer is minimal services: no garbage cans, no hookups, no showers, no reservations taken. The 11 sites do have fire rings and picnic tables, and there is a trail along the river, which is a prime steelhead stream. You can catch these big fish right there; I have. There are two accessible toilets. Pets are allowed on leash. There is a seven-day limit on camping.

Contact: Washington Department of Natural Resources. **Driving directions:** From Clallam Bay, head south on State Route 112, continuing straight in 6.2 miles where it becomes SR 113. At 16.2 miles from Clallam Bay, go left on US 101. Follow it east 1.9 miles to the campground entrance on the right (south) side of the highway. From Port Angeles, head west about 41 miles on US 101, then take a left into the signed campground entrance.

BACKCOUNTRY CAMPING

The backcountry shoreline here is the only part of Olympic National Park's wilderness beaches where camping is limited using a permit system, due to the area's popularity. From May 1 through September 30, you must make a reservation via the park's Wilderness Information Center to camp anywhere between Yellow Banks and Point of Arches, including the entire Ozette Loop. This is also the only major area of the park's beach strip where fires are restricted, to minimize damage to habitat. Fires are not permitted anytime from the Wedding Rocks headland on the Ozette Loop south to Yellow Banks, a stretch of about 4 miles.

HIKING

CLALLAM BAY/SLIP POINT
TIDE-POOLING AT ITS COLORFUL BEST

The dazzling tide pools at Slip Point on the east side of Clallam Bay rival others on the Northwest Coast in richness and diversity. Although 17 miles along the Strait of Juan de Fuca east of the ocean, these tide pools exhibit the characteristics of the unprotected outer coast, washed as they are by the tides and swift currents that drain the Salish Sea. Slip Point is one of the best places anywhere to see the pretty purple sea urchin—thousands of them. There is interesting history here as well, though few know it. Intrepid coastal trekkers willing to hike over rugged, slippery tidal rocks and boulders can also explore wild, seldom-visited shoreline landscapes of the strait to the east, if they choose a minus tide and time the visit to avoid getting trapped by the flood on the return. The tide pools here are relatively unprotected (as in no park or preserve status) and so in my opinion they are at risk, demanding a gentle touch. Please do not remove live creatures from their niches. Look, take photos, touch gently if at all.

A tide pool at Slip Point full of pretty purple urchins

Distance: 1.5 miles round-trip to explore tide pools; 2 miles round-trip to Slip Point, including short stroll to and from Clallam River mouth
Elevation gain: Almost none
Difficulty: 2; 3 if you explore east of Slip Point
Map: Washington Department of Ecology, Coastal Atlas, https://fortress.wa.gov/ecy/coastalatlas (under "Find a Public Beach," search for "Clallam Bay State Park")
Contact: Washington State Parks and Clallam County
Notes: Day use only, no camping. Dogs permitted on-leash; don't let them run wild on the exposed rocky tidelands, which is prohibited and, anyway, would be rough on their paws. The shoreline east of the point is public, designated State Beach 426, stretching 8+ miles to Pillar Point; it's really rugged and you need a low tide to explore. A minus tide is best for exploring tide pools.

DRIVING DIRECTIONS

This hike is reached through Clallam Bay County Park, which is actually on state park lands managed by Clallam County. In the town of Clallam Bay, precisely where State Route 112 turns sharply to the west, go north into the signed Clallam Bay County Park parking lot, usually open dawn to dusk.

THE HIKE

You'll walk through little-known history en route to the colorful Slip Point tide pools, including the site of a Klallam Indian village, now but a silent memory, swallowed up by the clash of cultures that followed the arrival of Europeans. A lighthouse tower also once rose from the shore here, but all that's left is the quaint Victorian-style lightkeeper's quarters, now the residence of the local county sheriff's deputy.

Bring the kids because they'll love this hike if the tide is out, and bring a bag for stones and shells. There are just a few agates to be found here, but a lot of pretty rocks, including small jasper and petrified wood pieces, and you can find shells of urchins, clams, and mussels, sometimes sea scallop. Please collect only small amounts for personal use. Bring the binoculars too because you'll see bald eagles and gulls, sometimes loons, harlequin ducks, rufous hummingbirds, and seals.

From the parking area, follow the blacktop trail past the restrooms to a footbridge over the Clallam River. Emerge on the heavily graveled shore of Clallam Bay just east of the mouth of the river, where the confluence of fresh- and saltwater attracts a host of gulls, often bald eagles, and sometimes shorebirds; head down there if you'd like to shoot a pic. Then head east along the gravel shore toward the old keeper's quarters and Slip Point. You'll find the footing very loose in the gravel; the backs of your thighs might feel it after this hike, as short as it is.

What happened to the lighthouse? With modern digital electronics, it was no longer necessary, particularly with the shipping lanes today well out in the strait. When the first light tower was erected in 1916, various craft of the Salish Sea's Mosquito Fleet made stops here, rounding shallow and rocky Slip Point, now marked by a green bell buoy, to a pier now long gone. The buoy is also a noteworthy beacon to salmon anglers; the chinook fishing off that bell can be phenomenal. I have put many kings in the boat while listening to its gong.

Somewhere more than halfway to the point, less then 0.5 mile from the parking lot, were several houses of the Klallam Indians who once lived on Clallam Bay, in a village called Hunnint. On the west side of Clallam Bay was the village of Klatlawas. The two together were called Xainant or Xanjinat, the *x* pronounced in guttural fashion, as in the German *ich*. Almost nothing is known of this specific band, which by the 1881 census had dwindled to forty-six people. They were a powerful group, noted for their skill in song and dance, the only band among the Klallams with the spirit power to hunt whales, like their Makah neighbors.

In July of 1790, Spanish naval officer Manuel Quimper sailed into the bay on a charting expedition. He was met by twelve canoes of Klallams, who towed his ship, *Princess Real*, to a safe anchorage. The Indians brought salmonberries and fish to the Spaniards—this would have been during the peak of the chinook salmon run. Quimper in return gave them pieces of metal cask hoops, iron being coveted by the Natives.

It doesn't take long to reach the pools at about 0.7 mile, and if it's a minus tide this place comes alive, each pool a complex, watery world of its own. Use extra care and caution while exploring the rocks and reefs, for two reasons. First, the rocks and especially the kelp and seaweed surfaces are extremely slippery. Second, the majority of the rocky surface is covered by living creatures, such as limpets, snails, barnacles, and mussels. These rocks hold vast beds especially of huge California mussels, the shells of which the Natives ground sharply into knives and harpoon points for whale hunting. Piles of mussel shell carpet parts of the shoreline here, in the nooks against the bluffs.

Using care not to crush anything, fully explore the tide pools, rich in orange sea stars, giant green anemones, smaller pinkish-red proliferating anemones, the armored black katy chiton, and most spectacularly, the curious purple urchin. The urchins especially are beautiful, with an ovoid endoskeleton, or "test," of up to 4 inches across, with dozens of purple spines radiating outward. They live in hordes, and a tide pool full of them is a dazzling world of purple brilliance. They have the uncanny ability to bore into the rocks, apparently with their five teeth, which ordinarily they use to eat algae and kelp. Over time the tide pool rocks become pitted with dozens or hundreds of urchin pockets, and you can see this quite plainly here. Sunflower sea stars and sea otters eat these urchins; sea otters were spotted here in the early 2000s, but not in the last several years—which is probably why the urchins are proliferating.

You'll pass beachfront homes on the way to and from the point. The unwritten beach hiker's code (mine anyway) demands that you respect the owners' privacy, so don't let your dog crap in their yard, don't leave litter, don't sit on the beach jabbering obscenities.

This isn't the kind of place for that anyway. It's the kind of place to feel the sea breeze in your hair, to listen to the waves rush up the shore, and to marvel at how nature's complexities can make your own seem irrelevant.

KEEP EXPLORING

If low tide allows, you might want to round the point and explore to the east along the strait, where upland bluffs plunge perpendicular to the rocky shore. This is not a great place to take the kids, though. It's super slippery, a rough boulder traverse, and an eerie world at times as you skirt the bluffs. Beach crabs and isopods use the low tide to climb up on rocks and logs, apparently to consume algae and rotting seaweed, scuttling away en masse as you approach, sometimes dropping off the boulders in retreat.

If you look close enough at the sandstone rocks and blocks at the base of the bluffs, you can find fossils embedded within, clams of common appearance, but also large, scallop-like bivalves. These are from an extinct clam known as pectens, from the Pliocene epoch 5 to 7 million years ago. Make sure to allow yourself enough time to get back around Slip Point before it becomes inundated by the incoming tide.

Back near the parking area, you can also wade the Clallam River if the flow is low, to explore the shore 1 mile to the west; that land is public, acquired by Clallam County in 2011 as Clallam Bay West Park. There are no facilities.

THE STRANGE TALE OF APOSTOLOS VALERIANOS, A.K.A. JUAN DE FUCA

The tale of Juan de Fuca, who lent his name to the great waterway that connects the Pacific Ocean to the inland seas of Washington and British Columbia, is one of history's most puzzling geographical debates. Most historians cast doubt upon the man, a Greek sailor whose real name was Apostolos Valerianos, and his story of exploring a fabled waterway some two hundred years before Spanish, English, and American explorers confirmed its existence. But it's an intriguing possibility. If nothing else, it did give us a lyrical name to the 95-mile-long strait.

The Northwest Coast was the last large stretch of continent on the planet to be charted, a task not completed until the late eighteenth century. One motivating factor—for Spain, England, France, Russia, and the young America—was the search for a possible inland passage, the so-called Northwest Passage, that would connect the Atlantic and Pacific oceans and avoid the long and dangerous voyage around Cape Horn.

Juan de Fuca claimed to have served the king of Spain as a pilot in the Americas for forty years. He said he had been commissioned by the Spanish viceroy in Mexico in 1592 to find the Straits of Anián, as the supposed passageway was then called. Between the latitudes of 47 and 48 degrees, Fuca claimed, he had found a broad passage inland, which he followed for twenty days until he reached the North Sea. As the story was reported, the entrance to this strait was marked by "a great Hedland or Iland, with an exceeding high Pincale, or spired Rocke, like a great pillar thereupon." Furthermore, Fuca claimed to have made several landings, finding people clad in the skins of beasts. He also said that he found the land "fruitful, and rich of gold, silver, Pearle and other things like Nova Spania."

Captain George Vancouver proved two hundred years later that there is no Northwest Passage, and Captain Charles Barkley, another Englishman, is credited with actually discovering the strait in 1787. Barkley did not follow it, but he did refer to it as "de Fuca's straits." So did English fur trader John Meares when he noted the waterway's probable entrance the following year. Even Vancouver used that name when he entered the strait and explored Puget Sound in 1792, despite doubting Fuca's report.

Historians have long since questioned Fuca's credibility, since he apparently at the time was seeking English employment, offering to pilot a new journey to the New World. Yet the entrance to the strait is very much marked by a great, stunning headland, Cape Flattery; as well as an island, Tatoosh. There is indeed a pillar nearby among the many sea stacks there, now called the Fuca Pillar. The strait reaches the sea a little north of latitude 48, remarkably close to what Fuca alleged 140 years before marine chronometers were invented. Enough of the account is credible that it can't be entirely ruled out.

There are other curious fables on the Northwest Coast. Documented Chinese accounts tell of a visit by a fleet of junks led by the Buddhist monk Hui-Shen in 499; he called this distant land Fusang. Some historians and archaeologists believe it likely that numerous storm-damaged Japanese junks washed ashore on the Northwest Coast over the centuries, stories bolstered by early explorers' accounts that the Native tribes knew of, possessed in limited amounts, and highly coveted iron, likely salvaged from such wrecks.

Who knows? But stories like these are fun to think about while sitting on a drift log on the coast, gazing out at the magnificent vastness of the Pacific.

DREAMING OF A HOKO RIVER STATE PARK

Someday, perhaps a culturally fascinating and spacious state park will be developed out of approximately 835 acres in five parcels owned by Washington State Parks, along and around the lower Hoko River west of Clallam Bay.

These lands hold the potential for a marvelous variety of quality recreation—camping, hiking, biking, birding and wildlife watching, fishing, paddling, and cultural interpretation. This economically depressed region desperately needs it. Today there is a grand total of zero fully developed state parks here. The Hoko parcels could serve as a marvelous centerpiece to broaden the region's tourism appeal, replete with a campground and a trail on an old logging rail line along the Strait of Juan de Fuca, linking the park to Sekiu.

But it doesn't appear imminent. State Parks is so broke it can barely maintain its existing developed parks. So Hoko languishes on the second tier of the agency's development priorities. Clallam County and the local Friends of Hoko River State Park are seeking grant money to develop the park.

The properties include almost a mile of shoreline on the strait in two separate spots; more than 2 miles of the lower Hoko River, including its archaeologically important estuary; and the extensive pasture lands of the 613-acre former Cowan cattle ranch along the Hoko and Little Hoko rivers. Both are important wild salmon and steelhead streams. The Hoko estuary once served as a seasonal village site of the Makah and was the scene of important archaeological excavations in the 1970s and 1980s.

Probably the biggest use of the proposed park lands now is providing access for anglers to the Hoko River, a fine little winter steelhead stream. But there are other recreation opportunities here too.

Little Hoko River hike: This easy and mostly flat 3-mile round-trip is on the former Cowan Ranch, found 0.5 mile up the Hoko–Ozette Road, which heads south from State Route 112, about 2.5 miles west of Sekiu. Look for a gated dirt road on the left. Follow the rough road once used by the Cowans to access distant pastures well up the Little Hoko. Past a turnstile at the gate, the road leads through maple and alder glades along the riffles and pools of the stream, important spawning areas for steelhead and chinook (closed to fishing for both). Less than 0.25 mile in, the road leaves the stream and winds along the edge of pastures, good places in the mornings and evenings to spot the local elk herd. Bears and even cougar have been spotted here as well. The road continues in this fashion until it dead-ends at the stream in 1.5 miles.

Sheep graze in the evening mist on leased pasturelands of the former Cowan Ranch along the Hoko River.

Strait of Juan de Fuca shore: This shoreline hike of 1+-mile round-trip is 4.4 miles west of Sekiu; find pullouts on the north side of State Route 112. Stroll leisurely along the sand and gravel shore for more than 0.5 mile, westerly almost to the mouth of the Sekiu River, watching for eagles, seals, and the occasional gray whale. This is a great spot to spread out a beach blanket, enjoy a picnic, and let the kids play in the sand.

Hoko River paddle: Find a primitive launch site at the river's mouth by turning north off State Route 112 about 4.2 miles west of Sekiu, onto Vista Drive; in less than 0.25 mile, go right (east) on Vista Lane to its end. The lower Hoko River is best paddled at high tide during low to moderate flows; tidal influence extends upstream more than a mile, beyond the SR 112 bridge to a large oxbow. The launch is on a side channel. Paddle downstream shortly to the main river and then go upstream; you can also paddle downriver to explore the mouth in a couple hundred yards. The archaeological excavations on the lower river explored both a wet site and a rock shelter, yielding ancient fiber baskets, hats, mats, nets, cordage, and curiously, stone "microblades" that were hafted in a row and used for dressing salmon, halibut, and other fish.

Find out more about this potentially terrific state park from Washington State Parks, including the park plan and maps (search for "Hoko River" on the state park website; see "Contacts and Resources" for all contact information).

OZETTE LOOP

TRIANGLE THROUGH TIME AND ALONG THE SEA

One of Olympic National Park's most popular hikes, the Ozette Loop is a journey through history and a primordial landscape, part deep dark forest, part open prairie, and part semiprotected but rough ocean shore. It's a terrific day hike but is best as a backpack of two or three days, because there's a lot to see and explore. The ocean side of this triangle-shaped hike is only 3.1 miles, the rest in forest and prairie that's interesting in places, monotonous in others, and some of it on slippery cedar-plank boardwalk. If the boardwalk is wet, and it is most of the year, pack tennis shoes to wear on the forest legs, since lug-soled boots are especially slippery on the stuff. Try to take short, flat steps.

Distance: 9.4-mile loop; about 10.5 miles if you explore the Ozette archaeological site
Elevation gain: About 100 feet
Difficulty: 3; 4 if done as day trip, due to length
Map: Custom Correct Ozette Beach Loop
Contact: Olympic National Park
Notes: Park entrance fee required for day use. Park wilderness permit and reservation (May 1–September 30) required for overnight stays; food must be kept in bear-proof container. Extremely busy in summer. Dogs prohibited. Fires prohibited from the Wedding Rocks headland south to Yellow Banks. Check tide tables to know the best times to hike the beach.

DRIVING DIRECTIONS

About 2.5 miles west of Sekiu on State Route 112, turn left (south) onto the Hoko–Ozette Road. Drive 21 miles to the Ozette Ranger Station at the end.

THE HIKE

From the ranger station, follow the trail to a footbridge over the Ozette River. One time I hiked here I saw a seal in the river just downstream of the bridge—3 miles upstream from the sea. River otters are seen here too. Cross the bridge and find a fork in the trail in a few hundred yards. You can go either of two ways, northwesterly to Cape Alava or southwesterly to Sand Point. I recommend you travel

ROCK ART: COMMUNICATION ACROSS THE AGES

One of the headlands on the Ozette Loop is the site of a fascinating and extensive collection of petroglyphs left by the Ozette people. I'm not going to specify the precise location, since over the last ten years damage has been done to them by humans and nature (you can get a map of the site from the Ozette Ranger Station or the park's Wilderness Information Center in Port Angeles). Several years ago one major panel was smashed in two, probably by a drift log during a storm. But human-caused damage is infuriating. The last time I visited, some ignorant fool had used something abrasive to scour away moss, perhaps to get a better photo, in the process damaging an important glyph. A youngster on a Boy Scout outing damaged another in recent years, according to park sources. And in one spot, some idiot with absolutely no respect scratched, "This is a not a . . ."

If you can't treat these images with respect, don't visit this place. Rock art is, after all, the only recorded history by the first Americans. Please don't touch the glyphs at all. Don't take rubbings. Anything you do to the images will only hasten their disappearance, and we'll all be poorer for that. Take photos, marvel at how the images reflect the surrounding environment and at what they represent—communication across the ages—and then leave them alone.

counterclockwise, taking the northwesterly leg of this triangle, which is much more intriguing.

Take the trail to the right, and shortly find yourself dropping into Hobbit-like brooks and nooks, crazy with skunk cabbage, ferns, red huckleberry, moss, and rotting cedar nurse logs. After a series of gentle ups and downs through this dankness, at 1.7 miles the way opens up into wet meadows and sedge fens dotted with scrub cedar, salal, and evergreen huckleberry.

Core samples taken by Western Washington University researchers show a pattern of repeated burning over centuries—these boggy prairies were created by humans. The Ozette people did this every few years to promote the growth of edible roots and berries and browse habitat for deer and elk. Later, two white men homesteaded here, Lars Ahlstrom and Peter Roose, and remains of their cabins and outbuildings can still be found. The Roose cabin, in fact, is intact and on the

National Historic Register. It's less than 1 mile off the trail, to the north. That's all I'll say, since it's a sensitive cultural site.

As you continue west, the prairies give way to old forest of western red cedar, all twisted, spikey, and gnarled and sporting nurse vegetation of ferns and moss on the limbs. Mixed in are Douglas fir and western hemlock.

About 3 miles in, shortly after entering these big trees, where the trail begins to drop, slow down and listen. The seashell is up to your ear. If it's fall through spring, you may distinctly hear a grunting, inharmonious melody of sea lions that bark territorial warnings to each other as they haul out on the hundreds of islets of the Flattery Rocks National Wildlife Refuge. These offshore waters and their extraordinary marine geology are also part of the Olympic Coast National Marine Sanctuary. As you near the shore, the conifer assemblage changes to a predominance of Sitka spruce, and you hear the sea's sounds and begin to smell marine air.

As the ocean comes into view at about 3.2 miles, you are now on the bluff above what for centuries was one of the busiest Native American villages on the Northwest Coast. To a trained eye the signs are everywhere, in the form of "middens"—shell and ash heaps, the refuse of countless meals.

This shore below is pretty important real estate, and always has been. It's most westerly location makes it the closest spot on land hereabouts to the migration routes of gray whales and, more in the past than now, humpback whales. Its maze of islands, islets, sea stacks, and reefs not only shelter it from the open surf but provide prime habitat for seals, sea lions, otters, and fish. If you're a people who make a living hunting marine mammals and fishing from dugout canoes, this is an ideal place. Here the Makah people's Ozette band built what was probably the largest Native American village located actually on the ocean anywhere along the Washington Coast.

That's what makes this hike special. The Ozette are gone, most of them moved to Neah Bay by the 1920s. But echoes of their souls still blow in the sea breeze, and if you get to know this place, you will feel it palpably.

When you reach the beach at Cape Alava, you'll find campsites spread northward several hundred yards and a stream for water; it should be filtered, treated, or boiled, since the protozoan parasite giardia is prevalent here. About 0.6 mile north is a seasonal park ranger cabin and, more interestingly, the Ozette Indian Reservation and the site of an important archaeological excavation in the 1970s. Check out the curious replica cedar-plank house filled with whale bones, all that's left of the dig and a place where generations of people lived, laughed, cried, and died. The dig revealed a complicated culture in which individuals specialized in different aspects of earning a living—as whale hunters, fishermen, weavers, canoe makers, spiritualists—and society was defined by classes of people, from nobility to commoners to slaves. If the tide is out, you can walk from the dig site out to Tskawahyah, or "Cannonball," Island; note the curiously round boulders at its base.

Then head south along the shore, which is not easy going at all, especially at high tide, with long stretches of loose gravel, slippery reefs, piles of kelp, and downed trees to go under, over, or around. The surf is minimized by the near-shore islands and reefs, and there are no long sandy beaches. The scenery is splendid, but this is not the most dramatic stretch of the park's wilderness beach. At the same time, the tide-pooling is great on a minus tide.

Two minor headlands can be rounded at a moderate tide or climbed over anytime. The first is Wedding Rocks headland at 4.3 miles (5.5 if you checked out the dig site). After rounding the second headland south of Cape Alava, the way becomes more gentle across a 1-mile crescent-shaped beach to Sand Point, where the loop heads inland and returns to Lake Ozette.

Look in the gravel piles for agates. I've found some here, as well as along the long beach south of Sand Point. Park regulations require that you take no more than a handful, but you'll have to work hard to find that many, since the agates are mostly small. Limited archaeological work found three other habitation sites in this vicinity, one dated to more than two thousand years ago.

Several campsites are tucked into the trees on the low bluff above the

USE CAUTION WHEN CAMPING ON THE BEACH

If you camp right on the beach, as opposed to at an established site on a bench above the beach, you must pitch your tent well above the high-tide line, and check the tide tables to ensure that the surf won't reach your tent. If it's stormy and/or the surf is high, don't take the chance: camp in a safe spot on the bluff instead. But if the weather is fair and the tides moderate, beach camping is preferred: it has less impact than camping on the bluff, where tents and footpaths eliminate vegetation. On the upper beach there is little vegetation, and high tides will wash away any trace of your campfire. Just be sure to check the tides, look at the last high-tide line, and use good judgment.

beach. Fires are not allowed here. If you stay, watch how the ebbing tides reveal extensive reefs, the boulders festooned with green and yellow seaweed. Sunsets can be spectacular. I recommend you climb out on the headland of Sand Point to watch the enormity of the ocean swallow that fiery golden orb.

An orange and black sign with a cross at 6.4 miles marks the route inland to the Ozette Ranger Station; it leaves the beach behind the campsites. You've got about 3 miles of nice forest, but without much variety.

OZETTE TO RIALTO BEACH THROUGH-HIKE

WILD TREKKING THROUGH OCEANIC BLISS

Insanely beautiful and wild, undeveloped, rugged ocean shoreline makes this one of the classic backpack trips in all of North America. You'll travel mile after mile of rocky headlands and crescent beaches, a big sky overhead and the big sea chaotically cluttered with offshore spires, daggers, pinnacles, and islets as far as the eye can see.

Distance: The park says 20 miles one-way, but I say 20+
Elevation gain: About 400 feet
Difficulty: 4
Map: Custom Correct North Olympic Coast
Contact: Olympic National Park
Notes: Park wilderness permit required for overnight stays; food must be kept in bear-proof container. Reservations required to camp north of Norwegian Memorial May 1–September 30. Dogs prohibited. Fires allowed only from Yellow Banks (about 5.1 miles in) south. Bring tide tables—you'll need them to navigate headlands.

DRIVING DIRECTIONS

About 2.5 miles west of Sekiu on State Route 112, turn left (south) onto the Hoko–Ozette Road. Drive 21 miles to the Ozette Ranger Station at the end. To leave a car at the south end of this hike, find Rialto Beach by heading west on SR 110 (Mora–La Push Road) from US 101, 2 miles north of Forks. In about 9 miles, go right at the Three Rivers store and café on the Mora Road (the north spur of SR 110) and follow it to its end in about 6 miles.

THE HIKE

Prepare yourself for an adventurous trek, with surprises around most every corner. This reach of the North American continent is like nature's textbook. You'll experience the ocean's moody ebb and flow, the brooding forest of the windswept bluffs, the stoic resilience of sea stack sentinels, and the urgency of the creatures that live on this edge of sea and sky. After 3 miles of forest, the hike is almost entirely on wilderness beaches and on the south end skirts the lithic kaleidoscope of the Quillayute Needles. You'll also pass at least three sites of ancient Native habitation. I won't say where, but here are hints: freshwater (for drinking), shellfish habitat, gentle surf (for canoe launching/landing).

But this ain't no place for wussies and weanies. You might think a hike on the beach with little elevation gain would be, well, a walk in the park. But these wilderness beaches are rugged, muddy, slippery, rocky, and wet, exacerbated by the fact that this coast—pummeled twice a day by high tides and regularly by wind and rain—is constantly crumbling. You can cross streams only when tides and rainfall allow. You'll find yourself climbing over slides of clay and rock and giant toppled spruce.

For most of the way, there is no specific trail. You find your own way, and the challenge is finding the best way. You'll wear out boots and packs here, due to the abrasiveness of the rocks and the corrosiveness

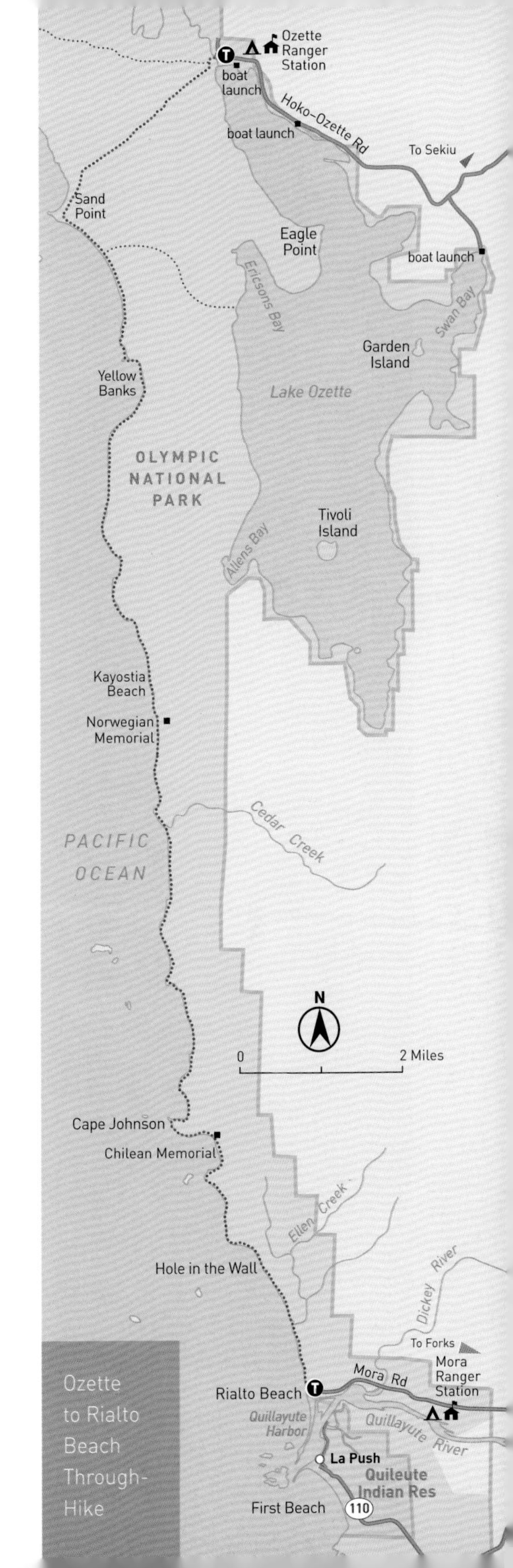

FINDING AGATES, THE SHINY JEWELS OF THE BEACH

Beach treasure glows amber in the sunlight.

Agates can be found all along the Washington Coast, although on some stretches they are rare or absent while other stretches are especially known for them.

The first thing you need to know is what they look like. Agate is a type of quartz, the result of silica- and mineral-rich water filling voids in other rocks, such as in cracks or even sometimes in the hollow of clam shells layered in sediments. Over time, chemical reactions cause the precipitation of hard, microcrystalline igneous quartzes of chalcedony or carnelian. The minerals lend the agates color and silica is of course translucent, like glass. Along the Washington Coast agates are usually white, rust or brown, orange yellow or gold, and often in these colors with a frosting of pearl white.

Beginning agate hunters often confuse other semitransparent stones with agates, known to regular hunters as sugar agates. They are abundant, worthless, and not true agates. To get a good sense of true beach agates, go to any coastal rock shop and ask to see unpolished beach agates. The Ocean Shores Interpretive Center has a very nice collection you can examine (see "Contacts and Resources" under "The Central Coast").

Once you get a sense for real agates, just get out there and look. Low tide is best, because it reveals more piles of stones where agates can be found. Mornings and evenings are best because the low angle of the sunlight often reveals their glow. When looking, walk at an angle that best puts the light on the beach. It's amazing how agates can sometimes just light up. If you do one of the north coast wilderness backpacks and really look as you hike, you should come home with a handful of pretty agates.

Teeth-like sea stacks and Hole in the Wall make this one of the most scenic beaches on the Washington Coast.

of saltwater. Ah, but to borrow a phrase from author Patrick McManus, it is a fine and pleasant misery!

OK, hoist your pack and head west from the ranger station, shortly taking the left fork to Sand Point. It's 3 miles to the ocean largely on slippery boardwalk; be careful. You'll emerge from the forest into tall salal shrubbery, with campsites on the right; stay on the main trail until it reaches the south side of Sand Point. From here a broad pebble/sand beach heads south for more than 1 mile to a minor headland, best hiked on the hard sand at a lower tide. Look for agates glistening in the sun as you go. Before long you'll see eagles overhead, seagulls fluttering at the edge of the surf, and you'll hear the raven's croaking caw.

In about 0.6 mile from Sand Point, 3.6 overall, note the round orange and black sign on the edge of the woods. That marks a 2-mile trail to Lake Ozette. Ignore it. It's used mostly by paddlers camping on the lake.

Reach the bedrock of the headland at 4.6 miles and round it if the tide is lower than 5 feet; if not, there's a tunnel above the high-water mark you can take. The footing is dicey in places, but it's a short stretch, beyond which you'll reach Yellow Banks, a series of eroded bluffs tinged with their namesake color.

From here south, campfires may be built. And you've put in 5.1 miles to this point, in addition to the long drive out to Lake Ozette. If you're planning on spending three nights on this hike, this is a good spot to stop. There's a stream for water about halfway along the Yellow Banks and ample room on the upper beach to pitch a tent.

The next 5 miles south include only one minor headland that can be rounded at any tide less than 6 feet (at 8.1 miles). But progress will slow to a crawl because much of the way is a rough, rocky hell, with long bluffs on the uplands pocked by stony alcoves and grottoes and serious stretches of algae-covered boulders, tide pools, large cobbles, and loose sand and gravel. A few years back, along this stretch I came upon the bloated carcass of a sea lion, its skull bare, and a mile farther, tracks in the sand showed the path of a cougar.

The way finally eases as you come to Kayostia Beach and the site of Norwegian Memorial, at 10.2 miles. There's a stream here for water and extensive camps in the forest.

A monument marks the tragedy of the three-masted Norwegian bark *Prince Arthur*. In a gale on January 2, 1903, the ship hit and grounded on offshore reefs. It was pounded repeatedly by huge waves that broke over the vessel, breaking its steel hull in two. Only two of its twenty-person crew survived. The Olympic Coast National Marine Sanctuary website (see "Contacts and Resources") has a terrific history of shipwrecks in this area, with a cool map.

At the south end of Kayostia Beach is a headland (at 11.3 miles) that can be rounded anytime except at high tide (5.5 feet and above), but it can be climbed over via ropes and "sand ladders," which are curious cable and timber affairs some ranger back in the day devised. They're fixed only on the top and are designed to ride out the slides that inevitably occur, remaining in place. You climb them with the assist of a rope also fixed at the top. Some of them are on steep, gooey, daunting slopes of clay and mud, but they do work.

Just south of this headland is the mouth of Cedar Creek (11.7 miles), easily crossed except at very high flows or high tides. A friend once found a winter steelhead—a large sea-run rainbow trout—floundering in the shallows of this small stream. Here begins a peculiar beach, where the gradient is steep and the surf often pushes and stacks foot-size cobbles into a narrow shelf against the uplands, on the high side piled with wave-burnished, sun-bleached drift logs—some of them giant old cedars with gnarly root bases. It's a chore following the shelf, but it's not much more than 0.25 mile, if that.

Less than 0.5 mile south of Cedar Creek, a smaller stream spills into the sea, marking the old Starbuck Mine site, one of several placer gold operations along this coast, all ultimately unprofitable. It was started around 1910, and by 1917 its operators reported they had extracted $5000 worth of gold and 5 ounces of platinum from the sand.

Just south of the site is a cool little headland, known locally as Coastie Head, reached at 13.4 miles. It can be rounded at low tide, but this is one worth climbing. The headland's saddle sports an old cedar shack, now listing southward, that was used by the Coast Guard as an observation post during World War II. The view from this head of surrounding sea stacks and islands is stunning.

South of Coastie Head you're entering the geologic oddity of the Quillayute Needles, a dizzying collection of pinnacles and spires that stretches southward for miles, culminating in the stunning Giants Graveyard south of La Push. At times it looks like a hundred chaotic Stonehenges offshore. These are the manifestation of plate tectonics, mostly volcanic in origin, shoved landward and upward over millions of years. They are then weathered into their current forms by a process known as differential erosion, in which the softer parts are washed away over time by the sea.

Scramble down the south side of the headland. From here south, despite a few more stretches of boulder negotiation, the hike just gets better. The scenery transitions from inspiring to absolutely sublime. The abundance of wildlife becomes intense. Tide-pool life is as rich and diverse as anywhere on this coast. Agate hunting is good. Camping is sweet.

The next few miles are mostly on easy sand beaches, with a low headland at 13.7 miles that must be climbed, but it's no problem. In another 1+ mile you'll find another head that can be rounded at any tide lower than 5.5 feet.

To the south is a rocky but pleasant half-moon cove, full of tide pools, followed in less than a mile by Cape Johnson at 15.9 miles. According to an old story, the Cape Johnson area long ago served as the seasonal camp of a family of Ozette Indians with eight sons, who together formed a full whaling crew. A sharp eye might spot signs of long shellfish use in this area or just beyond.

Cape Johnson can't be climbed. It can be rounded only at tides of 4 feet or less, through a tough patch of boulders, but it's not long. Once around the cape you'll

A backpacker looks in the tide pools after hiking through Hole in the Wall.

enter a beautiful sheltered cove, Big Bay, protected by rocks and reefs and a pretty cone-shaped, spruce-topped island on the south corner.

A granite marker on a bench above the beach, at 16.6 miles, marks the common grave of the twenty people who died in November of 1920 when the schooner *W. J. Pirrie* smashed against Cake Rock to the south. The dead, most of them Chilean, included the captain, his wife, and their baby son. It's ironic that Chilean Memorial stands here, because the next few miles of this hike are one of the prettiest stretches of the entire Washington Coast—it's not a sad place at all. There are a few campsites on the bench near the memorial, but most backpackers camp on the beach here—be darned sure to check the high-tide level.

The bay of Chilean Memorial is a great place to spend some time. Bring binoculars if you can. Seals haul out in fair numbers on the rocks of the bay. Harlequin ducks dabble in the shallows. Eagles are almost as common as ravens. River

CAN THE OZETTE SOCKEYE BE SAVED?

One species that is not doing well in the Lake Ozette area is a genetically distinct race of sockeye salmon that might once have numbered 30,000 annually. Preserved by drying and smoking, the "blueback" provided the Ozette people critical winter sustenance. It is now federally listed as a threatened species, with average annual returns of about 1000 fish.

State and federal biologists refuse to point a finger at the specific cause, but I will. Perhaps 85 percent of the lake's watershed has been logged over the last eighty years, and even twenty-five years ago logging practices were causing significant damage to spawning habitat. Streamside buffers were nonexistent or inadequate to prevent damage to riparian zones; clear-cut sizes were far too large; and, along with logging-road construction, this caused severe erosion that smothered spawning beds. Culverts along logging roads blocked fish passage to important spawning beds. The official version is on the Washington Department of Fish and Wildlife website (see "Contacts and Resources" under "Fishing Information and Regulations"). Despite restoration efforts largely by the Makah tribe, the bottom line is that the precious genetic lineage that remains might not be sufficient to save the Lake Ozette sockeye from extinction while the habitat recovers.

otters, which also live and fish in marine waters, are seen here and along the entire coast.

And if you watch the tide pools and kelp beds patiently when the tide is up, you might observe the much larger sea otter, a marine-specific species that's always a thrill to see. This is the animal that generated an intense fur trade along the Northwest Coast in the late 1700s, when this coast had not even been entirely charted. The Cape Johnson area has been noted in recent surveys for its concentration of sea otters.

There are patches of rocks and boulder piles to negotiate in this bay while heading south, but the route is passable at all tides. Rounding the south point of Big Bay—you can hike out and explore the island on a minus tide—you'll emerge onto a pretty gravel beach with campsites on the upland bench, at about 17.2 miles.

At 17.8 miles, the beach transitions into a rock shelf piled with large boulders, making for really tricky going, with one spot that can't be rounded at any tide higher than 5 feet. This shelf is no fun when a high tide pushes you right up against the bluff of glacial till, but it's pretty cool when the tide is up moderately, because the water surges into deep and narrow channels cut from the rock shelf over the ages. This stretch is less than 1 mile but takes some time.

Finally you round a corner and the rocks peter out into a gravel beach and then, there it is! About 0.5 mile south, at 18.8 miles, is Hole in the Wall, a famous portal near the end of a rock wall that resembles the back of a stegosaurus. As you head south toward the hole, if the tide is down, first look at the reef in the little bay here and the curious wavy patterns on one large tabletop rock shelf. This is a most spectacular piece of coast, the kind of primal and emotional place where people want their ashes scattered.

In fact, behind the bluff that hosts Hole in the Wall is another common grave, the victims of the three-masted bark *Leonore*, wrecked on nearby rocks in 1893. In this bay just north of the hole you can find metal pieces of some shipwreck, like a large rusty capstan, but I'm not sure which wreck.

When you reach Hole in the Wall, stop to look just beyond at the two beautifully angular nearshore sea stacks, topped by a few weathered spruce. Then, if the tide is higher than 5 feet, you'll have to climb around this steep rock face on a short trail, the route marked by the standard orange and black sign. If the tide is lower than that, hike right through the hole. Don't be tempted to negotiate Hole in the Wall at a higher tide; friends and I once watched a couple skirt disaster here, one of them taking a dunk in the waves, backpack and all. They were OK, but shaken.

Once south of this headland, you're just shy of 1.5 miles from Rialto Beach and the parking lot at the mouth of the Quillayute River. Campsites are scattered from here south for about 0.5 mile to Ellen Creek; people also camp on the beach just north of Hole in the Wall. The camps are all great for a quick overnighter, or for introducing kids to backpacking, due to their proximity to the trailhead and the sheer beauty of this locale. Of course, this is an extremely popular area as well, so don't expect solitude except perhaps in the dead of winter.

South of Ellen Creek, loose gravel makes the walking a bit tough. But it's a short stretch to the parking lot. And just a few miles down the road out is the café at Three Rivers Resort, where the nice people who operate it make pretty darned good burgers and shakes. For me it's a mandatory posthike stop.

PADDLING

LAKE OZETTE

A FRESHWATER WILDERNESS

If you're a light sleeper, the nighttime sounds of the wilderness might send chills up your spine while you're camping on this fine sheet of water, the third-largest natural lake in Washington State (at 7787 acres, behind lakes Chelan and Washington). Canoe and kayak opportunities are superb on Lake Ozette; virtually all of it is inside Olympic National Park and most of it is extremely wild, even though industrial logging on the hills to the east mars the viewscape. A trail near one of the major campsites on the lake leads to the ocean, a nice side trip. And there are three rough boat launches on the lake's north end. Despite plenty of camping spots—an idyllic boat-in only campground and at least six other smaller but sublime wilderness campsites scattered around the lake—Ozette is largely overlooked and thus offers excellent opportunities for solitude.

Paddling into the clouds on a calm morning on Lake Ozette

Distance: 8 miles round-trip from ranger station to Ericsons Bay
Difficulty: 2, when winds are calm
Map: Custom Correct North Olympic Coast
Contact: Olympic National Park
Notes: Park wilderness permit required for overnight stays; food must be kept in bear-proof container. Dogs prohibited. The lake has a long north–south fetch and waves can get big; people have drowned here. Carefully check forecasts, and for extended trips bring a battery-operated weather radio. Bring all necessary safety gear, especially a Coast Guard–approved personal flotation device.

DRIVING DIRECTIONS

About 2.5 miles west of Sekiu on State Route 112, turn left (south) onto the Hoko–Ozette Road. Three rough boat ramps on the north end of the lake are all just off this 21-mile road. For the Swan Bay launch, turn left at about 17 miles onto Swan Bay Road and drive 0.8 mile to its end. Almost 2 miles farther west along the Hoko–Ozette Road, find a primitive launch site on the lakeshore. The last launch is at the end of the Hoko–Ozette Road, between the ranger station and the Lake Ozette Campground. Your destination on the lake will determine which is best to use; for Ericsons Bay, use this last launch.

THE PADDLE

Lake Ozette is wild, really wild, even though you can see results of clear-cut logging to the east, even though a unique species of salmon native to the lake is on the brink of extinction, and even though a century ago more than a hundred homesteading families lived here. The haunting wail of a loon sang me a lullaby one night, and the next night the muffled, throaty hoots of a great horned owl roused me from slumber. Sticks sometimes snap in the forest at night, while a chorus of frogs can rise and fall from dusk to dawn depending on the season.

Although several private in-holdings sit along the northeastern shores, the entire western shore of the 8-mile-long, glacially carved lake is dense, uninhabited coastal rain forest, with Sitka spruce and western red cedar the dominant trees. And most of the lake is barely more than a mile inland of the Pacific Ocean.

It's an easy 4-mile paddle from the launch at the ranger station to the campground at Ericsons Bay on the northwest corner of the lake, near shore most of the way. This is the primary destination for paddlers, a beautiful location with campsites tucked into the forest along a pretty gravel shore. The sites are all primitive with no facilities, save for a fine enclosed pit toilet on a knoll in the forest. Ericsons Bay is large enough to comfortably hold ten or more tents but would be crowded at that if you're used to more isolated camping. Ericsons Bay is also an attractive spot because less than a mile south along the shore is the eastern end of a trail to the ocean that's still passable, although it sees little maintenance and is typically in miserable shape. It leads 2 miles over mucky bottoms, often on slippery and rotten cedar boardwalk, and through groves of big red cedar and head-high salal thickets, reaching the surf about 0.5 mile south of Sand Point.

Other smaller campsites with no facilities whatever include Eagle Point—a bit more than 2 miles from the ranger station at the north end of the lake—a sweet little spot where in years gone by the Ozette people camped in summer while fishing for sockeye salmon. In a large bay on the east side of the lake are campsites at Benson Point and lovely Garden Island, which still hosts exotic plants left by settlers. Three spots at the south end of the lake are on the tree-covered mound known as Tivoli Island, at Birkestol Point due south, and on Allens Bay, where a trail now abandoned once snaked 2.4 miles through the dense forest to Norwegian Memorial on the coast.

Today when you paddle the quiet waters of Lake Ozette, it's hard to visualize that most of the suitable sites around the 30-some miles of lakeshore were once inhabited, largely by Scandinavian immigrants beginning in the late nineteenth century. Ole and Sarah Ericson eked out an isolated existence on the bay that bears their name. Homes, barns, and outbuildings were built of sawn cedar logs. Sheep and cattle were brought in, vegetable gardens planted, wild berries picked, fish caught, deer, elk, and bear hunted. It was a hardscrabble life, and many left by the turn of the twentieth century. A second wave came not long after and persisted at varying levels until 1940, when President Franklin D. Roosevelt authorized the acquisition of the Lake Ozette area and a thin strip of land along Washington's north coast for parklands.

Almost nothing exists of the homesteads today. The wildlife remains, however, undoubtedly more abundant than ever in most cases. Arriving at Ericsons Bay, Lorna and I found a bald eagle splashing and bathing in the shallows. Eagles were our almost constant companions for three days. Returning from a hike to the coast, we paddled to our campsite under a huge spruce tree; two eagles roosted in its lower branches seemingly unconcerned. Rufous hummingbirds chased each

The pretty shoreline of Ericsons Bay, site of a boat-in only campground

other around the salmonberry bushes, sometimes buzzing and zinging within a foot of us. The second morning we saw two bears on a swampy point 0.3 mile down-lake from our campsite; Lorna wishfully said she thought they were just raccoons—and I let her think that.

I wish it was worthwhile to bring a fishing rod here, but the lake isn't known for fishing, its native species reduced by habitat damage and competition from introduced species, such as bass. All things considered, Lake Ozette is an unrecognized dreamscape for paddling, its often flat morning surface mirroring puffy clouds and big trees, its afternoon breeze softly whispering what is and what used to be.

RETURN OF THE SEA OTTER

The warmest, fuzziest wildlife story on the Washington Coast is that of the sea otter, a large member of the weasel family with fur so dense and lustrous it played a pivotal role in the exploration of this remote corner of the continent.

Sea otters were prized even before Captain Cook sailed to China from the Northwest Coast in 1778 and discovered that sea otter pelts would fetch extremely high prices there—"soft gold," it was called. For thousands of years Native peoples avidly hunted the sea otter, making long, striking robes from the pelts. After Cook's discovery, sea otters were actively hunted for decades by both Indians and white people, to virtual extinction along the Washington Coast by 1911. Reintroduced in 1969 by a transplant of fifty-nine otters from Alaska, sea otters are now more abundant here than they have been in perhaps 150 years. Today, aerial surveys indicate they might number about fourteen hundred. So it's a special treat to see them.

Male sea otters off Washington average a little more than 4.5 feet long and 83.5 pounds. They don't look that big in the wild because they typically float on their backs, with only their head and belly showing. Since they don't have an insulating layer of fat as do seals and sea lions, their fur is the most dense in the animal kingdom. They're ravenous critters, eating 20 to 25 percent of their body weight each day in clams, crabs, mussels, and sea urchins. They range in Washington primarily from the Strait of Juan de Fuca south to Destruction Island (where population density is highest), just south of the Hoh River near Kalaloch. Other concentrations are at Duk Point near the mouth of the Ozette River, at Cape Alava and Sand Point (two corners of the Ozette Loop), and at Cape Johnson and Perkins Reef, just north and south of La Push, respectively.

While the otter population is growing, serious concerns remain. The biggest threat is the potential for oil spills. Because they have no insulating fat, otters keep their fur impeccably clean by frequent preening. A coating of oil would prove fatal. Lack of genetic diversity in Washington's population is another concern. They are listed by the state as an endangered species and federally as a species of concern.

Sea otters are almost never seen on land, but river otters like this one are often seen on the shore and in the sea along the coast.

Inexperienced observers often mistake river otters for sea otters. Despite their name, river otters also live and feed in marine waters. They're far more abundant but thinner, typically darker brown, and are often seen on the beach. It's very cool to watch either type of otter!

THE NORTH COAST

CHAPTER 5

THE QUILEUTE INDIAN VILLAGE OF LA PUSH marks the epicenter of Olympic National Park's glorious 70-mile wilderness beach and its unparalleled hiking opportunities, as well as where the northernmost of Washington's great coastal rain-forest rivers—the Quillayute—meets the sea. Just to the south, two more classic rain-forest rivers, the Hoh and the Queets, lend their considerable flow to the Pacific, tumbling from the crown of the Olympic Peninsula, the glaciers and icefields of 7980-foot Mount Olympus, and the associated pinnacles and spires known as the Valhallas.

Between the Hoh and the Queets is an extraordinary stretch of windswept and often misty Olympic National Park shore, anchored by the oceanside village of Kalaloch, which most visitors blow right through. That's a considerable mistake. The beaches are beautiful, in places stunning, the geology and rockscapes intriguing, and most of this stretch is more accessible than the rest of the park's wilderness shore.

An overlook at the Beach 4 trailhead north of Kalaloch provides a terrific view of Starfish Point and the Pacific.

One curiosity on the beaches here is intense concentrations of drift logs in many places, such as at Ruby Beach and around Kalaloch Creek. Some of them are massive, wave-burnished beasts. Where did they come from? Those classic rain-forest rivers—the logs are the manifestation of the inextricable connection between the ocean and the rivers. The ocean sends the precipitation that grows these behemoths, often causing high flows that topple and send them to the sea. The ocean also sends the salmon that spawn, die, and fertilize the forest. And so on. The visitor to this coast is therefore compelled to explore the rain forests: the Hoh and the Queets in this chapter, the Quinault in the next.

The approximately 33-mile stretch of shore from the Quillayute River past the Hoh to the Queets is as compelling recreationally, scenically, and geologically as anywhere on the Washington Coast. The hiking, fishing, camping, critter watching, and beachcombing are all superb. Plus, the uncanny configurations of tide-washed stone along this coast reach their scenic apex in the stunning Giants Graveyard and Quillayute Needles. If you skip this part of the Washington Coast, you will miss much of the very best.

LA PUSH AND THE HOH RIVER

THE OCEAN BEACH HIKING HERE is magnificent: wild, even otherworldly, set amid groves of misty sawtooth sea stacks along often sandy shores, punctuated by headland ramparts. This area offers something for every type of hiker, from easy day hikes to an adventurous backpack. There are ample opportunities for camping too, mostly in the rain-forest valleys, and fair breaks for surfing and surf kayaking on First and Second beaches. And just inland a bit is the northernmost of Olympic National Park's terrific rain-forest hikes, including a couple easy classics around the Hoh Rain Forest Visitor Center.

For centuries the lifeblood of the Quileute people has been the Quillayute River—the tribe and river spellings are different—and its three major tributaries, the Calawah, Sol Duc, and Bogachiel. The same can be said for the Hoh tribe and river of the same name just to the south, as well as for the Queets tribe and

The trail to Third Beach near La Push travels an often-misty forest of Sitka spruce.

A LANGUAGE ALL THEIR OWN

The Quileute people are portrayed as werewolves or "shape-shifters" in the popular *Twilight* books, much to their chagrin I would imagine, but historically they were considered a strong, fearless tribe and linguistically were unique among Native Americans. Together with the associated Hoh tribe and the small breakaway Chimacum band on the inland waters (now long gone), the Quileute spoke the Chimakuan tongue. This "language isolate," as linguists call it, was unrelated to any other known language and, curiously, it had no nasal sounds (m, n). Intuitively this is significant, but no one knows how it came to be. With Native languages now vanishing worldwide, the tribe has published a dictionary online (see "Contacts and Resources") and undertaken to restore Quileute words to everyday usage, to help maintain the tribe's legends and identity.

river a bit farther south still. These three rain-forest rivers—the Quillayute, Hoh, and Queets—splash down from the northern Olympic Mountains and adjacent foothills and remain among the most productive salmon and steelhead waters in the Pacific Northwest. Several miles upstream from La Push, the meandering Bogachiel joins the turbulent Calawah; together they flow several miles before taking on the crystal waters of the Sol Duc River and becoming the Quillayute. I've caught many steelhead and a few salmon from these rivers, and all three flow through my vision of heaven. Add the Hoh and the Queets, and the sum is an angler's eternal paradise.

Although the Quileute depended heavily on the rich salmon runs, they also hunted whales on the open ocean and were especially noted by their neighbors as the best seal hunters on the coast. The Hoh are a distinct band, but both tribes' ancestors spoke the same Chimakuan tongue and the two groups are friendly, collaborative, and intermarried.

Steep and rocky James Island, just off La Push, in the olden days served as a fortified village the Quileute took to when approached by hostile tribes from the north. Early explorers noticed both the main village and the camp atop James Island. British fur trader John Meares, sailing south from Cape Flattery in 1788, reported that "although the village of Queenuitett was obscured from view, we could very plainly discern the town of Queenuitett, which . . . is situated on a high perpendicular rock, and is joined by a

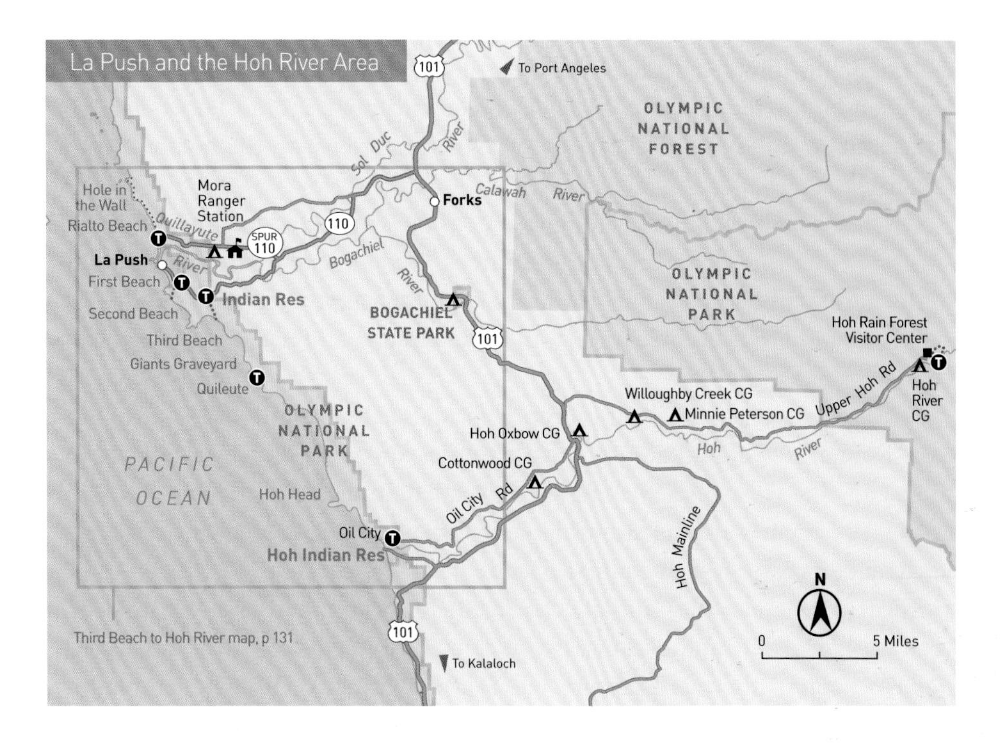

narrow and impregnable causeway, twenty feet in height, to the mainland, which is an entire forest. With our glasses, we observed a multitude of houses, scattered over the face of the rock." Meares may have confused the Quileute village name with that of the village and river Quinault well to the south. Other early explorers referred to what we now call La Push as Goliu.

The Quileute remain a proud people, as I discovered one day a few years ago. Tribal members hand-knit raw wool caps and sell them at the tribe's resort in La Push. The hats are similar to the better-known knitted wool garments of the Cowichan people of Vancouver Island. I foolishly blurted to the Quileute woman behind the counter, "Oh, are these Cowichan caps?"

"No," she said with a look of cool stone. "They're Quileute caps."

Feeling ever the ignorant *ho-kwat*—coastal tribal terminology for "white people"—I sheepishly tried on one with a traditional whale pattern, and I bought it right then and there.

GETTING THERE/STAYING THERE

Accommodations and services—restaurant, stores, gas, fishing tackle—are available in the traditional West End timber town of Forks, which somehow retains its rough-and-tumble character despite a slow process of gentrification recently hastened by the fame of the *Twilight* books and movies. Find Forks along US 101 about 56 miles west of Port Angeles, the major city on the north Olympic Peninsula.

On the south end of Forks along US 101 is the Forks Chamber of Commerce Visitor Center (see "Contacts and Resources" for all contact information), next to the Forks Timber Museum. There are some very nice B&Bs and resorts with cabins in and around Forks and from there west to La Push; check the chamber's website.

For La Push itself—from the French *la bouche*, or "the mouth"—turn onto State Route 110 (Mora–La Push Road), 2 miles north of Forks, and follow signs to its end. The village is a striking place, nestled on the south bank of the Quillayute, which curls around stunning James Island as it spills into the sea on the north end of crescent-shaped First Beach.

The tribe operates the Quileute Oceanside Resort on the shore of First Beach, with very nice accommodations. If you can afford it, get one of the luxury cabins. For boaters, there is a picturesque marina with gas, moorage, and launch ramp. The tribe also runs a quaint and cozy restaurant, the River's Edge, in an old wooden Coast Guard lifeboat station, with great views across the river to James Island.

Olympic National Park's Hoh Rain Forest is south of Forks. Head 12.6 miles south on US 101. Then turn inland on the Upper Hoh Road and drive about 18 miles to its end at the visitor center and campground.

FEES AND PERMITS

Olympic National Park charges an entrance fee at the Hoh Rain Forest. Pay with an annual park pass (Federal Interagency Pass, $80; or the Olympic-specific pass, $30, available at the WIC and entrance stations) or by the day at the entrance station ($15 per vehicle; $5 by foot, bike, or motorcycle; good for seven days).

Any overnight visit in the park backcountry requires a wilderness fee of $5 for the party, plus $2 per person per night. Obtain permits at the park's Wilderness Information Center (WIC) in Port Angeles (see "Contacts and Resources" for all contact information) or the Mora Ranger Station (open intermittently in summer only). You can also self-issue a permit by picking up a fee envelope at park trailheads and ranger stations, mailing it in after your hike.

Mora Campground is set in a forest of big spruce and hemlock.

The park's Hoh Rain Forest Visitor Center is near the campground entrance and provides brochures, trail reports and other information, interpretive displays, and hiking permits. It's open daily only in summer, with variable hours.

CAMPING

MORA CAMPGROUND

Set in a grove of big Sitka spruce and hemlock trees on a bench above the Quillayute River, this year-round Olympic National Park campground offers many cozy sites, but some lack privacy. A pond just across the Mora Road helps attract quite a variety of birds. I awoke one spring morning to a serenade of varied thrush, winter wrens, redwing blackbirds, ducks, and geese—a lovely chorus.

This campground's main drawback is that there is little to do here without driving, other than two short nature trails. It is, however, an excellent base camp for exploring the area's superb attractions. It has running water and restrooms, but no showers. The 94 sites are first come, first served ($12/night), and a few can handle RVs up to 35 feet. There are no hookups, but there is a dump station ($5). Rangers lead beach and tide-pool walks in summer.

Contact: Olympic National Park. **Driving directions:** From US 101, 2 miles north of Forks, turn west on State Route 110 (Mora–La Push Road). In 7.7 miles, at the Three Rivers store, turn right on the Mora Road (the north spur of SR 110) and follow it 3.2 miles, taking a left at the campground sign.

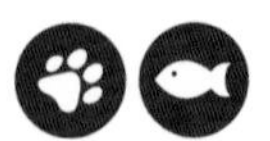

BOGACHIEL STATE PARK

A 123-acre way station sort of campground on the Bogachiel River, this small state park offers 26 standard sites ($12–$42/night), 6 sites with power and water hookups, and 2 hiker/biker sites. Two restroom buildings offer showers. Most sites don't come with much privacy, only a few are close to the river, and you can hear traffic from the highway.

Contact: Bogachiel State Park. **Driving directions:** Drive some 5.2 miles south of Forks on US 101. Signs mark the turn into the park on the west side of the highway.

HOH RIVER CAMPGROUND

Sandwiched by the riffles of the famed Hoh River and surrounding rain forest, this is one of Olympic National Park's nicer campgrounds. About a dozen of the sites are set directly on the river, which provides a sweet lullaby when you hit the sack. You'll have plenty to do here. The river is right there, with ample drifts and pools for fly- or spin-casting and plenty of space for wading or just lolling about. Two nature trails offer an excellent introduction to the mossy mysteries of the temperate rain forest, and the long route to Mount Olympus via the wonderful Hoh River Trail also starts here. Wildlife is abundant, with very high chances of seeing the majestic Olympic elk as well as eagles and otters (maybe the occasional bruin or wildcat too).

All 88 sites are first come, first served ($12/night), no hookups. There is a picnic area, an RV dump station ($5), and running water. There are no showers, but restrooms are heated in winter, for which my bottom was grateful one chilly February morn. In summer, rangers conduct campfire programs on rain-forest ecology and other nature topics.

Contact: Olympic National Park. **Driving directions:** From Forks, drive 12.6 miles south on US 101 to the Upper Hoh Road. Turn inland and follow it about 18 miles, past the park entrance station at 13 miles.

HOH OXBOW, WILLOUGHBY CREEK, AND MINNIE PETERSON CAMPGROUNDS

These Washington Department of Natural Resources (DNR) campgrounds along the upper Hoh River are all lovely spots and totally free. But like other DNR recreation sites, they suffer from a lack of maintenance and services. Due to budget shortfalls, the agency can't even afford to collect the garbage. That means unsightly piles of trash are not unusual. Since the campgrounds are unsupervised, they're sometimes used by the drinking/smoking/partying crowd. I don't mean to be judgmental; I was young once. But sometimes you'll find neither a family atmosphere nor occasion for quiet reflection along the otherwise beautiful riffles of the Hoh. That said, if you time it right, these campgrounds can be wonderful.

Hoh Oxbow, with 7 sites, is at the downstream end of the stunning canyon of the Hoh. It also serves as a boat launch and can be super busy during fishing seasons, especially winter to midspring and in late summer and fall. ADA-accessible toilet facilities; no running water. **Driving directions:** Oxbow is 14 miles south of downtown Forks, just north of the US 101 bridge over the Hoh, on the east side of the highway.

Willoughby Creek, right on the river with only 3 primitive sites, is especially nice, although it is close to the road. Pit toilets; no running water. **Driving directions:** From Forks, drive 12.6 miles south on US 101 to the Upper Hoh Road. Turn inland and head 3.6 miles east. The campground is on the south side of the road.

Minnie Peterson, named for a Hoh pioneer, consists of 8 sites. ADA-accessible toilet facilities; no running water. **Driving directions:** From Forks, drive 12.6 miles south on US 101 to the Upper Hoh Road. Turn inland and head 4.7 miles east. The campground is on the north side of the road. **Contact for all:** Washington Department of Natural Resources.

COTTONWOOD CAMPGROUND

This campground is right on the lower Hoh River, and years ago I watched my father hook and play a big, mint-bright steelhead right up to the bank here, where it slipped the hook and got away. The last time I visited, the campground and its 9 sites were in sorry shape, garbage strewn about and one wooden picnic table busted up apparently for firewood. But hit it at the right time and you'll enjoy your stay. A DNR campground, Cottonwood has no services except a pit toilet.

Contact: Washington Department of Natural Resources. **Driving directions:** From Forks, drive about 14 miles south on US 101, to between mileposts 177 and 178. Turn west on the Oil City Road and follow it for 2.3 miles, taking a left at the campground sign onto Road H4060 and following it less than a mile.

HIKING

RIALTO BEACH/HOLE IN THE WALL

IF YOU CAN DO ONLY ONE OLYMPIC NATIONAL PARK BEACH HIKE, THIS IS IT

The best day hike on any wilderness beach of the park is right here, the 2.4 miles from Little James Island at the mouth of the mighty Quillayute River north to the reef-lined bay beyond the sea arch known as Hole in the Wall. Shi Shi Beach and mind-blowing Point of Arches are hard to beat, true, true. Some might say the same of Ruby Beach. But Rialto Beach packs all the best of these beaches into one short stretch: Miocene islands and sea stacks that invite ebb-tide exploration, tide pools and surge channels rampant with marine life, broad agate beaches swept by growling surf, gargoyle piles of old-growth drift logs, and a stegosaurus-like sandstone hogback with a passageway clear through it. On a gray winter day, with a stout ocean swell rolling in, a hike here will feel almost as primordial as a walk on the dwarf planet Ceres. Those with limited mobility can also witness the thundering surf here via a wheelchair-accessible path from the parking area to the beach.

Distance: 3 miles round-trip to Hole in the Wall; 5 miles round-trip including a hike south to Little James Island
Elevation gain: Almost none
Difficulty: 2

The sea arch known as Hole in the Wall is set in a stegosaurus-like rock fin.

Map: Custom Correct North Olympic Coast
Contact: Olympic National Park
Notes: Park wilderness permit required for overnight stays; food must be kept in bear-proof container. You must camp north of Ellen Creek. Dogs permitted on-leash only from trailhead to Ellen Creek, otherwise prohibited. Loose gravel makes for difficult walking in places, but the trip is short.

DRIVING DIRECTIONS

From US 101, 2 miles north of Forks, head west on State Route 110 (Mora–La Push Road). In 7.7 miles, at the Three Rivers store, take a right on the Mora Road (the north spur of SR 110) and follow it to the parking area in about 5.1 miles.

THE HIKE

From the parking area, follow the accessible path through piles of driftwood and emerge on the beach. Look south: the pretty islands James (big and little). Look north: a broad gravel beach below jumbled piles of giant driftwood and a mile off, two tectonic spires of sandstone. Look west: surf that seems to roll and thunder like nowhere else on this coast, perhaps due to the gradient of the beach and the gravel shore. Or maybe it's just that the several times I've hiked here, always in the off-season, the swells have usually been up and surly.

Hike north, and in less than 1 mile of loose footing, reach tannin-stained Ellen Creek. In winter and spring, she can really roll, and you might have to clamber over driftwood log jams to get across. In summer or fall she can be either hopped or easily waded. Now the scenery gets really cool as you approach pointed sea-stack sand castles that are 80, 90, maybe 100 feet high and tickled at the toes by the swirling surf. Find very nice camps in the upland woods.

If you've packed chocolate and red wine and you're hiking with your honey, pull up a drift log—this is a very sweet spot. Or continue north into a little bay past the sea stacks, beyond which is the sandstone rock face framing at its seaward end the fascinating Hole in the Wall. If the tide is down you can hike right through it. If not, you can climb a short trail inland and around the wall. The reef-protected bay north of the wall also harbors a few campsites, and when the tide is down there is excellent tide-pooling, crazy with colorful sea stars, anemones, chitons, mussels, limpets, snails, crabs, and tiny little blind blennies flitting through the sea fronds.

KEEP EXPLORING

If you're a strong day hiker, you can make your way north for a rough and rocky 2 miles to the pretty bay of Chilean Memorial before turning around (see "Ozette to Rialto Through-Hike"). Check the tides, since one point along the way can't be rounded at tides higher than 5 feet.

To explore the James islands, head south from the beach near the trailhead, shortly reaching the jetty on the north bank of the Quillayute River, directly across from the village of La Push. You'll need a minus tide to best explore this stretch, to reach Little James and get good looks at the entire James group. If you've got a very low minus, say minus 1.7 feet, you'll be able to follow the shore on the west side of the jetty all the way to the usually submerged spit that connects Little James Island to the mainland.

If not, you'll have to scramble atop the jetty rocks—use care; they can be slippery and are big and jagged on the edges. However, being atop the jetty allows you to see the very lower end and mouth of the Quillayute, a very active place. You might see Quileute fishermen tending their gillnets. On a mid-April trip, I saw several harbor seals and two or three enormous sea lions chasing steelhead and/or spring chinook. I was pleased to see them catch none, but it was fascinating watching them rolling, splashing, and surfacing in their fruitless pursuits. At least half a dozen bald eagles perched nearby, apparently waiting for the marine mammals to catch a fish so they could pursue leftover morsels.

The jetty is flat on top for much of the way, and about two-thirds of the way along its length you'll be able to scramble down and reach the ocean shore, close to spruce-topped Little James. You can walk right up to it on a minus tide, and interesting tide pools circle its northwest side. Gunsight Rock and other stone sentinels rise from the sea just to the south. The biggest one is James Island itself, *Akalat* in the Quileute tongue, or Top of the Rock. In days gone by it served as a fortified village where the tribe could take refuge and defend itself during skirmishes with hostile tribes. It's said to have also served as a burial ground for Quileute chiefs.

The end of the jetty is about 1 mile from Rialto Beach; retrace your steps to return.

JAMES POND AND SLOUGH TRAILS

SHORT AND SEMISWEET

Two short nature trails at Olympic National Park's Mora Campground are best done together, both lovely but unspectacular. Both travel mature rain forest of large Sitka spruce and western hemlock, the understory rampant with the lush foliage of sword ferns, salal, and huckleberry, the ground carpeted by clover-shaped wood sorrel, heart-shaped false lily of the valley, and the curious brown fronds of step moss.

Distance: 2.2 miles round-trip
Elevation gain: About 40 feet
Difficulty: 1–2
Map: Custom Correct North Olympic Coast
Contact: Olympic National Park
Notes: Dogs prohibited

DRIVING DIRECTIONS

From US 101, 2 miles north of Forks, head west on State Route 110 (Mora–La Push Road). In 7.7 miles, at the Three Rivers store, take a right on the Mora Road (the north spur of SR 110) and follow it 3.2 miles, turning left at the campground sign. The Mora Ranger Station, typically staffed only in summer, is just on the east side of the campground entrance and is the trailhead for both trails.

THE HIKE

Bring binoculars on the short James Pond Trail, since the pond offers decent birding in the morning and evening. This pond might well be an ancient channel of the Quillayute River, long and narrow, strewn with logs. From the ranger station, find the path across the Mora Road to the north. It makes a 0.4-mile loop through deep green shrubbery and forest, which goes by quickly, since frankly there's not much to see.

Once back at the trailhead, take the Slough Trail, which leaves the east side of the ranger station parking lot and follows a bench above the Quillayute River through old and pretty spruce forest for about 0.5 mile before reaching an intersection. The left fork heads about 0.2 mile to the Mora Road; skip it. The right fork descends about 40 feet to an abrupt end at the slough. It's nice forest, but no scenic highlights. Simply retrace your steps.

SECOND BEACH

A MUST-DO WALK TO CRAZY OCEAN ROCKS

This exquisite 1.3-mile-long Olympic National Park beach is laced by the offshore rocks known as Quillayute Needles and bookended by impassable headlands, each graced by a sea-cut sandstone arch. Second Beach is easily reached, great for casual hikers, and a terrific place for a picnic. A couple campsites are tucked into the forest uplands, but most who camp here do so on the beach, above the high-tide line.

Distance: 4 miles round-trip if you explore the entire beach
Elevation gain: 200 feet
Difficulty: 2
Map: Custom Correct South Olympic Coast, but you'll hardly need it
Contact: Olympic National Park
Notes: Park wilderness permit required for overnight stays; food must be kept in a bear-proof container. Dogs prohibited. Pit toilet available. Use caution when exploring coves, reefs, and rocks so you don't become trapped by the incoming tide.

The islands and sea stacks at Second Beach are part of the huge lithic assemblage known as the Quillayute Needles.

DRIVING DIRECTIONS

From US 101, 2 miles north of Forks, head west on State Route 110 (Mora–La Push Road). Go about 13 miles, almost into La Push, and find the well-marked parking area and trailhead on the left.

THE HIKE

Pick a minus tide for hiking this beach if you can, because it will mitigate Second Beach's big drawback: it's just too short, blocked on the south by imposing Teahwhit Head and on the north by intriguing Quateata Head. You can't round either on foot anytime. But with a good low tide, you'll be able to fully explore the reefs, tide pools, and rock formations on both ends, which include two sea arches that lend visual poetry to this beach. And a primordially melodious beach it is, totally untamed and unchanged, appearing as it did in April of 1792 when Vancouver voyaged past.

The captain's naturalist, Archibald Menzies, could very well have been referring to this specific beach when somewhere just north of Destruction Island he wrote, "The whole shore we saild along this forenoon is steep and rocky and entirely lined with a vast number of elevated rocks and islets of different forms and size."

The remarkable assemblage of curiosities includes not just the arches but also such stone figures directly offshore as Crying Lady Rock, the dagger-shaped Quillayute Needle itself, and the islets known as Cakesosta Rocks. Second Beach is a veritable textbook of coastal geology, with chapters on tectonics, glaciation, changing sea levels, and erosion.

Climb a short hill from the trailhead into second-growth spruce forest and hustle through a plateau. With what's ahead, it's not worth taking your time. In about 0.5 mile you'll begin descending to the beach and soon see the rocks and islets. Pick your way through the driftwood at the bottom of the hill and emerge on the sand.

On your right, less than 0.25 mile north, is Quateata Head. You'll immediately notice the narrow oval arch partway along its long, sloping stone fin that angles down to the sea. This is the result of differential erosion, the sea having long ago scoured a soft spot out of the fin. At the foot of the arch is a reef-protected bay that provides cool tide-pooling on a minus tide. On an incoming tide, watch how the surf shoves the sea right through the arch. When seas are calm, keep an eye out for sea otters in the little bay and surrounding waters, since this reach of the coast represents one of their densest population concentrations in Washington. Scan the straggly spruce trees on the higher part of the fin for roosting bald eagles.

Almost in front of where the trail reaches the beach is a large nearshore block of volcanic rock, unusual for this area dominated by the sandstone of the two headlands that bookend the beach. The headlands are believed to be outcrops of a section of the earth's crust between two fault zones.

Just south of the volcanic block and a bit farther offshore is a spruce-topped islet surrounded by numerous other sandstone formations, one of which is the Crying Lady. I've read that the biggest island is the lady, but of them all, the one that appears to me most like a woman in tears is the upright, thumb-shaped rock immediately to the south. On a minus tide you can explore many of these islets and rocks. Farther offshore is the group called Cakesosta Rocks, perhaps from the Quileute word *kikc'ostal*, or "canoe-landing place." This is a major rookery site for a variety of shorebirds, notably gulls.

To the south of where the trail meets the shore is a mile of broad sandy beach, barricaded by huge Teahwhit Head and its labyrinth of projecting rocks. One of them defines a large triangular sea arch. It's best seen from the north a bit, because when you get closer the angle of the view puts other rocks behind it and the arch is harder to distinguish. The waves can roll in impressively on this south end of the beach, and sometimes the wind will whip wisps of spray off their tops as they break.

Small coves and pocket beaches around the north side of Teahwhit Head can be explored on a minus tide, but make sure that the tide has not turned. It would be very easy to get trapped behind a point by the incoming tide, and you'd be in an ocean of hurt.

That's not a good way to remember this beach. A better way would be to find a drift log upon which to perch on a clear evening, so you can recollect the sight of the falling sun silhouetting those needles. Since the approach trail is so short, you should be able to make it back to the trailhead by dark; bring a headlamp just in case.

FISHING THE LA PUSH, HOH AREA

For many people, the world in this region revolves around one thing: the mighty steelhead trout. For sure, there are a lot of other fish to catch here, including salmon, halibut, rockfish, and cutthroat. But perhaps the La Push–Hoh area's greatest angling attribute is being home to some of the best steelhead trout rivers in the world.

There are big steelhead rivers: the Bogachiel, Sol Duc, and Hoh. And small ones: the Calawah, Dickey, and Goodman Creek. Hatchery runs of smaller but feisty steelhead run early, from late November into February. And big runs of wild-spawning, native steelhead—some individuals reaching 30 pounds—run later, from late January into April.

Now, there's something that must be said right up front: Killing any wild steelhead in Washington State is a big issue. As a matter of conservation, many anglers simply won't do it, even where it's allowed.

The Hoh River descends into the Hoh Canyon.

The Washington Fish and Wildlife Commission has ruled that each properly licensed angler in Washington may take *one wild steelhead per year, and only one, and only from a handful of rivers*, all on the coast. Sad to say, this region has a long tradition of poaching, and more than a few anglers kill more than one steelhead per year. Respect is never due anyone who cheats, and by that I mean people who take wild fish illegally. Follow the rules, and learn which rivers to fish and when by checking with the Washington Department of Fish and Wildlife (see "Contacts and Resources").

One more word of caution: You will not be welcomed by your fellow anglers if you launch a motorized boat on any river here other than perhaps the main Quillayute. There's no written rule against it. It's a local tradition: drift boats, pontoon boats, or rafts only. Anglers who violate this custom by taking their jet sleds on the Hoh, Bogachiel, or any other river in this area risk having their tires slashed or rigs otherwise damaged. Don't get ticked at me, it's not my doing. However, I do favor the tradition of nonmotorized boating—not the vandalism though—and if you want to fish here you need to know the reality.

By the way, for the uninitiated, the way an angler determines whether a steelhead or salmon is of hatchery origin or of wild stock is by looking for an adipose fin. That's the small, smooth one on the fish's back between the dorsal fin and tail. All state hatchery steelhead, chinook, and coho are marked before they're planted in the rivers as fingerlings or fry by having the adipose clipped off. So if you catch a fish without an adipose fin and the season is open, you may whack it without compunction—bon appétit!

If you're looking for guides or charter boats, a good place to start is the Forks Chamber of Commerce or the Olympic Peninsula Visitors Bureau. See "Contacts and Resources" for all contact information, including for fishing regulations.

Here's a month-by-month description of fishing opportunities in this region:

January: This month is all steelhead, a transition period when the hatchery runs are waning but still viable, with the wild runs well underway by the end of the month. That means almost every river in the region is a good bet: the Hoh, Bogachiel, Calawah, and by midmonth the Sol Duc, for its wild-stock hatchery run and then its pure wild run. Even the little creeks, the ones that are open to fishing, can kick out steelhead in January.

February: True-blue steelhead anglers get all excited at the thought of fishing during the shortest of months, especially after a freshet. The hatchery run is pretty much done, and usually by midmonth serious numbers of wild steelhead begin showing up. Needless to say, it rains hard and often in winter, and rivers regularly rise so much and get so turbid that the fishing just isn't any good. But there's a magic period after the rain ends and the rivers crest and drop, when the clarity of the water improves to, say, 3 or 4 feet. Bright steelhead have moved in from the ocean, encouraged by the high flows, and fish that are fresh in bite most readily. If you're coming to this coast specifically to catch a big wild steelhead, begin marking your calendar on the last week of February. Most smaller streams close to steelhead fishing at the end of the month.

March: Then mark the entire month of March, because the peak of the wild steelhead run arrives sometime during these four-plus weeks. First, though, check your sportfishing rules pamphlet and the Washington Department of Fish and Wildlife's emergency regulations. Many smaller streams close to fishing at the end of February, and the state often closes other rivers usually open in March when run forecasts indicate a weak wild return. All the classic rivers are at their prime for native steelhead now, from tidewater to their upstream reaches, including the Calawah, Bogachiel, Sol Duc, and Hoh. By now anglers on the Sol Duc fishing downstream of the state salmon hatchery are taking some spring chinook. Lingcod fishing opens in the ocean usually at midmonth, but weather and seas are often problematic.

April: The wild steelhead run is beginning to wane in the lower rivers. But fishing can be good, with the weather warming and crowds thinning out. It's prime time for springers in the Sol Duc. Check the Fish and Wildlife rules pamphlet, though. The Hoh usually closes to fishing at midmonth and most other streams at the end of the month. Saltwater anglers out of La Push are now heading out daily when weather allows, for lingcod and rockfish. Surf perch anglers start seriously watching the forecast for calm periods.

May: This is the slowest month of the year in the rivers, but a busy month for bottomfishing in the ocean whenever weather allows. In the rivers, the lower Sol Duc is about it, open primarily for spring chinook, with anglers also taking some late winter steelhead, mostly downstreamers. The Hoh usually opens midmonth for salmon and steelhead (both under wild-release rules), but it's early yet. Offshore, halibut fishing typically opens midmonth, with good catches usually filling the catch quota and ending the season quickly. But rockfish and lingcod fishing remains open and is typically outstanding, with acres and acres of appropriately rocky habitat. Surf perch are an option.

June: The summer-run steelhead season commences in the Bogachiel, Calawah, Sol Duc, and the Hoh, all of which receive returns of marked hatchery fish that respond well to the fly, as well as to baits and lures. Summer steelheading is often best in June in the Bogachiel and Calawah, due to a combination of run timing of the "Skamania" stock used and river conditions, with flows usually still up and optimal. Summer steelhead catches usually peak later in the Sol Duc and Hoh, neither of which produce a lot of fish. Bottomfish action continues in the saltwater, and salmon fishing usually opens in the ocean late in the month, often starting off strong. Chinook salmon fishing often opens in the ocean and can be good. Surf perch fishing is often excellent.

July: Sea-run cutthroat trout begin moving into rivers and creeks from the ocean in numbers worth fishing, livening things up for fly-flippers and other stream anglers by adding an option to steelheading. A hatchery run of summer coho begins heading up the Sol Duc as well, along with lesser numbers of wild summer coho, but they're harder than hell to catch. A few summer chinook are now sneaking into the Hoh. In the ocean, the salmon season is going strong, with chinook and coho catches often spectacular but usually best some miles out and to the north of La Push. Bottomfishing continues.

August: This month is almost the same scene as July, except that in odd-numbered years pink salmon are added to the ocean salmon catch, and in the bigger rivers fall chinook begin trickling in from the sea. River fishing can be tough, though, due to low summer flows.

September: If they haven't already due to catch quotas being filled, ocean salmon seasons close after Labor Day, and rivers are now often running so low that fishing is tough. But when conditions allow, summer steelhead, sea-run cutthroat, summer/fall chinook, and even a few coho can be taken. It's actually not a bad month for bank fishing—the same can be said of August—since with flows down you can walk the whole bank and reach most drifts, and boat traffic is minimal.

October: This is the peak of the salmon season in the rivers, especially if rains raise flows, with the chinook run peaking early in the month and the coho run nearing its peak by the end of the month. A few fall-run wild steelhead sneak into the Hoh now.

November: This month is pretty much a coho show in the rivers, with a few late chinook around. By the last week of the month, the front end of the hatchery run of winter steelhead will appear, especially in the Bogachiel and lower Calawah rivers. These are bright fish fresh from the sea, usually smaller, from 4 to 8 pounds, but on strong run years they can arrive suddenly after a freshet in good numbers.

December: The hatchery run of winter steelhead typically peaks around the third week of the month. On good years there will be a lot, and while many wild fish purists poo-poo hatchery steelhead as inferior, I've caught "three-salt" hatchery steelhead more than 12 to 14 pounds that fought like screamin' meemies. Plus, you can bonk them for the barbecue or smoker.

THIRD BEACH TO HOH RIVER THROUGH-HIKE

ROAMING THE WILD AND RESTLESS OLYMPIC SHORE

If you tackle this often rugged and always spectacular stretch of coast between Third Beach and the Hoh River without falling madly in love with the wilderness coast of Olympic National Park, you'd better stick to golf or gambling. You're not cut out to be a coastal hiker. What I love about this hike is that it combines everything exhilarating about this restless shore: tough slogs over gooey headlands, rocky grottoes and secret pocket beaches, long and easy sand and gravel beaches, shoes-off river crossings, a maze of sand-castle sea stacks, wildlife intensity, and the unmistakable sense of those who came before.

Distance: 17.1 miles one-way
Elevation gain: About 500 feet
Difficulty: 4
Map: Custom Correct South Olympic Coast
Contact: Olympic National Park
Notes: Park wilderness permit required for overnight stays; food must be kept in bear-proof container. Dogs prohibited. Tide tables necessary for navigating headlands.

Huge drift logs like this wave-shredded red cedar at Third Beach are toppled and delivered to the seashore by high flows on nearby rain forest rivers.

DRIVING DIRECTIONS

From US 101, 2 miles north of Forks, head west on State Route 110 (Mora–La Push Road). In a little more than 10 miles, find the marked Third Beach trailhead on the left. For a car shuttle, the south end of this hike is on the north bank of the Hoh River near its mouth, a place called Oil City (even though there's no city). Drive south from Forks on US 101 about 14 miles, turn right (west) on the Oil City Road, and find the trailhead at road's end in 12 miles.

THE HIKE

The first 1.4 miles is gently downhill on a good path through pretty rain forest of cedar and spruce—blow through it, man, the ocean is just ahead and absolutely intriguing! Come to the beach, passing at least one campsite, clamber over the driftwood, and look south. That myriad of islets and sea stacks is called the Giants Graveyard—crazy rocks as far as the eye can see! They are sandstone remnants of the earth's crust, deposited some twenty million years ago, shoved, lifted, and folded by intense tectonic force and stress and then eroded by the elements over time. And look, on the bluff at the end of the beach: a pretty waterfall spilling into the sea.

You can explore north only a short 0.5 mile before dead-ending at impassable Teahwhit Head. But do it. The last time I was there I found among the driftwood

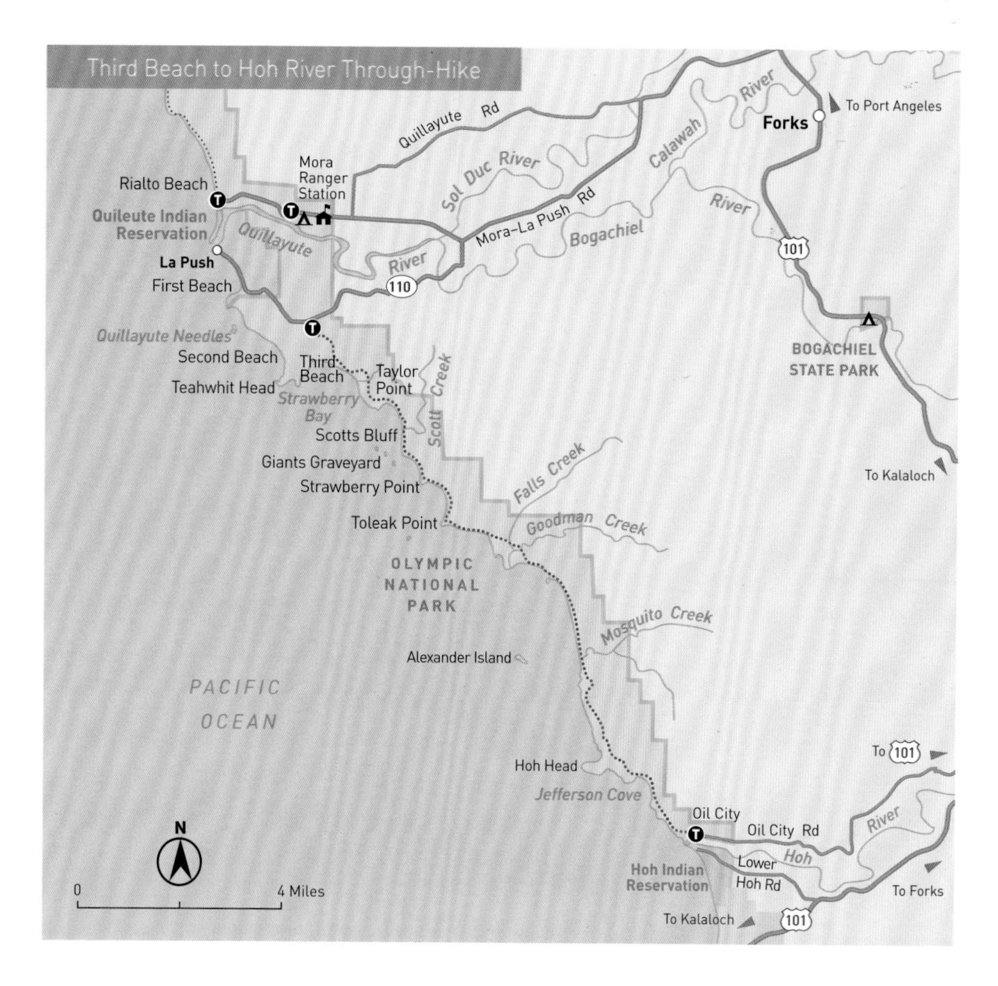

piled at surf's edge a huge iron wheel, the relic of an effort between 1899 and 1902 to drill for oil, toppled from the bluff above.

Then head south and savor an easy 0.5 mile of sandy beach, because it ends at the bluff with the waterfall, Taylor Point, and the route is up and over it. In late 2013, rangers reported that a slide had covered about 75 yards of beach just north of Taylor Point and that crossing the debris was difficult; they recommended going around it, requiring a tide lower than 5 feet. Check for ongoing or new slides on the park website before setting out.

Just beyond, at 1.8 miles from the trailhead, note an orange and black trail marker just short of the bluff. Incredibly, the route first climbs a nearly vertical wall of soggy clay and mud. You look at it and think, "That can't be!" But that is the stairway to heaven, brothers and sisters, starting with a bit of hell.

Onward and upward! Invented by rangers, sand ladders are designed to get hikers up steep and unstable slopes while minimizing erosion.

Last time I hiked this it was in late January, and this wet bluff had sloughed severely at the bottom. It seemed like there had been a sand ladder, a loose cable and timber structure designed to float over Mother Nature's geologic twists and turns. But it was gone. Only two ropes remained, tied at the top of the slide about 70 feet up. My hiking companions and I put on gloves and climbed, and it proved not so bad. Once above the slide, the route was intact, mounting a sand ladder and winding up through a cut to emerge atop Taylor Point.

Older guidebooks reported that Taylor Point could be rounded along the shore, with some difficulty, on a minus tide. But all sources, including the park, now say the point can't be rounded on any tide. You must climb over it. That's not a bad thing, because the forest atop it is interesting and pretty, the trail weaving through head-high salal and salmonberry, dense sword ferns, and thin hemlock and spruce trees. If you're allergic to the color green, you'll come down with hives here.

It's more than 1 mile over the point, and you cross the little stream that becomes the waterfall not long after you hit the top. At the south end the route drops back down with a fixed-rope assist (thank you, rangers!) at 3 miles, to a mostly rocky cove, with some tricky boulder hopping. If the tide is up, you must clamber up and over the big rocks, at one point following a short tunnel through a sandstone wall.

You then emerge onto a crescent beach, easily followed for less than 1 mile to Scotts Bluff. You can round this bluff at tides lower than 1 foot, or climb it. The route over the top is less than 0.5 mile and passes the site where a quaint cedar shelter once stood. The park removed it sometime after the mid-1970s, the start of an ongoing policy dictating the removal of most wilderness structures not deemed historic. But I remember it well, because I slept there on the first of my many nights backpacking along this wilderness coast, sometime around 1976 or 1977. C'est la vie.

Drop down to the beach at 4 miles to find several camps around Scott Creek, all exquisite spots to perch and ponder while looking out over the Giants Graveyard at the world's largest sea. As the planet rotates on a clear evening, watch the sun cast shadows between these stone bones of planet Earth as it drops with a golden flourish.

But there's a lot of good stuff ahead, and easy beach walking for the next 3+ miles south, with decent agate hunting. This is also a terrific stretch to search for glass fishing floats that sometimes wash ashore from Asia. I saw a photo taken by a well-known local beachcomber some years ago after a fierce storm: glass floats of various sizes were scattered across one beach in this stretch, more than twenty of them.

The next point south can be rounded on any tide lower than 4 feet, or easily climbed, and then at about 5.4 miles reach pretty Strawberry Point. This minor point can be rounded on any tide and is an exquisite camp spot, with nearshore sea stacks that can be explored at lower tides. Between Strawberry Point and Toleak Point at 6.4 miles is a crescent-shaped sand beach of about a mile, with a curiously tilted cone-shaped stack also very close to shore. On the entire stretch between Scott Creek and Toleak, watch for seals, sea lions, porpoises, gray whales (particularly in spring and fall), and most especially, sea otters.

Stunning Toleak Point once served as a seasonal encampment of either the Quileute or Hoh tribe. When I first came here in the late 1970s, a bench just above the beach made a splendid camp spot, precisely where the village had stood. The bones of whales and seals were scattered in the surrounding bushes. Since then, however, the ocean has devoured this low terrace and most camping is now on the beach above the high-tide line. It remains a superlative spot, with a picturesque island and associated sea stacks ringing the point.

Just south is a year-round creek for water, and on the bluff above is an old wood shelter no longer habitable whatsoever. Long ago I spent two February nights here in the open-ended shack. Late the first night I heard a rustle near where my hiking buddies and I had left an almost empty plastic garbage sack. This was well before the requirement that all food and odiferous items be kept in a bear-proof canister. Anyway, I flipped on my flashlight and caught the tail end of a spotted skunk high-tailing it for the bushes—not exactly a pleasant perspective. Hoping I had scared it off, I snuggled back into my sleeping bag, only to hear the rustling noise a few minutes later. I flipped on the flashlight and it fled again, and rather than risk causing a serious stink, I knotted the plastic bag and tossed it into the bushes outside. There wasn't much in the bag anyway, and in the morning we found it undisturbed.

Nowadays, a ranger camp is set up nearby during the peak season. Year-round is a pit toilet, open to the elements and nicely positioned on the hill so that the sitter might enjoy a grand view of the offshore sea stacks.

The easy walking continues on pleasant beach for about 1 mile to the headland of Goodman Creek, at 7.3 miles, which must be climbed via a 1.5-mile inland trail. Goodman Creek is a fair-sized stream with a decent run of winter steelhead—I caught a dandy buck of 11 pounds in it once—as well as sea-run cutthroat and salmon. It also has an interesting mouth. Over the final ⅛ mile before it meets the sea, it flows through a rock gorge with steep walls 30 to 50 feet high. This curious geology raises the question of how the creek cut through the gorge. Why didn't the flow eons ago just go around the rock?

Ponder that as you ford not only Goodman Creek just above the entrance of this gorge but also its tributary just upstream, Falls Creek, which true to its name descends in a lovely double cataract. You can't cross either stream at high tide, which pushes upstream about 0.5 mile, or during rain-induced high flows. You can sometimes find a log to cross over Falls Creek, but at Goodman I've always had to doff the boots and wade.

The headland trail ends at 8.8 miles, at a beautiful sandy beach that leads about 2.2 miles south to Mosquito Creek, at 11 miles. This stream offers the sea about half as much flow as Goodman Creek and produces a small run of winter steelhead, along with cutthroat. It also can't be crossed during high tide or high flows. Just north of the creek a level bench once embraced beautiful campsites where the Coast Guard maintained dog kennels and a patrol station during World War II. The bench is now gone, consumed by ferocious seas during a storm about thirty years ago.

Beach camping is good here, however, except during extreme high tides, and a spacious camping area remains on the bluff above the south bank of Mosquito Creek. It's well worth camping here, especially when daytime tides are low enough to explore the beaches to the south. One sunny and sublime May evening, my best friend Scott and I sat on a huge drift log here, swigging on a bottle of Crown Royal and watching gray whales spouting and rolling just offshore, apparently feeding.

To complete this hike you must take a 3.5-mile inland trail that leads around massive Hoh Head. It's nice forest, but the trail is often muddy with minor ups and downs and, well, it gets boring. Before a slide occurred, hikers at very low tides could take the beach south for 2 miles before climbing a steep and wet bluff to get atop Hoh Head. That cut the inland trail down to about 1+ mile. You can't do that anymore; that bluff is now impassable. But that 2-mile stretch of beach can still be explored (you'll need a tide of less than 0.5 feet to get around the first point south), and it's full of cool coves, pocket beaches, sea stacks, tide pools, and a sea cave. It's very wild—particularly now that it can't be hiked through. In addition, Perkins Reef just offshore of this stretch is known by biologists for its concentration of sea otters.

At the south end of Hoh Head, the inland trail drops precipitously to rocky Jefferson Cove, at 14.5 miles. From here it's 2.6 miles to the Oil City trailhead on the north bank of the Hoh River. There are two minor headlands that require tides lower than 2 and 3 feet to round and can't be climbed. Despite the rocky nature of this stretch, one time I found a softball-sized glass fishing float here, partially covered by kelp.

This hike is like that, full of surprises, superbly rewarding. You gain a sense of the primal ebb and flow of life in this wilderness, and it puts your own life in perspective. Please treat it for what it is, an absolutely precious part of America, a priceless legacy for future citizens of this country and the world.

SPRUCE NATURE TRAIL AND HALL OF MOSSES

WHERE MAPLES GROW BEARDS AND SPROUT MICROCOSMS

A mind-boggling proliferation of life upon life in myriad shades of green lushness greets walkers on these two short and easy but mesmerizing loop trails, both beginning at the Hoh Rain Forest Visitor Center and campground and best done together. If you want a short introduction to one of the finest remaining examples of temperate rain forest in the United States, you won't find a better one. You might well see elk, otters, eagles, and/or salmon.

Distance: 2 miles round-trip
Elevation gain: About 100 feet
Difficulty: 2
Map: Custom Correct Seven Lakes Basin–Hoh or brochure from the visitor center
Contact: Olympic National Park
Notes: Park entrance fee required. Canines? *Nein!*

DRIVING DIRECTIONS

From Forks, head south on US 101 for 12.6 miles. Turn east onto the Upper Hoh Road and follow it upriver a little more than 18 miles. The park entrance station is reached about 13 miles along the road.

The bones of a coho salmon—found along a spring-fed creek near the Spruce Nature Trail—deteriorate and lend their nutrients to the forest.

THE HIKE

Chills almost crawl up your back when you hike coastal rain forest, because it's often dark, damp, and moody, the trees big, old, burdened, and seemingly brooding. Perhaps most spectacular is the signature species of the temperate rain forest, the magnificent big-leaf maple. The largest North American maple, it reaches for light, sometimes 100 feet or more high. Its canopy seems as wide as its height, the branches broad and sweeping, some upward and some laterally, and usually laden with other species—mosses, lichens, ferns—that in sum can weigh four times its own foliage.

But when you understand that each part of this incredible proliferation of foliage is interdependent—each lending its attributes to some and borrowing from others—you realize that this is not a sad forest at all. Abundant red alders add to the soil nitrogen, an important growth nutrient. The maple's profuse leaf, blossom, and seed litter enriches the forest floor with potassium, calcium, and ultimately fertile, moisture-retaining humus. The canopy of the maples, alders, cottonwoods, and spruce creates an ultrahumid environment where a crazy variety of mosses, liverworts, and ferns proliferate. Walk these two trails and you'll get a powerful sense for what happens in a place where it rains 12 to 14 feet a year.

Find the trailhead just east of the visitor center. On your right is the start of the Spruce Nature Trail and the Hoh River Trail—the latter heads well inland and then upward toward Mount Olympus—beyond the scope of a book about the coast. But the Spruce Nature Trail loops through an environment that is ever so linked to the ocean, following a creek where coho salmon can be seen spawning in fall, later adding their life's essence to the rain forest—and making quite a big stink.

This is a spring-fed creek, absolutely crystal, limpid, and lovely. Lime-green sword ferns sprout prolifically along its banks, anywhere not covered by the detritus of the forest. Downed alders and spruce span the creek bank, all draped with pale olive club moss or hanging moss, while spruce boughs litter the forest floor. The understory of this forest is surprisingly open, thanks to browsing elk, and dominated by ferns and ground mosses.

The dominant conifer here is spruce, as the trail name implies, and some of them are of imposing proportion, easily 6 feet through at the butt. In about 0.25 mile, you'll reach the bank of the Hoh River at a wide bend, offering upstream views of its meandering and frequently changing course. Impelled by intense rains and the meltwaters of Mount Olympus's glaciers, the Hoh goes wherever it may, and always has. The trail follows the river upstream for less than 0.25 mile before veering back toward its start, entering a cool glade of maples festooned amazingly with mosses and licorice ferns. Your shutter will be snapping here; you'll get the best results with a fast lens. But don't dally because there are even better angles up ahead, down the Hall of Mosses.

Reach the intersection with the Hoh River Trail again at 1.2 miles, and just before you reach the ranger station, find the signed start of the Hall of Mosses. This little loop starts by crossing the creek near its spring-pond source and then climbs a ridge above, offering views over same. Look, but keep moving; the real show is ahead and it'll spike your wow meter. Keep to the left at a trail intersection (the other way is the other end of the loop) and shortly come to a little spur, defined by a fence, on the left, in about 0.4 mile. You're entering the hall, a glade of impressive big-leaf maples draped with long green-brown curtains of curly moss. The fence is designed to keep the feet of the masses out of the hall's inner sanctum.

But don't fret: the trail passes the heart of another churchly glade just ahead. Return to the main trail and soon find yourself strolling under big and amazing maples sporting a multitude of mosses and ferns. Hanging club moss (*Selaginella oregana*) is the main one, descending 2 or 3 feet. But you might also see tree-ruffle liverwort in creeping mats, balls of the true hanging moss (*Antitrichia curtipendula*), wispy cattail moss, and dense, shaggy coil-leafed moss. These mosses and liverworts are bryophytes, or nonvascular species, lacking well-developed water-conducting systems. Who needs 'em in this sodden setting?

Vascular species thrive here as well, such as the delicate, feathery licorice fern, one of many epiphytes here—plants that grow on plants—sticking out everywhere on the wet spines of maple trunks and branches. Wow. Get out your tripod, try to capture it all in a box. Morning and evening light are best.

Soak in this rain-forest glen and marvel at the tenacity of life. Measure your own luminosity against its sheer insistence. It's a curious perspective. Then move on down the trail, which shortly closes the loop before descending to the creek crossing and point of origin in 0.8 mile.

SALMON: "KING," "SILVER," "HUMPY," WHAT?

Salmon are tightly woven into the fabric of coastal culture, and their remarkable life history is well known throughout the Northwest. Born in rivers and creeks, they migrate to sea, sometimes thousands of miles, to feed and grow before returning to struggle upstream, spawn, and then die. But people who don't fish are often puzzled by the various species and names. So here's a basic primer on our five native Pacific salmon species, plus the similar and important steelhead trout.

Chinook, a.k.a. "king," "spring," "blackmouth": Largest of the Pacific salmon, in Washington mature *Oncorhynchus tshawytscha* range from 10 to more than 60 pounds; the state-record sport-caught king was 70.5 pounds (at Sekiu). Many consider chinook the tastiest salmon (particularly spring-run kings), rich, earthily pungent, reminiscent of the sea. Chinook life history is diverse: they leave natal rivers anywhere from immediately on emergence from the spawning gravel to two years later and spend from one to five years at sea, returning to rivers as adults almost year-round, mostly March through November. They are incredibly prized by anglers and are sporting when taken on hook and line, due to their size, strength, and variety of escape maneuvers.

Coho, a.k.a. "silver," "hooknose": *Oncorhynchus kisutch* is the second most important salmon to anglers, a sporting, acrobatic fish when hooked that grows to 8–12 pounds at maturity, typically spending one and a half years in rivers of birth before heading to sea for eighteen months to two years (the state record is 25.34 pounds, at

Sekiu). Oil-rich, but not as heavily as chinook, they are superb table fare, with a distinct pungent but gentle marine flavor.

Pink, a.k.a. "humpbacked," "humpy": An exaggerated dorsal hump develops on mature males. Smallest of the Pacific salmon, *Oncorhynchus gorbuscha* averages 4–5 pounds (the state record is 15.4 pounds, at Stillaguamish River). In Washington waters, by some quirk of evolution, the majority spawn only on odd-numbered years; almost none are seen in even-numbered years. It's not considered the best salmon for eating, but properly handled (immediate bleeding, icing) pinks are quite palatable, with a vague nutty flavor. Easy to catch, sought by sport fishermen, they migrate past Neah Bay and Sekiu but don't spawn in most coastal rivers.

Chum, a.k.a. "dog salmon," "keta," marketed as "silverbrite": Lowest-quality salmon for eating and least important recreationally, dog salmon spawn in many coastal rivers and are taken primarily for the sport of it. The second-largest salmon, *Oncorhynchus keta* average about 10 pounds (the state record at 25.97, at Satsop River) and are strong and powerful. They don't bite well in saltwater but are caught in many rivers.

Sockeye, a.k.a. "red," "blueback": Extremely high-quality table fare, sockeye have only two coastal runs (Quinault and Ozette rivers), although millions pass through the Strait of Juan de Fuca each summer. Rich with oil and delicately but distinctly flavored, *Oncorhynchus nerka* average about 5 pounds (the state record is 10.6 pounds, at Lake Washington). The famed Quinault blueback is struggling but holding on, while Ozette sockeye are diminished, protected under the Endangered Species Act. Sockeye can be taken in saltwater with the right tackle (a chrome dodger and blue or red hook, fished bare); there is potential for significant sport fisheries off Neah Bay and Sekiu.

Steelhead trout, no real nickname: *Oncorhynchus mykiss* is a salmonid but also a rainbow trout that migrates to sea, arguably the finest game fish on the Washington Coast. Incredibly strong, averaging 5–14 pounds (the state record is 35.06 pounds, at Snake River). It has a highly varied life history, spending one to three years in rivers before heading to sea for one to three years. Particularly wide-ranging, steelhead from the Washington Coast have been captured and tagged by Japanese research vessels 6000 miles across the Pacific. Steelhead don't die after spawning as do true salmons; some spawn two or three times. Most return to rivers early winter into spring (the so-called winter-runs). Certain races enter rivers late spring into fall (summer-runs). They spawn in virtually every river on the coast and are excellent eating.

The chinook, or "king," is the largest salmon. Note that this big king, taken at Sekiu, lacks an adipose fin between the dorsal fin and tail, which indicates it is of hatchery origin.

A rosy tint decorates the gill plate of this female steelhead, caught and then released in the Hoh River. Note the adipose fin on its back, which indicates it is of wild origin.

Another popular game fish on the coast is the pretty cutthroat trout.

KALALOCH AND THE QUEETS RIVER

MY INTRODUCTION TO THE MAGICAL bliss of the ocean and the Washington Coast came while staying in one of the older cabins at Kalaloch with my parents, brother, and sister some fifty years ago, back when the village was operated as Becker's. We'd stay for a week every year, in spring or summer. I can still see my mom standing by the stove frying razor clams or surf perch, her black hair wavy and short, or sweeping the door stoop free of the sandy mess left by her brood. I can picture my dad walking back to the cabin, hip boots folded at the knee, fishing pole in one hand, a bucket of perch in the other, a cigarette dangling from his lips and contentment etched across his face. As I look back a lifetime later, it seems like yesterday, and I feel the allure of the ocean stronger than ever.

The rustic Kalaloch Lodge, built in the 1950s atop the bank of Kalaloch Creek, offers views of the mighty Pacific.

But many never come to know Kalaloch's charms. This relatively short ribbon of ocean beach is a long way from major population centers, on the western edge of the continent, almost four hours from Seattle by any route. And at first glance it's just a long, sandy beach—nice enough, but lacking the geologic drama of beaches to the north. That's not exactly accurate. Inspiring sea stack scenery, tectonic contortions, and other lithified curiosities are found here. But ironically, the same characteristics that cause this beach to be overlooked are what make it so intriguing.

First, this stretch of shoreline is paralleled for several miles by that iconic West Coast ribbon of asphalt known as US 101, so a lot of hikers see Kalaloch as too tourist-oriented and skip it. The upside? There are seven easy approaches to the beach along just 11 miles of highway.

Second, much of this part of the coast looks the same—long sandy beaches seemingly lacking diversity, especially in the Kalaloch Lodge and campground vicinity. So visitors assume they've seen it all. But there are plenty of harder-to-reach spots that are lightly visited, which happen to be among the most exquisite. Most folks miss the quiet rocky coves of spots like Browns Point, or the lonesome, wild, and headland-hindered 4-mile stretch between Beach 4 and Ruby Beach. Some of these are very sexy beaches where you just might find yourself alone with your sweetheart and the surf. But you might have to hike a ways to reach them, wade a couple streams, and pay heed to the tides to get around a few points.

Finally, the long sandy nature of these shores creates ideal conditions for a lot of activities. Beachcombing after a storm can be superb. The open sandy shore welcomes flotsam and doesn't shatter the beachcomber's trophy, those precious glass fishing floats rarely used to hold up nets today but still kicked out of the North Pacific currents. The few locations marked by rocks and sea stacks offer amazing tide-pooling, perhaps as rich as anywhere on the coast. The best spots on the entire Washington Coast for dipnetting surf smelt are right here, precisely because these coarse sand and gravel beaches offer optimal spawning conditions. Surf perch fishing is as good here as anywhere because of the open habitat of the breakers. Wildlife watching is fabulous. You can see eagles diving into the surf for smelt, also otters, dolphins, and seals fishing for them as well. Whale-watching is unobstructed and optimal here. In spring, you can often sit at your South Beach or Kalaloch campsite with binoculars and watch an endless stream of gray whales spouting and rolling.

Furthermore, this wide-open shore makes for inspirational ocean watching. You really get a sense for the vastness of the ocean here, or as Kipling put it in

"The Sea and the Hills," "the sight of salt water unbounded—The heave and the halt and the hurl and the crash of the comber wind-hounded." If you sit for a spell, the back-and-forth Zen of the tides and waves can feel like those breakers are tossing the dawn of time right into your lap.

Even more remote is the rain-forest valley of the Queets River, well worth visiting. The valley is heavily populated by Olympic elk, and they're often seen here. But the Queets River is best known for its superb fishing for winter steelhead, some of which reach trophy proportions—25 to 30 pounds.

History is rich here too. At either end of this part of the coast are two Native tribes, the Hoh and the Queets, often regarded as outlying bands of larger groups—but if you ask them, they will tell you they are their own people. The Hoh live at the mouth of the river of the same name; they spoke the Chimakuan tongue like the larger Quileute tribe to the north.

The Queets live on the Queets River, some 15 miles to the south of the Hoh. The Queets spoke a Salishan dialect like their neighbors to the south, the Quinault. But both the Hoh and the Queets have been here on their own for millennia, fishing the sea, the shore, and the two bountiful rivers, hunting the inland forests, gathering roots and berries, making a living and guarding their lands zealously.

All of the coastal tribes of Washington engaged in warfare. I'm not an anthropologist, but competition for territory and resources seems a plausible explanation. They were fierce people ready to take on all comers, also occasionally hostile to the strange white people who sailed the coast starting some 250 years ago. The Hoh were among the most notorious, killing and/or capturing several crew from the Russian *Sv. Nikolai* when they attempted to flee south after their ship foundered near La Push in 1808. Earlier, in 1787, English fur trader Captain Charles Barkley lost six crew members to the Hoh.

In this region, you can hike along the likely spot where this all happened. To me, knowing that history makes the region come alive.

GETTING THERE/STAYING THERE

Kalaloch is easy to find, directly on US 101 about 35 miles south of Forks and 65 miles north of Hoquiam. The turnoff for the Queets Valley is about 15 miles south of Kalaloch.

Kalaloch's first lodge was built just south of Kalaloch Creek by Charles W. Becker Sr., sometime in the late 1920s. Becker's Ocean Resort opened with a lodge and several cabins on the bluff above the beach. Today's Kalaloch Lodge was built in the early 1950s to replace the original, which burned down in 1943 (see "Contacts and Resources" for all contact information). Open year-round, it is the only lodge directly on the north Washington Coast and one of the few area accommodations in close proximity to the ocean. Lining the bluff just south of the lodge itself are two rows of cabins, all extremely popular.

Services are limited on this remote part of the Washington Coast, with only two small stores, at Kalaloch and the tribal village of Queets. Olympic National Park maintains an information center at the Kalaloch Ranger Station, open daily in summer but rarely any other time. When it is open, you can get park maps, brochures, and fishing regulation pamphlets.

FEES AND PERMITS

There are no Park Service entrance fees at Kalaloch or in the Queets Valley.

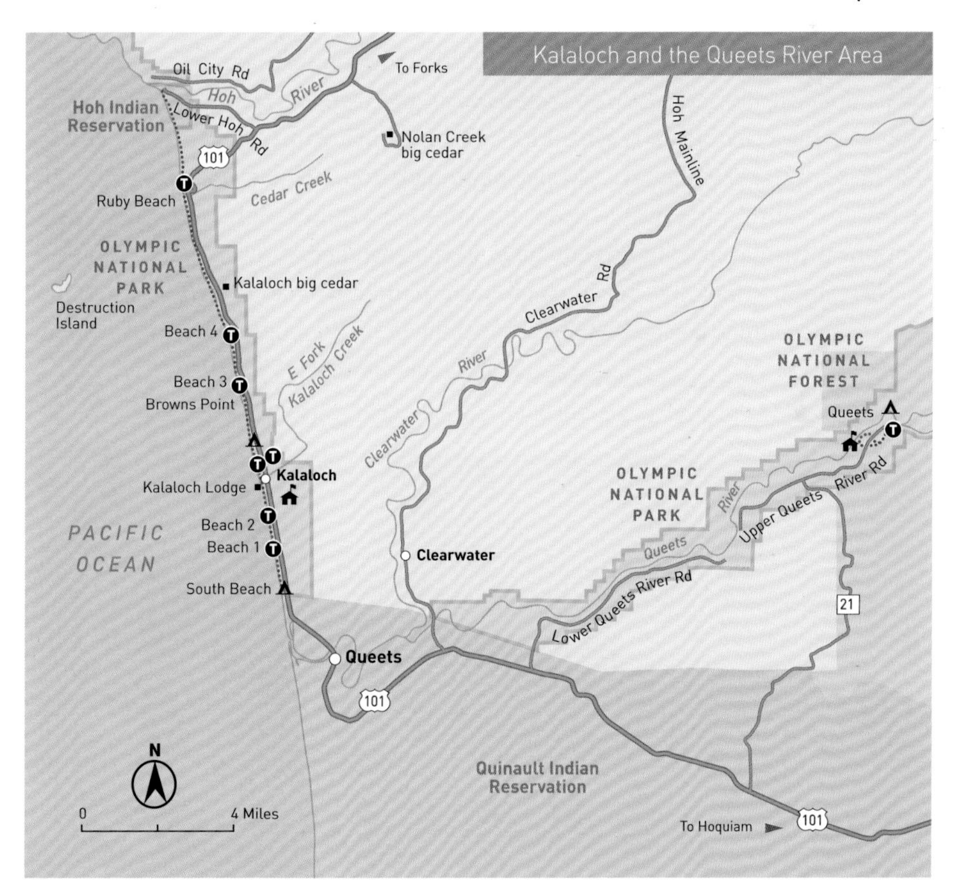

CAMPING

KALALOCH

Hands down this is the finest campground on the Washington Coast (Cape Disappointment State Park is a close second), set in a quaint spruce forest on a low bluff directly above the roaring Pacific Ocean. Rangers lead campfire programs and beach walks in summer.

This is the only campground in Olympic National Park where reservations can be made, but summertime only (mid-June–early September). During that time it can be busy in the extreme, with the best sites reserved and the rest taken by noon or 1:00 PM, check-out time being 11:00 AM. The campground has 170 campsites and is open year-round, but only three of the six loops are open in the off-season. All campsites offer large, sturdy picnic tables and iron fire rings with grills. Running water is available and restrooms (no showers) are open year-round. During the off-season, campsites are $14 per night, and you self-pay at stations near the restrooms. During the busy season, the sites are $18 per night and you pay at a kiosk near the day-use lot directly beyond the entrance.

There are no hookups, but most sites can handle RVs up to 21 feet, and a few spots can accommodate up to 35 feet. Speaking of no hookups, please be courteous

Sunsets at Kalaloch can be dramatic, like this one silhouetting Destruction Island.

USE CAUTION ON DRIFT LOGS AND KEEP A CLEAN CAMP

A few precautionary notes must be added here. The Kalaloch beaches are popular for families and lined with massive piles of drift logs, many of them huge, fed to the sea by the big rain-forest rivers Hoh and Queets. Those logs have killed people. When the tide is high and up into the wood, waves can fling 2-ton logs like an angry black bear snapping sticks. This is not a good time to be on the beach.

At any tide level, if a log is in the water, being pushed and pulled by the surf, for god's sake don't play on it or around it. Looks like fun, you might think, but you're wrong, maybe dead wrong if it rolls over you.

There are critters here too. Occasionally cougars are seen on the beaches and the Park Service will post precautionary signs, as well as in the Queets Valley, but they are rarely any problem (see "Chew on This: Critter Concerns" in chapter 2). Raccoons are a persistent nuisance at the two beach campgrounds. They are just doing what comes naturally. People are the real problem. Secure all food, drink, and any other stink in your car or in one of the food lockers the Park Service provides.

Please use your head when you visit this awe-inspiring shoreline. If you do, you'll discover a natural salve for the soul. If you're weary of city life, this place is absolutely therapeutic.

if you come with a generator. Remember that most of your neighboring campers will not appreciate listening to or smelling your gas motor. If you must use a generator, please be sure to shut it down between 8:00 PM and 9:00 AM.

Contact: Olympic National Park. **Driving directions:** Kalaloch Campground is on the west side of US 101, 35 miles south of Forks and 65 miles north of Hoquiam.

SOUTH BEACH

The 55 sites in this Olympic National Park campground circle an open grass and gravel area and offer absolutely no privacy, but most have a stupendous view across the Pacific Ocean to the very curve of planet Earth. Sites perch atop a low bluff over the breakers and combers, with little vegetation to obstruct the views. If you get one of the bluff-edge sites, you can sit at your camp and watch gray whales rolling and spouting just outside the surf (best in spring). You'll see eagles soaring along the bluff and if you look closely, seals at the edge of the surf. You are definitely going to want to bring binoculars.

This campground is extremely popular among RV, trailer, and pickup-camper travelers. I'm a tent camper who enjoys a degree of privacy, so I've never camped at South Beach. But I have picnicked here and stopped to watch whales, and I'm always knocked out by the view.

The driftwood-lined, cobbled ocean beach is just a tiny scramble below. Because the campground is just north of the Queets and about 10 miles south of the Hoh—two of the world's finest temperate rain-forest rivers—the drift logs here are often immense remnants of old-growth red cedar and Sitka spruce. When swells are down, surf perch fishing is great.

The campground is usually open Memorial Day weekend through mid-September; first-come, first-served; $10 per night. The campsites all have picnic tables and fire rings. There is a restroom, but it's not wheelchair accessible. Running water is available. Most sites can accommodate RVs up to 21 feet, and a few can handle up to 35 feet.

RAZOR CLAMMING

Razor clams on the Kalaloch beaches seem sensitive to minor changes in ocean conditions. The population here fluctuates more than at Washington's four other traditional razor clam beaches to the south, so seasons in this area have been restricted in recent years. Digging has been closed since 2010 due to low numbers.

Those of us who have enjoyed razor clam digging at Kalaloch—the first time for me was more than fifty years ago—have high hopes for a rebound. After all, these fascinating golden-shelled dwellers of the ocean sands have been providing sustenance to human beings for thousands of years.

When the season is open in the Kalaloch area, digging is allowed only from South Beach Campground north to Browns Point, not quite 4 miles. Check with the Washington Department of Fish and Wildlife for current information (see "Contacts and Resources").

Contact: Olympic National Park. **Driving directions:** South Beach Campground is on the west side of US 101 a couple miles south of Kalaloch, some 63 miles north of Hoquiam and 36 miles south of Forks.

QUEETS

This enchanting little year-round Olympic National Park campground, set in a mossy rain-forest grove on the bank of the Queets River, is often overlooked because it's so far off the beaten track. Steelhead fishermen use it winter into spring, when the big native fish run. Whitewater kayakers stay here when spring flows are up. In summer and fall, when the river can be forded safely and the fabulous Queets River Trail can be reached—it's on the far bank—hikers use it as a first night's camp.

But the Queets Campground is a sweet spot simply for camping and exploring one of the park's lesser-known rain-forest valleys. Some of the Sitka spruce you'll camp near are humongous. One in particular just east of the campground loop is the biggest you'll ever see, a serious old specimen, almost 15 feet thick at the butt and 248 feet tall. One of the most impressive big-leaf maples I've ever seen spreads its giant limbs over one campsite, a platform for ferns, moss, and huckleberry bushes growing in a separate world 25 feet high. The Sams River Loop circles through the campground, and in the fall you can often see spawning salmon both on the Sams and the Queets.

This is a primitive campground, way off of US 101 via winding gravel roads. It has just 20 sites, pit toilets, no running water other than the river, no hookups, no reservations, and is not recommended for RVs or trailers. There is a rough boat launch. The Queets is precisely my style of camping—if you want the comforts of home, then stay there.

Contact: Olympic National Park. **Driving directions:** About 15 miles south of Kalaloch on SR 101, turn north on Forest Road 21 (well marked). In about 7 miles, it veers left to become FR 2180 and turns to gravel. In 2 more miles, turn left at the Upper Queets Road sign on an unnumbered road, reaching the Olympic National Park boundary in less than a mile and descending to the Upper Queets Road. Turn right, heading east, and in less than 3 miles, pass the Queets Ranger Station (usually unstaffed). Find the campground on the left in another mile at the end of the road.

Scenic Abbey Island and associated sea stacks at Ruby Beach are the eroded remnants of a former headland.

HIKING

RUBY BEACH TO HOH RIVER

THE CROWN JEWEL OF KALALOCH

Rich tide pools, towering sea stacks, and one long, lonely sandy beach with a historic massacre site lift this hike into the must-do zone for anyone who wants to really know the Washington Coast. But you don't have to hike all the way to the Hoh to get the best of it. Ruby Beach itself is the most scenic beach in the Kalaloch area, with a concentration of rocks, sea stacks, and tide pools—a wonderful spot for a picnic or beach fire.

Distance: 6 miles round-trip
Elevation gain: 60 feet
Difficulty: 2–3
Map: Custom Correct South Olympic Coast
Contact: Olympic National Park
Notes: Dogs permitted on-leash. Check tide tables; don't get trapped at high tide north of the creek and a nearby headland. If you do hike north, conditions must be right, flows down and the tide low, since you have to wade Cedar Creek, which spills into the sea at Ruby Beach. Tide-pooling requires a zero or minus tide.

DRIVING DIRECTIONS

Find the large parking area on the west side of US 101 about 7 miles north of Kalaloch. Signs on the highway give ample warning.

THE HIKE

Bounce down a wide gravel path and almost immediately see through the spruce and alder forest to an amazing collection of stone sentinels on the shore below, lined by an infantry of drift logs, a creek snaking through it all to the sea. Soon emerge on the south bank of Cedar Creek, scarcely a brook in summer but often swollen with rain in winter to the point of being impassable. Follow it several hundred yards to the sea, and look—there's a pooka in the sea stack nearest to shore! Centuries of punishment by the waves has bored a hole clear through. And just north, on the other side of the creek, see spruce-topped Abbey Island, the king of these stacks.

This creek mouth wanders depending on the hydraulics of heavy winter flows and storm-driven oceanic landscaping of the beach. Sometimes the creek hugs the north bank and winds through the stacks to the sea; sometimes it flows straight into the ocean. Tides and flows must be down for you to cross the creek.

First, however, pause and contemplate this nifty little group of impressive sea stacks. The nearest one has the hole. If the tide is low enough, you can climb up into it; pose your boyfriend there for a pic. This is perhaps the most played upon sea stack on the Washington Coast. But also, look back at the bluff just north of the creek. It's rock too, the same as that of the stacks. Unlike the purely sedimentary bedrock just to the north and south, these rocks are primarily volcanic in origin, but mixed with sedimentary rocks and fused by tectonic pressures into what is known as volcanic breccia. But what's interesting is that if you look at the upland bluff and the sea stacks together, it's quite apparent that they are the remnants, the skeleton so to speak, of a former headland. The sea has eroded away softer material over time, leaving this charming assemblage of stone.

If you've got a minus tide, you're in for a treat. Wade the creek and explore the pools around the stacks to the north, as well as Abbey Island. A fantastical world of sea life awaits. It's everything you would expect: red and purple sea stars, a myriad of rock barnacles, gooseneck barnacles, mussels, snails, limpets, and big green, gooey anemones. Some of the smaller rocks sport amazing Medusa-like hairdos of tube worms. Tiny fishes flit and flash through the pools.

Now look north. It's 2.8 miles to the mouth of the Hoh, along a beautiful sandy beach with the gentle shape of a scythe. Not a lot of people venture up there, and you might find yourself alone enough to run naked with the surf. Or spread out a blanket and enjoy a picnic. Remember, though, that about 1.5 miles north of the creek you reach the boundary of the Hoh Indian Reservation, and you should respect tribal sovereignty by being on your best behavior.

North of Abbey Island, the shoreline is much less picturesque but nonetheless intriguing. As you hike, notice the "glacial till" on the upland bluffs above, some as much as 150 feet high. During the Pleistocene epoch some 17,000 to 20,000 years ago, glacial lobes extended down the valleys from the frozen Olympic Mountains, and as they melted and retreated, their flows washed extensive beds of silt, sand, and gravel down to the coast. In places, deep and unstratified deposits suggest deposition directly from glaciers—evidence that at least one lobe of the great Cordilleran ice sheet extended down the valley of the Hoh at least as far west as the present-day coast. Less than 1 mile north of the creek, notice landslide activity from the bluffs and in places "drunken forests" of tilting and toppled trees.

As you near the mouth of the Hoh, you're likely passing the site of the second recorded massacre of white explorers by indigenous people on this coast. The first was in 1775, when Spanish skipper Juan Francisco de la Bodega y Quadra sent seven crewmen ashore from his 36-foot schooner *Sonora* near the mouth of the Quinault River; none returned. Twelve years later, British fur trader Captain Charles Barkley anchored his 400-ton, twenty-gun *Imperial Eagle* inside what is believed to be Destruction Island. This is the big, flat-topped island 3 miles offshore and 2 miles south of Cedar Creek. You can easily see it from anywhere on this hike. Sent ashore in the ship's longboat for freshwater, mate Miller, purser Beal, and four others were apparently attacked and killed by the Native peoples. They never returned to the ship. An interesting footnote is that Barkley brought along his seventeen-year-old bride, Frances, who might well have been the first white woman to see the Northwest Coast.

Barkley's log was lost, so much of the story is uncertain; perhaps the boat headed directly for Cedar Creek. But what has filtered through the mists of time is that somewhere in this vicinity about 230 years ago, six sailors met their fate. Nothing remains today, of course, except perhaps six restless souls eternally wandering the pristine shore.

At 3 miles overall, reach the mouth of the lovely Hoh, and then retrace your steps to Ruby Beach. By now you're probably wondering how the beach got its name: tiny garnets in places, mostly south of Cedar Creek, give the sand a slight tinge of ruby red.

BEACHCOMBING FOR SEASHORE TREASURES

Who knows what treasures wash in with the tide? Perhaps the wooden hatch of a fishing boat, a wayward life ring, a Chinese earthenware urn, or a prized glass fishing-net float. All of these things are eagerly sought by those who comb the beaches of Washington and the entire Northwest Coast, many objects riding the clockwise currents of the North Pacific for years until storm winds blow them ashore.

The ocean shoreline is a natural place of curiosities, and for many people beachcombing is a casual pursuit, something to do while wandering the magical edge of land and sea. They look for sea glass—broken bits of various colors burnished by endless friction of waves, rocks, and sand—or interestingly shaped driftwood for garden landscapes, or rocks that just look pretty.

For others, beachcombing is a passion. They wait for ideal conditions that send ashore glass floats of many sizes, colors, and even shapes, as well as other cool flotsam. These folks can be specific in the rocks they pursue, seeking out agates especially, but also jasper, petrified wood, and fossils. It's like a treasure hunt, and when you find something rare—like a glass float—it's a special thrill.

Unfortunately, most of the stuff that washes up these days is depressingly plastic, with a high percentage of senseless beverage containers. Let me say this right now: in my opinion, anything plastic that is not reusable should be outlawed, internationally. Cheap plastic beverage containers are the worst; they're made with petrochemicals, last damned near forever, and yet are often thrown away after a single use—recycle, dammit!—often into the sea by ignorant fishermen or the crews of ships. They litter virtually every shoreline everywhere these days. At least glass bottles break and disintegrate at a more rapid rate.

One thing that makes beachcombing in Washington so fascinating is that you can find things from all over the northern half of the vast Pacific Ocean, the world's largest body of water. Glass floats, for example, were made and used by Russians, Americans, Japanese, Chinese, Koreans, and others. I've found not only glass floats washed ashore after storms but also other odd stuff, like coconuts. Suntory whiskey bottles from Japan are common, or used to be. I've also found bottles from Vietnam, Russia, and Ukraine. One of the coolest beachcombing finds I've ever seen was a Chinese urn found by the father of a dear friend, the late Barbara Northup of Lake Quinault.

Beachcombing is best after strong storms. What you want are sustained westerly winds, and especially northwesterly winds. These knock floats out of the clockwise flow of our part of the ocean, including the Kuroshio, North Pacific, Alaska, and California currents. The famed Manila galleons and other sailing ships centuries ago used these currents to cross the Pacific between the Philippines and the New World. Floats get trapped in this circle, sometimes for decades, before being blown out.

The best beaches for finding glass floats are those of low gradient, so the floats find a perch at high tide and don't roll back into the sea, and of sand or fine gravel, so the floats don't break on the rocks. Based on that, you'd think the long sandy beaches

A very large glass fishing net float of Japanese origin lies exactly where it was found on a Kalaloch-area beach after an April storm.

of the south Washington Coast would be the best, and indeed a lot of floats and other cool things wash ashore there. However, the rocky north coast—much of it remote wilderness beaches inside Olympic National Park—can be very good for beachcombing as well. The main reason is that there's less competition. The south coast is more populated, and you can drive most of it for much of the year. When my father was co-owner of a salmon charter business in Westport during the 1970s, he and my mom would drive the beaches in his four-wheel-drive International during storms, on nighttime incoming tides, using a spotlight plugged into the lighter socket to find the floats. Locals still use that technique.

On the more remote beaches where driving is prohibited, you can hike untouched stretches after storms and find floats. I've found single glass floats while backpacking the park's beaches days after storms, washed up into the driftwood or partially hidden in piles of wood and kelp.

Treasure, of course, real treasure, is always in the back of the mind when beachcombing, and finding some is a slim possibility. Several years ago, silver dollars dating to the nineteenth century were found on Copalis Spit; the speculation was that they were from a ship wrecked nearby and had been washed ashore by storms.

But all that glitters is not gold or silver. Agates are a more realistic treasure to search for. These semiprecious, translucent stones are not worth much, but they're fun to find. They're often quite beautiful, and a few I've found are spectacular. Agate hunting is best during or right after the storms of fall though spring. But you can find them anytime. Every time the tide comes in, it shuffles the piles of rock and gravel where agates are found, often revealing ones that were buried.

You can also find jasper, usually in satin-like sheens of brown and red, and frequently pieces of petrified wood. The latter looks just like wood, is typically mixed with other stones, but with a noticeable hard look.

Other types of fossils are sometimes found along the coast, occasionally right on the beach but more often associated with upland sediments. I've found fossils of pectin clams, a large scallop-like bivalve, near Sekiu. Fossils of other clams, snails, and crabs are sometimes found, and I met an avid beachcomber from Forks who has found fossilized shark teeth as well as a woolly mammoth tooth.

The things you might find are just another manifestation of the ocean shoreline's truly dynamic nature.

BEACH 4 TO RUBY BEACH

THE WILDERNESS WITHIN KALALOCH

Pack a beach blanket, cheese, bread, chocolate, and a jug of wine, because this is the most remote stretch of ocean shore in the Kalaloch area and it offers a near certainty of solitude. Except maybe in the summer tourist season, you'll probably not see anyone in the middle 2 miles of this hike—just lonesome, exquisite, pristine ocean shoreline, a mix of sand, gravel, cobbles, reefs, and creek crossings. Bring your surfcasting rod and binoculars: surf perch fishing at numerous spots is good anytime the surf is gentle, and the wildlife watching is always good.

Distance: 9.4 miles round-trip
Elevation gain: About 70 feet
Difficulty: 3+
Map: Custom Correct South Olympic Coast
Contact: Olympic National Park
Notes: Dogs permitted on-leash. If you leave a car at either end, you can through-hike this route. There are several creek crossings, all easy except during rain-boosted high flows. Two points, one less than 0.5 mile south of Ruby Beach and the other about 1.4 miles south of Ruby Beach, can only be rounded at tides lower than 3 and 4 feet, respectively, and you can't go up and over.

DRIVING DIRECTIONS

Find the big Beach 4 parking lot on the west side of US 101 less than 3 miles north of Kalaloch—a sign provides ample warning. The Ruby Beach parking area is less than 4 miles to the north.

THE HIKE

From the Beach 4 parking area, scurry down the trail through salmonberry and huckleberry thickets to a babbling brook with tiny waterfalls. Follow the path to a rocky point just above the shore.

Stop here momentarily and ponder the tilted stratification of this outcrop. It's crazy, as if some giant flipped this bed of rock on its side! Dead on, Mr. Science. See how the parallel wavy lines of strata are almost vertical? These are layers of sandstone, part of what geologists call the Hoh rock assemblage, fused and cemented eons ago after they were deposited and then gradually tilted by tectonic pressures, until the top layer faced west. These are the same pressures that make this coast, in the span of geologic time, exceedingly active. You're standing on the grinding edge of two moving plates in the earth's crust. Here the heavier volcanic rock of the eastward-bound Juan de Fuca Plate dives beneath the North American Plate, in the process sheering off associated lithified sediments (sandstone and siltstone), which are then accreted, crumpled, and piled up. This is a tangible manifestation of the forces that make a massive subduction earthquake along the coast simply a matter of time.

Clamber down off the outcrop, hit the soft beach, and head north, reaching rocky Starfish Point in a few hundred yards. Watch the waves as you go. The coarse sand of the beach is prime surf smelt spawning habitat, and all the critters

A BANNER DAY BEACHCOMBING

The fickle winds of fate and the Pacific often dictate beachcombing success, so it pays to watch the forecast.

My best trip treasure hunting came after at least three days of westerlies at 20 to 30 knots, followed by two days of northwesterly wind at 25 to 35 knots, with gusts to 45 knots. Serendipitously, my wife and I found ourselves with two days off (as in unemployed) at the very end of that forecasted blow, and so we packed the truck and headed for the coast. In an afternoon and morning of hiking some of the more remote beaches, we found six glass floats ranging from the smallest I'd ever seen, about Hacky Sack size, to the largest I'd ever seen, bigger than a beach ball at 15.59 inches in diameter.

I'd never found more than one glass float at a time, and Lorna had never found any, so for us that trip was a huge thrill. That storm also washed ashore dozens of plastic floats in various sizes and colors, many with Asian lettering; a Russian steel float; crab pot floats; coconuts; and bottles from Japan, China, and Russia. I heard later from an avid beachcombing friend that the storm had shoved ashore glass floats up and down the Northwest Coast. A great beachcombing storm track of that proportion happens, I would guess, every five to ten years.

The pristine shore north of Beach 4 offers opportunities for solitude. Hoh Head is visible in the distant mist.

hereabouts know this well. From May into September, the bald eagles keep their keen eyes on the waves; river otters and harbor seals patrol the surf; and gulls, terns, and other seabirds fly low over the rollers. When smelt are around, the show can get pretty interesting.

Especially in spring but even during summer, you can also often see gray whales spouting and rolling just outside the surf. In addition, just offshore around Destruction Island live the single largest concentration of sea otters on the Washington Coast, more than four hundred of them. They mostly stay around the island's kelp forest and associated rocks and reefs to the northeast. But at times they move in to feed on clams, mussels, and maybe urchins around rocky nearshore areas like Starfish Point, so keep an eye out.

Incidentally, Starfish Point is the precise spot where a mysterious ailment known as sea star wasting syndrome was first detected in the summer of 2013. It has significantly reduced sea star populations in many areas along the West Coast and in Puget Sound. The good news is that the syndrome, of undetermined cause, never significantly reduced sea star populations along Olympic National Park's wilderness beaches. Furthermore, according to Park Service scientist Bill Baccus, significant recovery from the syndrome has been noted in the Starfish Point population of sea stars. At a minus tide or less, you can wander around the rocks and check out the plentiful purple and orange stars. Then continue on your way: round Starfish Point, where at medium-plus tides on big seas, the waves smash impressively into the rocks, sending geysers of spray skyward.

North of Starfish Point, about 1 mile of pretty sand and gravel beach stretches north, backed by wooded uplands and divided by two small streams. The northern of these streams sometimes disappears beneath the sand and gravel at lower tides, reemerging near the surf; its north bank serves as the path of the unmarked Beach 5 approach, about 1 mile into this hike.

Once you're another 0.5 mile or so north, spread out the blanket anywhere and break out the surf rod. I've caught a mess of perch here and have been alone enough to do whatever comes naturally. When the weather has been warm, I have thrown off my clothes and run around under the sun like a crazy coyote during a full moon.

At 2.3 miles you'll reach Steamboat Creek, the biggest of the several water crossings on this hike. It's typically a breeze, rarely more than knee-high. If you have

GLASS FLOATS, THE BEACHCOMBER'S PRIZE

Glass fishing net floats are spherical and sometimes oblong objects of a simple and soothing beauty, the older ones blown by hand, and range in size from barely more than an inch in diameter to huge orbs 19 inches across. They can be beer-bottle brown, sea green, aqua, clear, gold, and ruby. They are a diminishing resource, since they are virtually no longer in use, long ago replaced by more durable plastic. But over more than a hundred years of their use, from the late 1800s right up to the 1990s, millions were lost in the North Pacific in shipwrecks or sinkings, during storms, after the nets snagged debris, or simply by breaking free of worn rigging. Beachcombing expert Amos Wood calculated in 1975 that 12 million lost glass floats were strung out in the Kuroshio and associated currents of the North Pacific. If 30,000 per year over the past thirty-five years were washed ashore by storms, sunk, or otherwise lost, that still leaves more than 10.9 million circling the currents. So they are still found along the Washington Coast after storms, along with a wild variety of plastic and even metal floats in many sizes, often with Asian lettering.

SMELT PROVE THAT RULES OF THUMB ARE MEANT TO BE BROKEN

One early June day that happened to be uncommonly warm, my wife and I decided to sit near the Beach 3 approach with a sixer of Rainier and wait for the tide to turn so we could fish for surf perch, which is best on the flood. While we sat there enjoying the sun and scenery, waiting for the tide change, she noticed two bald eagles standing on the beach at the edge of the surf about 200 yards north. Occasionally they would lift off and dip toward the waves. She put the binoculars up and said excitedly, "They're catching smelt!"

I told her that couldn't be, since the tide was still going out and anyone who's ever smelt a smelt knows they only run on the incoming tide. But she insisted it was so, and another look through the glasses confirmed it.

I put the 300 millimeter lens on my camera and slowly walked toward them, using the upland bluff to shadow my approach. Sure enough, we learned that eagles are expert fishers for surf smelt—and that smelt sometimes come in on an ebb! I waded out and could feel the smelt running against my bare legs—I actually trapped one with my foot. Another angler down the beach, who happened to have a dip net, saw the commotion and came up and bagged a limit of smelt in about fifteen minutes.

We've also seen seals and otters catching smelt in the surf, and we've seen them catch perch as well. The otters we've seen here have been river otters. But there are very good chances to spot sea otters as well, since a large concentration of the furry mammals spends most of its time around Destruction Island a few miles away.

the time, climb onto the driftwood at the mouth of the creek and look upstream. You should see rusty relics of the creek's namesake shipwrecked steamer.

It's also worth pausing here to look directly west at Destruction Island, first named Isla de Dolores (Island of Sorrows) in 1775 by the Spanish naval officer Juan Francisco de la Bodega y Quadra. The long-held assumption is that the island was so named because of an attack by Quinault Indians that killed seven of the crew aboard Quadra's schooner *Sonora*. But neither Quadra nor his commanding officer, Bruno de Hezeta, captain of the frigate *Santiago*, said so in their journals. In fact, the island might have been named two days before the attack. At any rate, the flat, 30-acre chunk of sandstone bedrock was likely once part of the mainland, left 3.5 miles offshore by an estimated six thousand years of coastal erosion. A 94-foot lighthouse sits atop it, first lit in 1892.

The shoreline bluffs here reach heights of more than 100 feet, largely glacial outwash of sand, silt, clay, and gravel. Up on the bluff just north of the creek, you'll also see an observation point with a cedar rail. Years ago the park operated a campground here, and the Beach 6 trail descended from it. Coastal erosion obliterated the trail some years ago, leaving a precipitous bluff. The park closed the campground too.

At 3.4 miles you'll reach a steep, cliffy sandstone headland that can't be rounded on any tide higher than 4 feet. Be sure to time your hike during a low. Just north, the bluffs slump, with dead trees tilted catawampus by the soil's movement, a "drunken forest." At 4.2 miles you'll reach a cave-pocked headland informally known as Wet Foot Point, and you'll need a tide lower than 3 feet to get around it.

Once on its north side, you'll be approaching a group of nearshore rocks that can be explored on minus tides, and the tide pools are thick with orange and purple sea stars, pink-fringed green anemones, gooseneck barnacles, regular barnacles, and large colonies of big black California mussels. A little more than a stone's throw north, you'll see the group of scenic sea stacks clustered around the mouth of Cedar Creek and just beyond, wooded Abbey Island, where the tide-pooling is

TIDE-POOL ETIQUETTE

Before you go, it's instructional to check out the Olympic Coast National Marine Sanctuary online (see "Contacts and Resources"), including its informative list of common tide-pool invertebrates and gentle reminders about tide-pool etiquette.

Probably the most important rule of thumb is to be careful where you step, using bare rock and sand whenever possible. It's OK to touch, but if a creature resists being removed, leave it there or you might harm it. If you do remove it, replace it precisely where it was, and handle it gently.

KALALOCH'S LOST BEACH APPROACHES

Years ago, there were four other beach approaches from US 101 between Beach 4 and Ruby Beach, trails to Beaches 5 through 8. The trails to Beaches 7 and 8 have been left unmaintained by the Park Service and are now overgrown, while the Beach 5 approach has been left unmarked but is being maintained by someone. The other, the former Beach 6 approach, was obliterated several years ago by a landslide that left only sheer bluff. I like it better this way. Tourists can still reach 12 miles of beach in the Kalaloch area by seven official approaches: trails at Beaches 1 through 4, at Ruby Beach, and via the two campgrounds. The lack of easy access makes the middle section between Beach 4 and Ruby Beach all the more lonesome.

even better, unbelievably rich. Your shutter will be clicking like mad—it's really pretty here.

You're now at Ruby Beach, at 4.7 miles. If you didn't leave a car at this trailhead, go as far as you care to and turn around. If you did, make your way to the creek and up the 0.2-mile trail to the parking lot.

RED CEDAR, THE RAIN-FOREST KING

Gazing up at a wizened red cedar, an immense, craggy castle of a tree with its spiky candelabra top scratching the sky and hosting a variety of hangers-on species, you wonder what it would say if it could talk. Tell me, oh shaman of the conifers, what have you seen in the thousand years since your seedling first pushed above the damp rain-forest floor? Did strong men wearing the skins of animals split planks from your side and fell your neighbor to shape it for riding the ocean waves?

Thoughts like this cross your mind—well, at least mine—when you see either of two western red cedars in the Kalaloch region that are, or were, among the very largest in existence. You might also feel sad because they look very old and dead, nothing more than a growth medium for hemlock and huckleberry sprouts. But look high and you'll see the flat green spread of the cedar's bough, a fraction of its total immensity but very much alive.

Before March of 2014, there were two red cedars in the Kalaloch region that were considered among the biggest in the world. But then the one along US 101 just north of Kalaloch, which had no doubt been observed by millions of visitors over the decades, split in two in a fierce storm. It was a massive beauty, an outstanding specimen, sadly now a shadow of its former self, but still impressive.

If one word could describe the western red cedar, it would be endurance; if two, the other would be function. No other species on the Northwest Coast is more enduring, and none so functional. It's amazing how *Thuja plicata* soldiers on through time. A softwood, as it ages and gains height, storms typically snap off its brittle top. It responds by sending surrounding limbs skyward, resulting in multileader candelabra-shaped crowns. Over hundreds of years, the red cedar's lower trunk swells to enormous girth, even as heart rot and sometimes fire render it hollow. Yet it survives—as long as it's not girdled, limb growth continues, becoming ever more sparse as centuries progress. A member of the cypress family, these trees are incredibly long-lived, although difficult to age because of the heart rot. Northwest big-tree expert and University of Washington forest ecologist Robert Van Pelt figures the Nolan Creek cedar north of Kalaloch is probably two thousand years old.

Perhaps even more amazing is the red cedar's host of useful attributes. Anyone who has spent time camping on the Washington Coast knows that it's remarkably eager to the flame. In the dead of a wet coastal winter, if you can find enough red cedar wood to split into shavings or kindling with a small knife, you can get a blaze roaring. The brittleness of the wood makes it highly resonant and valued as a top for fine acoustic guitars. The wood is so light and straight-grained that it makes superb and beautiful shingles and fine house siding; and it's so rot-resistant that it's highly valued for fencing and decking. The first people on the coast made hats, skirts, and rain capes from cedar bark, pillows and diapers from its shredded bark. They made baskets and cord from its roots, boxes by steaming and bending the wood, and large house planks split sometimes from living trees. They used cedar logs for carving house crests and totems and for house posts and beams. From whole logs they carved canoes, some enormous war craft 60 feet long that could carry fifty armed men.

Ancient red cedars develop a haunting appearance. They're like old wooden castles, dark and spooky inside, nursing other species outside, like ferns, huckleberry, and hemlock. And there are many such specimens on the Washington Coast, 10 to

The author standing well up on the swell of the Kalaloch giant red cedar

19 feet thick at the base. The grand champion is at Lake Quinault just off the North Shore Road.

The two near Kalaloch likely sprouted sometime between the birth of Christ and Leif Eriksson's alleged landing on Vinland (North America) a thousand years later. The one that split presides over a magnificent grove of old cedars inside Olympic National Park, just north of Kalaloch. The other, the Nolan Creek cedar, towers ignobly over a large patch of replanted conifers in the middle of a Washington Department of Natural Resources clear-cut south of the Hoh River. The loggers left the monster cedar, put up a plaque declaring it the world's largest—though it apparently is not—and cut down all the trees around it. Some of those familiar with this history say the tree has been dying a slow death ever since, its trunk now bleached white by the sun, only a scattering of green limbs still sprouting green near its gnarly, multitrunk, 178-foot top. But Van Pelt, who rates it the third-largest known western red cedar, believes it could last several more centuries. It definitely is worth seeing, at least if big cedars stoke your wow meter like they do mine, to marvel at its 19.4-foot-thick buttress.

Driving directions: The Nolan Creek cedar, also called the Duncan cedar, is reached via a logging road that leaves US 101 about 6 miles south of the Hoh River bridge and 5.5 miles north of the Ruby Beach parking area north of Kalaloch. Signs along the highway mark the turn to the south onto gravel Road N1000, with three right turns on Roads N1100, N1112, and N112, respectively. You'll reach a parking area about 4 miles from US 101. The roads are all in fair shape and you should be able to reach the beast in the family car.

The cedar that split is about 4 miles north of Kalaloch, just off US 101. Watch for the "Big Tree" sign and turn east onto a gravel road, driving about 0.25 mile to its end. Follow the trail a hundred yards or so to what experts say was one of the largest western red cedars in the solar system. Van Pelt had rated it as the fifth largest, based on wood volume; it's 19.6 feet in diameter at breast height. Likely more than a thousand years old, it's hollow and rotting, with an incredible, twisted, gnarly crown. It had been measured at 123 feet, with a candelabra shape of twelve major trunks separating from the butt about 25 feet up.

KALALOCH TO BEACH 4

THE MISTY SHORE THAT BECKONS

Two miles of often misty, always sandy, and surf-pummeled shore lead north from Kalaloch Campground to the sandstone headland of Browns Point, a curious spot with offshore rocks and tide pools, tilted strata, pocket coves, and a cool little arch. Beyond that is a miracle mile of mostly open shore between Beaches 3 and 4, where you can watch all manner of creatures making their living. Along this shoreline I've dug razor clams, caught surf perch and Dungeness crabs, dipnetted smelt, and watched eagles, otters, seals, sea lions, dolphins, and whales.

Distance: 6.2 miles round-trip
Elevation gain: None, unless you exit at Beach 4, then about 70 feet
Difficulty: 2–3
Map: Custom Correct South Olympic Coast
Contact: Olympic National Park
Notes: Dogs permitted on-leash. Browns Point headland can only be rounded at tides lower than 3 feet.

DRIVING DIRECTIONS

Find the Kalaloch Campground on US 101, 35 miles south of Forks and 65 miles north of Hoquiam. Turn west into the campground and straight into the day-use lot. You can also access this stretch from the Beach 3 approach, less than 3 miles north of the campground on US 101, and from the Beach 4 access about 4 miles north of the campground, the latter with a large parking lot and pit toilets. Highway signs clearly mark both approaches.

THE HIKE

Find the short trail to the beach at the west end of the parking lot, and carefully scramble over the driftwood to emerge on a broad sandy beach. There might not be a better place to take in the vast fetch of the Pacific Ocean than right here. Although the low bluff uplands are lined with crazy, wind-warped spruce forest, it's the sea that steals the show. On a calm day the waves are gentle but roll in ceaselessly in mesmerizing fashion. After a stormy day or night, beachcombing can

A small sandstone arch at Browns Point curls above a block of tilted strata.

be great here, since other than the Kalaloch Rocks just to the south and Browns Point to the north, there's nothing here to block incoming flotsam.

If you can, hike this beach at low tide. The wet, hard-packed sand is ideal for running, jogging, or just walking. The last time I hiked here was during a minus tide in May, the sky thick with characteristic morning mist cloaking an insistent sun. That created an eerie sort of light, and as I walked north along the wet edge of a soft surf, it illuminated thousands of busy razor clams siphoning and expelling below a thin sheen of seawater. As I walked, they felt the vibration of my steps and withdrew their siphons, so that looking back I could see a trail of "shows"—precisely what you look for when digging razor clams.

So, follow the sand and clams north on an easy beach open to the giant sea, in about 2 miles reaching one of the most special little spots in the Kalaloch area, Browns Point. This headland is a series of bedrock outcrops of what is known as the Hoh rock assemblage. The rocks were deposited in the ocean some 15 to 22 million years ago in turbid waters, consolidated as siltstone and sandstone, and then moved eastward over time, being twisted and tilted in the process. You can see these tilted strata, overlain by sand and gravel laid down by glacial outwash during the Pleistocene. Between the outcrops are a series of quaint little coves, two

Two bald eagles wait for opportunities while fishing for surf smelt just north of the Beach 3 approach.

of them separated by a cool sea arch about head-high. It makes a nice frame for a snapshot.

Tide-pooling is also very good here on a minus tide, the rocks harboring a huge variety of mussels, barnacles, chitons, sea stars, and pink-fringed anemones. You need a tide lower than 3 feet to get around Browns Point, which effectively marks the northern limit of Washington's razor clam population. On the north side of Browns Point is Beach 3, at 2.5 miles.

The 1-mile stretch from Browns Point north to Starfish Point (another outcrop of Hoh rocks), past the Beach 3 and 4 approaches, is a very cool piece of shoreline. This is the best beach on Washington's outer coast for dipnetting surf smelt. It's also an excellent beach for red-tailed surf perch fishing, anytime the swells are less than 4 feet, with just the right gradient.

This is also a fabulous beach for wildlife watching, for packing in a small cooler of beer and your binoculars and then just sittin' and lookin'. Be sure to pack out your empties, since I'm convinced there's a ring of white-hot fire reserved in hell for heathens who litter, particularly in a place as scenic and pristine as Olympic National Park.

Make your way north, passing a large honeycombed boulder about midbeach. The next rocky outcrop on the uplands marks the trail to the Beach 4 parking lot, some 3.1 miles from the Kalaloch Campground. Turn around anytime and head back to Kalaloch. But linger, listen, watch, breathe in the salt air, and contemplate things beyond yourself. This beach might provide a perspective you've never considered.

FISHING THE KALALOCH AND QUEETS AREA

No other part of the Washington Coast offers such a diversity of fishing opportunities as the Kalaloch area's intriguing mix of shellfish, surf fish, and river fish. You can dipnet the delectable little surf smelt here, and when the weather is fair, that's a sloppy-wet blast. This stretch of coast is as good as anywhere to cast for red-tailed surf perch, a pleasant way to really experience that dynamic edge of sea and land. You can also dig razor clams when populations are strong enough (they haven't been the last few years). Chances of catching a trophy steelhead are as good on the Queets River as anywhere—all wild steelhead with an intact adipose fin must be released alive—and salmon, mostly coho, are caught as well.

Salmon and steelhead in this priceless river system—the Queets itself is almost entirely within Olympic National Park—can get big, really big. Years ago as a cub reporter for Aberdeen's *Daily World*, I did a story about a Queets fisherman, the hereditary chief of the tribe, and spent a day on the lower river with him working his gillnet. It was September and most of his catch was coho salmon, but when we unloaded his fish at the old wooden Queets fish house (since replaced), there on a pile of crushed ice was a 65-pound chinook another tribal fisherman had netted that day. It was massive, long and thick, its jaws had twisted with maturity into a hideous grin, and it was black as night. I'd never seen anything like it, never any salmon as big nor as black. I think this is characteristic of very large, mature coastal king salmon; in the old they were referred to here as "black salmon."

While in their ocean phase, salmon are bright as shiny chromed metal, often with snow-white bellies. As they mature and near the freshwaters of their birth, they undergo sometimes drastic physical changes, the jaws of the males often hooking, or kyping, and their overall coloration changing dramatically.

You can access most of the Queets on foot and can often enjoy a solitary angling experience on this wild rain-forest river. If you manage to hook one, so much the better! Sea-run cutthroat can also be taken in the Queets and its tributaries, including the Clearwater and Salmon rivers, and even in the creeks that spill into the ocean.

Due to the differing jurisdictions, regulations are complicated in this region, and anglers must thoroughly familiarize themselves with Olympic National Park fishing rules, especially on the Queets, and the separate state regulations for the tributary Salmon and Clearwater rivers, both of which are mostly outside park boundaries. You

Four decent-sized red-tailed surf perch, caught at Beach 4, will make a fine meal.

can fish under much more liberal regulations on the reservation waters of the Queets and Salmon, but only if you hire a Quinault tribal guide. See "Contacts and Resources" for all fishing regulation contact info.

Here's a month-by-month synopsis:

January: During calm periods, surf perch fishing is often good in the Kalaloch area. Winter steelhead have reached the lower Queets and its tributaries, the Salmon and

Clearwater rivers, and by late in the month some big native fish show up. Even smaller streams such as Kalaloch and Cedar creeks kick out a few winter-run steelhead.

February: Surf perch fishing can be good during calm periods of low surf, and fishing for wild steelhead improves in the Queets and Clearwater.

March: This is prime time for the big wild steelhead of the Queets and Clearwater. Surf perch are an option when the surf is mild. If the population rebounds, razor clam digging should be open during appropriate minus-tide series, from Browns Point south past Kalaloch to South Beach Campground.

April: Exactly the same as March, but steelheading is entirely closed by the end of the month.

May: This is a perfect time for surf perch, except during windy weather and high surf. Razor clamming will be open if stock abundance allows.

June: It's prime surf perch time! It's also entirely possible that surf smelt will show up at Beaches 3 and 4.

July: Surf perch and smelt are your options now. There are likely to be some sea-run cutthroat in streams.

August: Same as July.

September: Ditto, with a few chinook arriving in the Queets system. Razor clam digging could be open at low-tide series if the population allows. Sea-run cutthroat fishing is an option in all streams.

October: Chinook salmon are now being taken in the Queets and Clearwater rivers, but they must be released in the Queets if they are wild, that is, with an intact adipose fin. Coho salmon begin arriving in both rivers as well and may be kept in both. Surf perch are an option. Razor clam digging could be open at low-tide series if the population allows.

November: Same as October, and a few winter steelhead arrive in the Queets and Salmon rivers.

December: Winter steelheading is now worthwhile in the lower Queets and Salmon.

KALALOCH TO QUEETS RIVER

HIKE IT OR JOG IT

Unless your goal is to hike as much of the Washington Coast as possible, or you're staying at the Kalaloch Campground or resort, I'm going to say this is one beach hike you can skip. I've hiked this stretch and I've spent a lot of time just south of Kalaloch, and I've enjoyed every single second. But each of the Kalaloch-area hikes to the north is better, with greater diversity and more interesting geology. Having said that, the beach-combing here can be seriously good after a storm, whale-watching is unobstructed and often very good, and surf perch fishing A-OK. This stretch also makes for a nice morning run if the tide is low enough to reveal the harder wet sand; the upper part of the beach is heavily shingled with beach cobbles most of the way. The one part of this beach you must not miss is the burl forest on the upland side, bisected by the trails to Beaches 1 and 2. In fact, the Beach 1 trail offers a short loop through the richest spruce burl grove I've ever seen, appropriately called the Spruce Burl Trail.

Distance: 7.5 miles round-trip
Elevation gain: 30 feet
Difficulty: 2
Map: Custom Correct South Olympic Coast
Contact: Olympic National Park
Notes: You can also approach this stretch through Kalaloch Resort, South Beach Campground, and the Beach 1 and 2 trails. The river mouth is on the Quinault Indian Reservation, and for the southern 0.5 mile of this hike, you must obtain a beach pass; check with the tribe for availability.

DRIVING DIRECTIONS

The trailhead is at the Kalaloch Campground on US 101, 35 miles south of Forks and 65 miles north of Hoquiam. Turn west into the campground and straight into the day-use lot.

THE HIKE

Hike the short approach trail from the day-use lot, picking your way through the driftwood and heading south, soon reaching Kalaloch Creek. Seagull concentrations can be intense here. Flip off your footwear and cross the creek near the surf, where the creek spreads out and shallows. If you've got a good minus tide, the Kalaloch Rocks will be exposed, less than ⅛ mile south of the creek. They're worth a look, full of colorful critters.

At about 1.5 miles from the campground, look for the orange and black trail sign. That's the marker for the Beach 2 approach. Go up there and hike into the upland forest. It's a most curious grove of thin-trunked spruce, most of them festooned vertically with multiple warty bulbous burls, the whole sprouting from a luxuriant green undergrowth carpet of salal, sword ferns, and vanilla leaf. It's quite a scene—you half expect a troll or a gnome or a menehune to jump out and bark, "Who goes there?"

Head back to the beach, continue south, and at 2.5 miles note the upland marker for the Beach 1 trail. Go up and circle the Spruce Burl Trail, even more intense with the curious round growths. No one knows why they form, but since they're most prolific on the edge of the sea, experts assume they're associated with the intense onshore flow and/or the salt air. If you choose, you can always hike the burl loop by driving to the Beach 1 parking area along US 101 south of Kalaloch Lodge.

Curious nodules known as burls grow on spruce trees along the approach trails for Beach 1 and Beach 2.

Back on the beach, in less than another 1 mile south, you'll see tents, campers, and RVs on the bluff at South Beach Campground, at least if it's during the late-May to early-September season when it's open. In less than 0.25 mile south, you'll reach the boundary of the park and the Quinault Indian Reservation. Most people turn around here.

If the tribe reopens its beach-pass program and you have a permit (available at tribal headquarters in Taholah), you can proceed, reaching a large spit carved by the Queets in less than 0.5 mile, attended by large flocks of gulls and other seabirds.

KALALOCH CREEK NATURE TRAIL

AN EASY FORESTED LOOP

This easy loop explores the dank and pungent world of a coastal creek, much of it on boardwalk and most of it away from the creek itself, winding through wet grottoes of skunk cabbage, salal, red huckleberry, and salmonberry.

Distance: 0.8-mile loop
Elevation gain: Almost none
Difficulty: 1–2
Map: Benchmark Maps' *Washington Road and Recreation Atlas*
Contact: Olympic National Park
Notes: Dogs permitted on-leash

DRIVING DIRECTIONS

Limited trailhead parking is just north of Kalaloch Lodge on US 101, on the west side of the highway. The trail enters the forest across the highway, on the east side, just north of the US 101 bridge over the creek, a short walk south of the Kalaloch Campground. You can also access this trail via a short path from the southeast corner of the campground.

THE HIKE

In the old days a dirt path followed the north bank of the creek some distance upstream, and you could find pleasant spots to sit and watch the flow. My mom and I once picked a coffee can full of red huckleberries here and then went back to the cabin at Kalaloch, where she baked one damned fine pie. I find the current loop much less interesting, but the hike is worth it if you're staying at Kalaloch and have already explored the area's phenomenal beaches.

SAMS RIVER LOOP

GIANT TREES AND MEADOWS WHERE ELK ROAM

Chances of seeing elk are high on this quiet loop through old homestead pastures and big mossy rain forest in Olympic National Park's Queets River corridor. The path is partially along the magical Queets and partly along its tributary, Sams River. This trail also passes the largest known Sitka spruce anywhere, as measured by wood volume. Much of the trail is a muddy, sloppy mess fall through spring and appears to be suffering neglect by the Park Service. If you're staying at the lovely Queets River Campground, you must do this hike, since it cuts right through the middle of the campground and also visits the Queets Ranger Station.

Distance: 3-mile loop
Elevation gain: 40–50 feet
Difficulty: 2
Map: Custom Correct Queets Valley or park map available at ranger stations and park website
Contact: Olympic National Park
Notes: Day use only. No hounds. Keep your bearings, as the tread is faint in places.

DRIVING DIRECTIONS

About 15 miles south of Kalaloch on US 101, find Forest Road 21 (well marked with signs in both directions) and turn north (left). In about 7 miles, the way veers left to become FR 2180 and turns to gravel. In 2 more miles, turn left at the sign for the Upper Queets Road on an unnumbered road, reaching the Olympic National Park boundary in less than 1 mile and descending to the Upper Queets Road in another 0.5 mile. Turn right. In less than 3 miles, reach the Queets Ranger Station (usually unstaffed) on the left. Park here.

THE HIKE

Here you'll see huge Sitka spruce towering above and old big-leaf maple bending with the weight of multiple other species on their limbs, while delicate vine maples grace the understory above a carpet of step moss, wood sorrel, and sword fern. This trail might not be as spectacular as those in the Hoh Rain Forest to the north, but you won't find crowds here. I like its combination of old homestead pastures where elk graze, stretches along the banks of the Queets and Sams, and the deep, mossy, mysterious rain-forest groves. It's exquisite how nature has landscaped this place in ways no human could. You hike through tunnels of arching vine maples draped by cattail moss. The ground cover is thick, damp, and lush, and much of the understory is open glade due to the browsing of hungry elk.

From the ranger station, head back out the driveway and cross the Queets Road to the signed trail. Almost immediately, you'll cross crystal-clear frog ponds on single-log bridges. Soon, you're deep into spruce forest and the trail becomes downright boggy (except maybe in late summer). In spring and summer, watch and listen for the tiny winter wren and its complex, melodic trill—this is a signature sound of the Pacific Northwest forest. Sometimes they'll sit on a limb nearby with their short upright tails, open their little beaks, and sing their hearts out. Usually you'll just hear the sweet song.

Soon the forest begins opening up, and at 0.4 mile you'll enter an old homestead pasture, slowly being reclaimed by spruce. Approach quietly and slowly, and you might see elk. Mornings and evenings are the best time. If you don't see these big beasts, rest assured that you will if you spend any time in this valley. You'll certainly see their tracks and nugget piles all over. In a corner of the pasture you'll see the remnants of an old orchard. The trail seems to disappear in the old pasture, but search the far side and you'll pick up the tread, which leads to a small but wide streambed at 1 mile, which might be flowing. Work your way across it and reach a grove of large, mossy, mature big-leaf maple. Then enter a hollow where in 2005, strong winds blew down much of the spruce forest.

Not quite at the halfway point, at 1.4 miles, the trail bends north and picks up the bed of the Sams River, its gravel pocked with elk tracks. Soon you'll reach the very end of the Upper Queets Road, which serves as the trailhead for the up-valley Queets River Trail. Follow the road to the left, and soon note two small cairns on the left (hopefully) marking a short way trail. Take it and in a few yards, greet with upward gaze an ancient emissary from the tree gods, *Picea sitchensis*, Sitka spruce. Although many claim that a Sitka spruce to the south on Lake Quinault is the world champion, this one takes the prize as measured by Robert Van Pelt, a forest ecologist at the University of Washington. No other specimen is as high, 248 feet, and no other contains as much wood as this one's more than 12,000 cubic feet. And a beast it is, 14.9 feet in diameter at the moss-covered swell.

From here the Sams Loop Trail stays on the Queets Road for less than ⅛ mile, passing the campground loop. At about 1.7 miles, at a sign, the trail veers into forest on the right. This leads through a spruce glen to a high bank on the moody ribbon of Mount Olympus's tears known as the Queets River. Gradually, the high bank drops toward the river, and at several spots you can reach the flow and dangle your toes. The trail then reaches and skirts another old pasture, now heaven on earth for big brown beasts with shaggy collars, dirty-white butts, and often very large pointy antennae. The trail evades this wet meadow, though, cutting through a maple thicket and arriving back at the ranger station.

SURF FISHING: DIPPING INTO NATURE

You might think that nothing could live in the rolling, crashing, relentless surf of the Pacific. But remarkably, a variety of fish do, and they also attract seals, otters, dolphins—and people—right into the surf, all after a meal. Two species are of importance in the Kalaloch region, surf smelt and surf perch. It's an absolute blast to catch them. Here's how.

SURF SMELT

Catching ocean surf smelt (*Hypomesus pretiosus*) is a marvelous, quirky fishery unlike any other and pretty much a total sensory experience. You're standing right in the surf, dipnetting, and if the weather is warm enough to go barefoot and wear shorts, you can feel those little buggers against your legs and feet as they swarm ashore. You taste saltwater on your lips, smell the sea, hear the waves, feel the spray. If you're successful—and you won't always be—the smelt are flipping like mad in the dip net. Some jump out before you get them, seals are often mere feet away chasing the same thing, gulls are diving on them, and eagles swoop down. When smelt show up, the food chain has been pulled, nature's dinner bell rung, and you're very much part of it all.

Then you get to go back to camp or cabin or home and cook up a plate of these rich delicacies—they're oily and toothsome. I like them gutted, beheaded, lightly floured, and hot-fried quickly in butter, then eaten with a bit of salt and pepper, a glass of pinot grigio—oh man!

You do need a dip net of some sort, and when the smelt are thick, just about any kind will work. You can buy cheap, hoop-shaped aluminum dip nets that work OK, and there are people in the town of Forks to the north who make functional, folding wooden ones for around $125. But some locals make their own of the traditional wooden Quileute/Quinault rectangular design, which can't be improved upon, in my opinion.

The Native design is simple yet ingenious, extremely efficient for the purpose. The frame is simply a long handle with a slight curve on one end and two crossbeams mounted on it. Between the ends of the crossbeams, a heavy cord is strung—natural fibers were used back in the day, but now more durable nylon is used. With the cord strung, a rectangular frame is created, from which a fine-mesh and deep-bagged net is attached with more cord. What you've got then is a functional net that presents a broad opening directly to the wave without much resistance to the flow.

The technique is to simply stand in the surf and dip the net into the oncoming waves. But conditions must be right, and most dippers wait until they see signs of smelt. Although smelt do approach the beaches in winter, the peak of spawning on the coast in summer, August being the prime month. Anytime from late May into September is suitable (see "Contacts and Resources" for fishing regulations). However, smelt seem to avoid the surf when swells are high, and you should as well, because attempting to stand in 6-foot waves is dangerous. If the marine weather forecast calls for ocean swells of 2–4 feet or less, go for it. Do keep an eye out. Even when conditions are good, every once in awhile a big one will wash in. I've seen people get rolled while smelting.

Back in the day, people dipnetted at many beaches on the coast. The Quileute, Hoh, Queets, and Quinault bands all relied on smelt, so the fish were abundant at least at times from La Push south to the Quinault River. Today, it's rare to see anyone dipnetting smelt anywhere other than reliable Beaches 3 and 4 just north of Kalaloch. The daily limit in Olympic National Park is 10 pounds per day (maybe one-third of a 5-gallon bucket), and that's plenty. The signal to get your net into the surf is provided by the local wildlife. If you see eagles, gulls, cormorants, and puffins diving into the surf, or river otters and harbor seals rolling in same, get down there!

FRIED SMELT: FROM DIP NET TO DELICACY

Smelt are called the perfect fish for panfrying, and I'd have to agree. They're small and so fit the pan well, they fry quickly and require only a turn, and the result is a crispy, butterflied morsel with a rich flavor that screams of the sea.

A limit of surf smelt and a dip net of traditional design, with the handle and crossbeams made of big-leaf maple

10–20 smelt, cleaned
1 cup flour
1 teaspoon garlic powder
Sea salt and fresh ground pepper to taste
2 tablespoons peanut oil
Lime or lemon for garnish (optional)

Manly men might eat them whole, but I prefer removing the head and guts. Then in a bowl, mix the flour (I use whole wheat), garlic powder, salt, and pepper. Roll those babies in there until coated evenly.

In a medium or large frying pan, heat the peanut oil to medium-high. Lay the smelt in the pan, and do not crowd! Cook five or six at a time so the oil stays hot. Cook about two minutes on one side, flip, and repeat. Drain on paper towels.

From the head end, grab the backbone and gently lift it entirely out of the fish, leaving a thin butterfly of pure bliss. Sprinkle on a little sea salt if necessary, serve with a wedge of lime or lemon and a glass of pinot grigio—and prepare to arrive in heaven.

SURF PERCH

The surf smelt's grand frère is the red-tailed surf perch, and it's uncanny to me that they both actually spend much of their respective lives directly in the crashing waves of the ocean. Their body shapes are much different, they're different species, and yet both are adapted to safely negotiate the churning brine. Perch are not as rich and flavorful as smelt, but the white fillets are delicate and tasty nonetheless. They are also super fun to catch.

Amphistichus rhodoterus—rhodo is Greek for "rosy"—is a pretty fish, silver-scaled with pinkish-red fins, almost round as a hubcap and sometimes almost as big. The Washington state record is 4.05 pounds, taken at Kalaloch. They range from California north to Vancouver Island and in Washington are fished primarily from the Kalaloch beaches south to the Columbia River. They seem to be fished mostly on the more open, sandy beaches, perhaps because those are more accessible to anglers.

While smelt are plankton feeders, surf perch are more carnivorous, foraging in the surf and sand for isopods such as rock lice or sand fleas, small snails, shrimps and crabs, and a variety of polychaete worms, such as tube worms. Tube worms were once the preferred bait for surf perch but over the years were over-harvested for that purpose. Today it is illegal to use tube worms for bait throughout Olympic National Park, where they are again abundant.

Not to worry, though, since a variety of other baits work just fine. Razor clam diggers who fish for surf perch save the very tip of the clam's siphon to use as bait, and that works well most of the time. What works as well as anything anytime the perch are biting is a piece of fresh prawn. That might seem expensive, but a single prawn can be cut into many perch baits.

This is a year-round fishery, limited only by weather and seas. When seas and surf are big, the perch don't bite, moving offshore to escape the chaos. But whenever Zeus relaxes and calm prevails, surf perch fishing can be a contemplative joy. You can almost always find a spot on the beach to be alone with the waves, the birds, your thoughts, your fears, your hopes, your dreams, and the perch.

Surf perch are not that challenging to catch, biting readily when conditions are good; and with an average weight of less than a pound, they're not usually big enough to test your tackle. One of the aesthetic issues of the fishery is that tackle must be relatively stout to cast out and hold in the surf, and the perch can't put up much of a fight. A lot manage to shake the hook and get away. But the bigger ones put a grin on your face; those of 2 or more pounds will race sideways between waves and make strong little runs.

You'll need hip boots or chest waders, or at least knee-high boots. The best rods are long, 9 feet or more, but with action that's not too heavy. You're going to be hurling a two-leader rig with a 2- or 3-ounce pyramid sinker at the end of the line. Leaders with bait hooks sized no. 3 or 4 are affixed to the line about 10 and 25 inches above the sinker, either with three-way swivels or tying loops in the main line. Bait those hooks and then simply stride out into the smaller waves while casting out as far as you can. The surf will roll the gear around some; take up any slack in the line so you can feel the bite. When surf is very gentle, you can use lighter rods and weights and really enjoy the spunk of these scrappy fish.

The limit is 15 perch per day (see "Contacts and Resources" for fishing regulations), but I get tired of filleting more than 7 or 8, and that's plenty for a great meal for two.

PERFECTLY POACHING YOUR PERCH

Surf perch are typically filleted like any other roundfish, leaving two skinless, palm- to hand-sized strips of delicate white flesh. You can lightly flour or batter them and fry them in hot peanut oil or butter, or broil them. But they poach oh so very well, a healthy alternative to frying, leaving a moist, tender, flavorful blanket for a bed of, say, long-grain white or brown rice, or a rice/quinoa mix.

6–8 perch fillets (1–2 pounds)
3 tablespoons extra virgin olive oil
1–2 tablespoons dry sherry
1 tablespoon shoyu (soy sauce)
2 cloves fresh minced garlic
1 tablespoon shredded ginger root
2–3 medium-sized prawns (optional)
Green onion, parsley, ground pepper, lemon for garnish (optional)

Simply put the perch in a sauté pan with the olive oil, sherry, and shoyu, topped with the garlic and ginger root. If you like, add some medium-sized prawns as well.

Cover and cook at medium heat for several minutes. Don't overcook! Lift the lid and check the progress once or twice.

Serve sprinkled with chopped green onion, parsley, and ground pepper—a wedge of lemon if you like, but I prefer a sprinkle more of shoyu—on a bed of rice, along with a glass of sauvignon blanc, or two.

Wow—or as my pops used to say, "Wow de dow!"

THE CENTRAL COAST

CHAPTER 6

WITHOUT A DOUBT, THIS IS THE most curious stretch of the Washington Coast: rocky, rugged, remote, and wild on the north end; open, sandy, way less wild but nonetheless gritty on the south end. This rough and tumble region, which marks the latitudinal center of the state's outer shore, is the home of Indians, fishermen, loggers, shake rats, free thinkers, retirees, and other regular folks in a setting of rivers, rain forests, giant trees, wild critters, big fish, big ocean sunsets, and vast clear-cuts.

All that is cool about the Washington Coast is here between the Queets River and Grays Harbor, some 35 miles to the south—along with all that is creepy. You can hike to scenic spots on the ocean and in the forest, find some of the best birding in all of Washington, catch big salmon and steelhead, dig the biggest razor clams in the state, dig your toes into the sand, and sing songs around a beach fire. At the same time, less obviously, there is poverty, drug abuse, and the highest rate

Merriman Falls drops 40 feet from the hills above the South Shore Road in the Lake Quinault area before curling toward the Quinault River.

of joblessness in the state (9.9 percent in April 2014). Ours here is not to dwell upon the latter. But it is a reality of the place.

Geologically there are also two faces to this transitional area, where the rocky north coast gives way to the sandy south coast. Spectacular Point Grenville on the Quinault Indian Reservation marks the southern end of the scenically stupendous and rugged north coast. From Grenville south, the beaches are long, sandy, less scenic, but still mesmerizing. Captain George Vancouver's 1792 description is still apt: "From [Point Grenville] as we proceeded to the north the coast began to increase regularly in height. . . . The shores we passed this morning . . . were composed of low cliffs rising perpendicularly from a beach of sand or small stones; had many detached rocks of various romantic forms."

The Quinault Reservation defines the north part of this chapter and includes 23 miles of some of the wildest, most scenic, and definitely the least accessible beaches of the state's outer shore. Most unfortunately, the Quinault tribal council in late 2013 closed this stretch of the coast to the general public. At the same time, the shore from the reservation boundary near the town of Moclips, south to Grays Harbor—known locally as the North Beach area—is the most accessible stretch of the coast, with multiple access points. You can drive most of the beach here in your vehicle.

Two mighty rain-forest rivers drain the southwestern Olympic Mountains and reach the ocean on the Quinault rez, the Queets and the Quinault. Together with the Humptulips River just to the south and several streams that flow into the Chehalis River and Grays Harbor, they deliver to the sea all the accumulated mountain snow and rain from the southwestern corner of the peninsula. And that's not just a little. It rains here a lot for much of the year, and hard. Rivers and streams define this place, as much as anywhere on the coast.

While the beaches south of the reservation are decidedly less spectacular, they are wide open and offer plenty to do. These long sandy beaches are the epicenter of the state's razor clam habitat and offer good surf perch fishing, great beachcombing, superb and diverse birding, and a handful of pretty cool hikes.

Just inland, the Lake Quinault country is an extension of the coast, a major recipient of the rain the ocean sends copiously, the result being forests of monster spruce, fir, and cedars, rain-forest valleys, abundant fish and wildlife, and interesting history. A network of trails, along with the lake, allow the visitor to experience it all most tangibly.

CULTURAL COLLISIONS: EARLY EUROPEAN LANDINGS ON THE WASHINGTON COAST

This reach of the Washington Coast includes the very spot of the first recorded landing of Europeans on what would become Washington State—and the location of the Quinaults' subsequent violent response. In July of 1775, two small Spanish ships set anchor some 5 miles apart off the lands of the Quinault. The command ship, the 77-foot frigate *Santiago*, lay to in what is now Grenville Bay. Just north, the 36-foot *Sonora* dropped its hook at high tide near the mouth of the Quinault River. In the early morning of July 14, the *Santiago's* captain, Lieutenant Bruno de Hezeta, along with the ship's surgeon, friar, and an armed escort, came ashore to claim this coast for the king of Spain. The ceremony was witnessed by at least two Quinault men.

The captain and crew of the tiny *Sonora* , meanwhile, discovered themselves trapped at low tide inside treacherous reefs, unable to move until the ocean flooded once again. During the wait, seven men were sent ashore to collect freshwater, cut a new topmast, and gather firewood. Battling whitecaps and breakers in the schooner's launch, the seven had barely struggled ashore when dozens of armed warriors set upon them, killing or capturing all and then battering the launch to bits for its metal fittings.

The schooner's captain, Lieutenant Juan Francisco de la Bodega y Quadra, who would later prove a bold and capable mariner, watched from the stranded craft horrified, his weapons out of range. But soon, canoes approached the *Sonora* with apparent ill intent, according to Bodega y Quadra. It's likely that some of these oceangoing canoes were longer than the tiny schooner *Sonora*. But as the lead canoe drew within range, the Spaniards fired their swivel gun and several muskets, killing several Quinaults. Later, Bodega y Quadra named nearby Cape Elizabeth in mournful commemoration, calling it Punta de los Martires, or Point of the Martyrs.

Some have suggested that the landing by Hezeta and the assault on the *Sonora* crew members was no coincidence at all. It's hard to imagine the Quinaults didn't feel threatened by these strange people who planted a cross in the sand. >>

<< Both locations are on the shores of the Quinault Indian Reservation, currently closed to the general public—but exquisite spots nonetheless, worth hiking should the tribe reopen its beach-pass program.

The *Sonora*'s ill-fated reception was not the last violent encounter between explorers and Native inhabitants on this stretch of coast. Seventeen years later, the American captain Robert Gray "discovered" Grays Harbor (and later the Columbia River), the next day ordering an attack on the local population, presumably the Chehalis tribe.

On May 8, 1792, while anchored at a depth of five fathoms inside Grays Harbor, Gray's 83.5-foot *Columbia Rediviva* was approached just after midnight by several canoes full of shrieking Indians. During the day, the crew had traded with these Indians, but as the canoes approached under a bright moon, the crew noted they were "a savage sett" well armed with bows and arrows.

"We fier'd several cannon over them but still [they] persist'd to advance with their war Hoop," wrote crewman John Boit. "At length a large Canoe with at least 20 Men in her got within one-half pistol shot of the quarter & with a nine-pounder loaded with langerege & about 10 Muskets load'd with Buckshot we dashed her all to pieces & no doubt kill'd every soul in her, the rest soon made a retreat—I do not think they had any Conception of the power of artillery—but they was too near for us to admit of any hesitation how to proceed."

Although this locale of Grays Harbor has since changed substantially, due to the construction of the north and south jetties at its entrance and the resulting accretion of sand islands and spits, today a hiker can walk perhaps not far at all from the likely spot of this event, on state lands at Damon Point near Ocean Shores. It's hard to pinpoint exactly where this occurred, since Boit's journal puts the ship at a very likely latitude but at a longitude impossibly miles up the Chehalis River.

LAKE QUINAULT AREA

YOU MAY EXPERIENCE A KINK IN YOUR NECK after visiting the Lake Quinault area. It's one of three major temperate rain forests on the Olympic Peninsula, the one most known for gigantic conifers—behemoth Sitka spruce, gargantuan western red cedar and Douglas fir, and western hemlock so tall the limbs don't start until 100 feet up. You'll be craning your neck, looking up and saying "wow!" quite a bit. Hiking the trails through these forests will make you feel really, really tiny—some might say that's a very important perspective.

Did I say rain forest? Bring your raingear, because here the heavens pour forth—this is one of the wettest places on the North American continent. Average annual precip is some 140 inches, and some years get close to 190 inches of total rainfall—that's 12 to 15 feet. Nonetheless, a lot of spring and summer days are warm and dry.

Although winds can and do blow in the afternoons, Lake Quinault is often a gentle and scenic place to paddle.

Two other things the Lake Quinault valley is known for are wildlife—elk, deer, bear, cougar, bobcat—and the venerable wooden Lake Quinault Lodge. Built in 1926 in a rustic style reflective of its surroundings, it's one of three great park lodges on the Olympic Peninsula, along with the Kalaloch and Lake Crescent lodges. FDR stopped here in 1937 while pondering protection for much of the peninsula, so it's hallowed ground for wilderness freaks, such as me. In 1998 it was added to the National Register of Historic Places.

If you do nothing else in this area, you must experience no. 1, the giant trees; no. 2, the wildlife; and no. 3, the fabulous old lodge. Depending on the weather and your inclination, you can visit this area casually, mostly by car with short walks; or hardcore, putting in miles on the trail cloaked in your raingear. One of the biggest trees you'll ever see is the largest Sitka spruce on planet Earth: 191 feet high, 17 feet across at the butt, and less than 0.25 mile off the South Shore Road on an easy trail—it's truly astounding. One of the three largest known western red cedars is about 0.25 mile by trail off the North Shore Road—it's hollow and spooky. A great way to see wildlife here is by driving the 31 miles around the lake and part of the upper Quinault River, looking carefully in the meadows (mostly

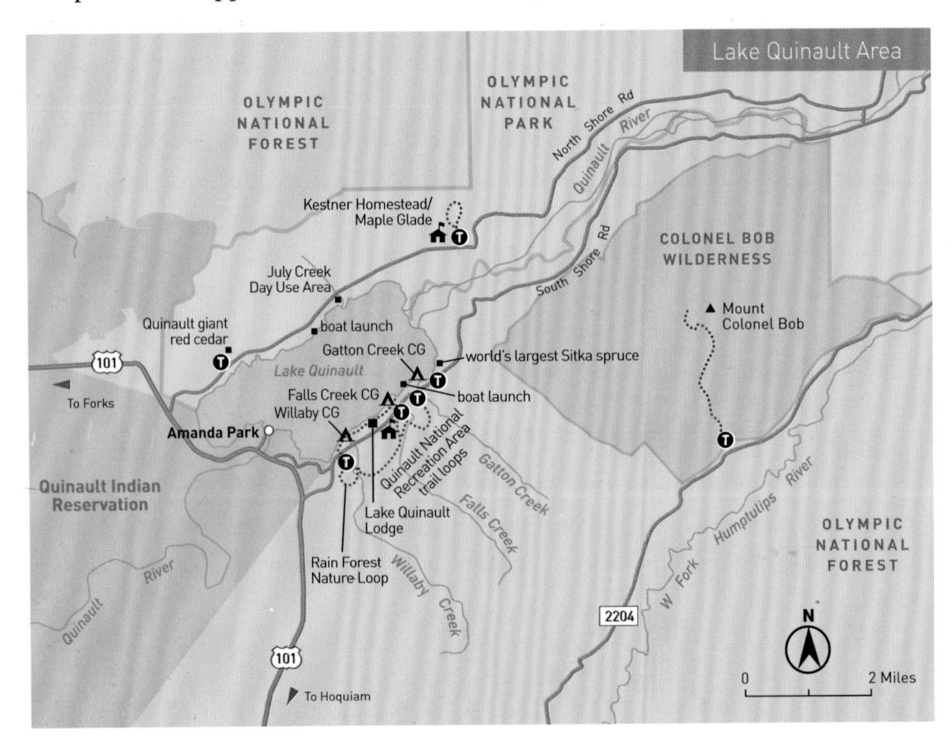

Driving all the way around Lake Quinault, through the river bottoms and old homestead pastures on its remote east side, is an almost surefire way to spot Olympic elk.

former homestead pastures) on the north side of the river. Bring your binoculars, camera, and longest lens.

For the more adventurous, the lake—about 4 miles long, 2 wide, and all 3729 acres of it inside the Quinault Indian Reservation—offers fine fishing for pretty cutthroat trout and Dolly Varden, a native char. I like to fish it by kayak, which lets me slip into nature and better observe wildlife such as loons, eagles, and otters. Fishing for sometimes huge steelhead can be good in the Quinault River, both in the lower river below the lake (tribal guide required) and the upper (see "Contacts and Resources" for fishing regulations).

Hiking in the area is intriguing, with a network of loop trails through giant trees totaling 10 miles, just off the South Shore Road. My favorite is a 4-mile traverse of imposing cathedral forests, a curious cedar bog, and cool waterfalls. There is a butt-buster of a hike here as well, to the 4492-foot top of Mount Colonel Bob, the crown of the little-known 11,961-acre Colonel Bob Wilderness. A former lookout site, this superb perch looks north over Lake Quinault and the Olympic Mountains.

The valley's history is interesting as well, from time immemorial—when the ancestors of the Quinault Nation arrived—to today. Like the Hoh and the Queets valleys to the north, the Quinault Valley was one of the last areas settled in the

Lower 48, the pioneers hacking out farms from the dense rain forest beginning in the 1880s. The Lake Quinault Museum, in a former post office on the South Shore Road (near the lodge), is worth a visit (see "Contacts and Resources" for all contact information). On the North Shore Road, Olympic National Park's seldom-staffed Quinault Rain Forest Ranger Station sits on a former homestead, which can be toured via the short Kestner Homestead Trail—a great place to see Olympic elk.

GETTING THERE/STAYING THERE

Amanda Park is the tiny village on the west end of Lake Quinault (store, café, liquor store), along the iconic ribbon of West Coast dreams known as US 101, 64 miles south of Forks and 40 miles north of Hoquiam. The North Shore Road leaves US 101 1.8 miles north of Amanda Park, the South Shore Road 1.2 miles south of that town.

There are three small US Forest Service campgrounds on the lake, all off the South Shore Road. Lake Quinault Lodge is the history buff's option; it has a motel wing as well (see "Contacts and Resources" for all contact information). A variety of other accommodations range from a lakeside resort (Rain Forest Resort Village), to vacation rental homes, to rustic lakeside cabins built decades ago (like the Lochaerie Resort). The Lake Quinault area website is a clearinghouse for area information, including accommodations, services, and activities.

FEES AND PERMITS

One curious twist in the Lake Quinault area is that management is split three ways: The Quinault tribe manages the lake itself. The National Park Service oversees Olympic National Park lands mostly on the north and east of the lake. And the US Forest Service is in charge of the Olympic National Forest lands on the south side of the lake, including the terrific trails above the South Shore Road. Appropriately, the Quinault Ranger Station on the South Shore Road is jointly operated by the Park Service and Forest Service.

You'll need a federal recreation pass (Northwest Forest Pass, $30/year; or Federal Interagency Pass, $80/year) to park at trailheads along the South Shore Road. These passes are available online or at the Quinault Ranger Station (see "Contacts and Resources" for all contact information). There is no entrance fee for national park lands in the area. To fish Lake Quinault, you must purchase a tribal fishing permit ($10/three days or $35/season), available at the Amanda Park Mercantile on US 101. A boat permit is also required, but nonresident boats may not be allowed on the lake due to invasive species concerns; be sure to check for current information.

CAMPING

WILLABY, FALLS CREEK, AND GATTON CREEK CAMPGROUNDS

Three small US Forest Service campgrounds nestle along the south shore of Lake Quinault, all near the mouths of creeks that tumble out of old-growth forests. All three have terrific sites right on the lake. But for my taste, they lack privacy and are too busy during the peak season. All are first come, first served, and maximum recommended RV size is 16 feet, except for 10 overflow spots at Gatton Creek.

Willaby is near the mouth of the creek of the same name. The campsites on the lake are sweet but close together, while sites on the upland side of the campground loop are close to busy South Shore Road. The campground is very close to the nicest trails on the south side of the lake, the 0.5-mile Rain Forest Nature Trail and the 4-mile Quinault Loop, both through fine old-growth conifer forest. Willaby is also a bit removed—but within walking distance—from the hustle-bustle around Lake Quinault Lodge, with the adjacent ranger station and Quinault Mercantile across the street. Willaby is currently open year-round, but in the past it has been closed seasonally and its status may change. There are 19 tent/RV sites (16 feet max), 2 walk-in sites, and 10 overflow RV sites. All cost $20 per night. Seven of the sites are deemed ADA accessible. There are two flush toilets and potable water but no hookups, no electricity. There is also a boat launch. **Driving directions:** The campground is 1.6 miles east of US 101 along the South Shore Road.

Falls Creek has two loops, with sites for 21 tents, trailers, or RVs (16 feet max) and 10 walk-in tent sites, all on a scenic point on the lakeshore. The campground operates seasonally, usually open just before Memorial Day weekend. Sites cost $20 per night for a vehicle spot, $15 for a walk-in; extra vehicles are $8 per night. There is potable water, a flush toilet, and boat ramp. **Driving directions:** The campground is 2.4 miles east of US 101 along the South Shore Road, adjacent to the Quinault Ranger Station.

Gatton Creek is a tiny campground at the mouth of its eponymous creek, with just 5 walk-in sites, at least a few of them beautiful spots right on the lake, along with 3 picnic spots. The parking lot also accommodates up to 10 RVs up to 24 feet long, but with no tables or fire rings. Gatton is open seasonally, usually beginning just before Memorial Day weekend. Sites cost $15 per night, another $8 for an extra vehicle. There is a vault toilet but no potable water. **Driving directions:** The campground is about 2.8 miles east of US 101 along the South Shore Road.

Contact for all three: Olympic National Forest

OTHER CAMPGROUNDS

Well up the Quinault Valley, in the rain forest along the two forks of the upper Quinault River—outside this book's coastal scope—are two primitive Olympic National Park campgrounds: Graves Creek (30 sites) and North Fork (9 sites). Rumor has it that the North Fork Campground could be on the budget chopping block.

HIKING

QUINAULT GIANT RED CEDAR TRAIL

BEHOLD THE CASTLE OF A GIANT RED CEDAR

In a stretch along the Washington Coast, about 50 miles as the raven flies, are three wizened old western red cedar trees that are among the largest of their kind, each at some point deemed the largest of the species on the planet. I'm not expert enough to name the champ, but like the Nolan Creek and Kalaloch cedars to the north, this hollow giant is impressive. It's surrounded by other cedar beasts and reached by a short trail through pretty rain forest.

Distance: 0.4 mile round-trip
Elevation gain: 80 feet
Difficulty: 2
Map: Park map available at ranger stations and park website
Contact: Olympic National Park
Notes: No canines

The Lake Quinault Giant Red Cedar, with other species growing on its aging bulk

DRIVING DIRECTIONS

From US 101, 1.8 miles north of Amanda Park, turn east onto the North Shore Road. Find the parking area and trail in 1.9 miles, on the left.

THE HIKE

From the trailhead, the rough, often muddy path climbs through the forest, sometimes on cedar boardwalk, soon reaching the giant after a few huffs and puffs. Note fallen trees along the trail, one in particular well up off the ground, supporting rows of western hemlock seedlings—a "nurse log."

Thuja plicata was a fundamental species to the Native tribes of the coast, providing the medium for canoes, houses, boxes, baskets, medicines, and many other things. The wood is light, easily split and worked, and amazingly rot resistant. But the largest old cedars are often mostly dead, and the Lake Quinault giant is a perfect example. It's hollow—you can walk into its center and look up and see light.

One time I hiked up the trail to find a bearded soul with his ear up against the trunk of this large forest ent. I asked, "What does it say?" He replied, "It's dead," and then turned and walked down the trail. Well, apparently he wasn't listening carefully. It isn't dead, not entirely. If you look high on its beefy trunk, you can see among other trees and bushes growing upon its limbs some cedar foliage still sprouting.

KESTNER HOMESTEAD AND MAPLE GLADE TRAILS

HIKING THE HISTORY OF A RAIN-FOREST HOMESTEAD

History is what makes this easy double-loop hike cool, giving some sense of what it must have been like to carve a homestead out of the dense temperate rain forests of the Olympic Peninsula. Anton Kestner arrived here in 1889, and one loop wanders his fields, barns, and outbuildings before crossing a crystal-clear stream to a smaller loop through a classic, moss-draped rain-forest maple grove. Your chance of spotting elk in the fields and nearby meadows is very high. This is a great hike for kids.

Distance: 1.8-mile loop
Elevation gain: None
Difficulty: 2

Map: Custom Correct Quinault–Colonel Bob or park map available at ranger stations and park website
Contact: Olympic National Park
Notes: Dogs prohibited

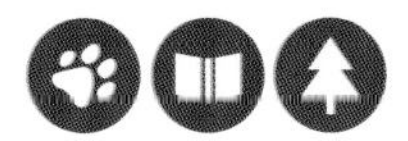

DRIVING DIRECTIONS

From US 101, 1.8 miles north of Amanda Park, turn east onto the North Shore Road and drive 5.5 miles east. Turn left at the sign for the Quinault Rain Forest Ranger Station, staffed in summer only.

THE HIKE

Early morning or evening is the best time for this hike, when the low angle of the sun lights up the mossy trees and you'll have a good chance of seeing the Olympic elk that browse in the old homestead fields. Find the trailhead at the ranger station and walk down the old road that led to the homestead, crossing Kestner Creek and reaching the homestead house in about 0.6 mile.

The trail then passes old barns and outbuildings, rusty trucks and farm implements, with glimpses to the surrounding forested hills. The trail leads to the Maple Glade Loop at about 1 mile; go left. The glade is not as spectacular as the Hall of Mosses along the Hoh River, but it's quite pretty nonetheless. The trees have green whiskers and beards of hanging Oregon selaginella moss and are decorated with licorice fern fronds and other mosses. The short loop returns quickly to the Kestner Trail; go left, cross Kestner Creek, and arrive back at the ranger station.

QUINAULT NATIONAL RECREATION AREA TRAIL LOOPS

OF WATERFALLS, CEDAR SWAMPS, AND CATHEDRAL RAIN FOREST

A series of connected trails on the old-growth hills above the South Shore Road, totaling about 10 miles, provide a marvelous tour of Quinault country's big trees, with options for multiple loop hikes along and across babbling rain-forest creeks, waterfalls, and small canyons. Some of the conifer stands are monumental. This mix of trail loops was

Hiking through the cathedral forest of giant conifers on the Rain Forest Nature Loop

hit hard by a powerful windstorm in 2007 that knocked down scores of big trees and seriously damaged the ambience of part of the Gatton Creek Loop, also resulting in the closure of a spur that once led to yet another near-record-sized ancient red cedar. In my opinion, the best of these trails is the 4+-mile loop that begins near the Quinault Ranger Station and climbs along Falls Creek.

Distance: 4.4-mile loop
Elevation gain: Less than 400 feet
Difficulty: 3
Map: Custom Correct Quinault–Colonel Bob or brochure from ranger station
Contact: Olympic National Park
Notes: Northwest Forest Pass or Federal Interagency Pass required to park at trail-

head. Dogs permitted on-leash. Restrooms and water available at the Rain Forest Nature Loop trailhead. Keep your map handy to navigate the many intersections and thus route options.

DRIVING DIRECTIONS

From US 101, 1.2 miles south of Amanda Park, head east on South Shore Road. In 2.3 miles, find a small parking area on the north side of the road, between the ranger station and Falls Creek Campground. Another access point at the other end of this loop is a Forest Service trailhead, 1.4 miles from US 101; if you only have time for the short Rain Forest Nature Loop, park here.

THE HIKE

People who really love the Lake Quinault area will want to explore all the loops that emanate from the South Shore Road. But the very best is the westernmost, a delightful route that gives you four stream crossings over pretty falls and cascades and the very best of the giant spruce, cedar, hemlock, and fir.

From the parking area 2.3 miles from US 101, find the trail heading up Falls Creek on the south side of the road. Through lush rain-forest vegetation with an understory of ferns, dogwood, and salmonberry, the trail climbs easily near the creek to a bridge. Stop and take some pics of the pretty swirling water, and then find an intersection just beyond, at 0.4 mile from your car. The left trail is part of the Gatton Creek Loop, so stay right and soon find another bridge, the trail veering west. In about another 0.25 mile, reach another bridge crossing a bubbling tributary, Cascade Creek. At 1 mile, reach yet another bridge, this one crossing Falls Creek again, the stream turning and curling insistently in pretty cascades (best during the full flows of winter and spring).

Beyond is an intersection; stay left, since the right fork leads back to the South Shore Road. As you continue west through big forest, soon the jungle closes in spookily, the ground becomes even more moist, and the trail becomes a boardwalk. At about 1.5 miles, the path transits a curious cedar bog, many of the trees dead and ghostly, the swampiness scented pungently with skunk cabbage. You almost expect a troll to jump out to ask you your business.

Just beyond the bog, at 1.7 miles, the trail reaches an intersection with a trail to nowhere; stay on the main path (right). The other fork once climbed into forest even more primeval, to a giant, near-record red cedar. The 2007 storm toppled so many giant trees over the trail that Forest Service managers blanched; there are no plans to cut the blowdown out and rebuild the trail, which also required a stream crossing difficult at high flows.

Your route soon turns toward the southeast and just gets better, the trees massive. At about 2.3 miles, just before a crossing of Willaby Creek, the trees seem smaller, mostly western hemlock. Ponder why. Soon, beyond the crossing, the big trees recommence and the wide path follows above the canyon of Willaby Creek. This is truly monumental forest. In one stretch, Douglas fir seem all of a consistent, giant size, like natural, towering colonnades.

You'll soon reach an intersection at 2.5 miles; on the left is one part of the 0.6-mile Rain Forest Nature Loop and most worthwhile. Take a detour, or continue on the main path above Willaby Creek, picking up the other end of the nature loop below; take it by going left. More phenomenal massive forest follows, including one impressive specimen in particular.

Finish the nature loop and arrive back on the main trail where you started, now 3 miles into your hike. Retrace your steps to the other end of the loop and drop down under the South Shore Road via a tunnel to Willaby Campground, at about 3.5 miles. From here, find the lakeshore trail part of the loop, passing by the Lake Quinault Lodge and the ranger station to reach your car near Falls Creek at 4.4 miles.

KEEP EXPLORING

For the Gatton Creek Loop, go left instead of right at the very first trail intersection 0.4 mile from the trailhead. This used to be a superb hike, full of giant trees, and is still nice. However, hit hard by the 2007 storm, it just isn't as magnifique. The way loops back to the South Shore Road in 2.1 miles at Gatton Creek Campground. Head west along the road about 0.6 mile to your vehicle.

Want more? Along the South Shore Road 11.4 miles east of US 101, take a right on a short spur to the Fletcher Canyon trailhead. This trail through deep, dark rain forest once climbed 4 miles to Moonshine Flat on the Mount Colonel Bob Trail. Some years ago, the Forest Service stopped maintaining it beyond 2 miles. It's steep, rocky (like Bob), and crosses many creeks through huge forest before pretty much dead-ending in shintangle beyond a crossing of Fletcher Creek.

WORLD'S LARGEST SITKA SPRUCE

AN EASY STROLL TO A SPRUCE MONSTER

This is really not a hike, the trail being only about 0.25 mile long, and a visit here isn't really about a trail at all, as pleasant as it is. It's about a tree, a monster tree, quite possibly the largest you'll ever see. If you leave the Quinault country without seeing this tree, you leave with business unfinished. Seriously, you MUST see this tree, recognized since 1987 as the world's largest Sitka spruce. The Quinault Sitka spruce is 191 feet tall, 58 feet, 11 inches in circumference, and about a thousand years old. Under the points system devised by the nonprofit group American Forests, it's listed as the standing champion Sitka spruce on the group's 2012 National Register of Big Trees.

Distance: 0.5 mile round-trip
Elevation gain: None
Difficulty: 1
Map: Park map available at ranger stations and park website
Contact: Olympic National Park, Olympic National Forest; the trail is on private land, but the folks at the Quinault Ranger Station can tell you about it
Notes: Dogs permitted on-leash

DRIVING DIRECTIONS

From US 101, 1.2 miles south of Amanda Park, take the South Shore Road east for about 3.2 miles. Just beyond the entrance to the Rain Forest Resort Village, find a sign and parking area along the road, on the right. The trail begins just across the road (on the north side).

THE HIKE

Skip down the short, flat trail—I believe courtesy of the nice folks at the Rain Forest Resort—on the north (lake) side of the road, and soon run headlong into the massive giant. This tree really is mind-boggling. The girth of its base is truly jaw-dropping, spread wide because it began life atop a nurse log (a tree that had fallen down), the spruce seedling sprouting and taking root around its host. It would take probably ten or eleven people to circle the spruce's base, hand to hand.

Pose on its massive base, snap a pic, and then think about this: when this tree took root, no white man had ever seen the lake, Columbus had not yet set sail, and this place was wilderness primeval, the Quinault people maintaining villages at the head of the lake (likely a seasonal camp) and at its outlet (the present-day Amanda Park). If this tree could talk!

MOUNT COLONEL BOB

BIG VIEWS AWAIT ATOP A BRUTE CALLED BOB

The inappropriately named Colonel is about the closest actual peak to the Pacific Ocean along the entire Washington Coast, at some 27 miles distant, the other major peaks of the Olympics all well inland. Named for Civil War veteran and famous agnostic Colonel Robert Ingersoll, who apparently never came anywhere near it, the mountain is a famously difficult hike, often steep and the tread a loose-rock hell that lengthens

A pretty subalpine basin just off the trail up Mount Colonel Bob

THE QUINAULT COAST: SO NEAR, SO FAR

The 23 miles of coast that define the western edge of the 208,150-acre Quinault Indian Reservation include some of the most magnificent ocean hikes you've probably never heard of and might never visit. They include two of the most historic spots on the Washington Coast as well as some of its most beautiful scenery and geologic curiosities. The Quinault coast is also wild, almost entirely undeveloped, with no highway along most of it.

Sadly, the Quinault beaches are not open to the general public and there are no plans to open them. But there is hope. Although for about thirty-five years beginning in 1969, all of the Quinault Reservation's ocean shoreline was closed to the public as tribal leaders expressed their independence from the manipulating chain saws of the federal Bureau of Indian Affairs, a beach day-pass program was instituted in the early 2000s. That allowed the general public to visit all but the most sacred Quinault beaches, for a modest fee.

Even then, many of the beaches were difficult to reach. But in late 2012, the tribe abruptly closed its beaches again, due to concerns about non-Indian activities on its shore. This is most unfortunate, because the general public stands to learn a lot about the land and the people by visiting the Quinault beaches. The tribe also stands to gain some level of economic stimulation by allowing low-impact use of its beaches, in pass fees if nothing else.

Of course it should be pointed out what the Quinault people gave up for the reservation: most of their land, their aboriginal ways, just about everything. The tribe should be protective of its beaches. They are precious, many are pristine, and they have in the past been threatened by development. However, I believe, perhaps wishfully, that these issues will be resolved sooner or later.

But to be clear: at this writing, you can't experience these places. I mention them because they are important and exquisite and to give hikers a heads-up should the beaches be reopened.

Point Grenville and environs are historically significant as the locale of the first recorded landing of Europeans in what is now Washington, and almost simultaneously the first recorded attack by Native Americans on Europeans in what is now the state. Just south of precipitous Grenville and its collection of pocket coves >>

<< is the spot where officers of the Spanish frigate *Santiago* landed to plant a cross and claim the coast in July of 1775. Just north of Grenville is where seven members of the accompanying 36-foot schooner *Sonora* met their fate at the hands of Quinault warriors—only hours after the cross planting.

Two day hikes past these spots—one from the village of Taholah south to Point Grenville and the other from Grenville Bay north to the point—are both intriguing and superb. Grenville was the most popular spot on the Quinault Reservation when the tribe operated its pass program, because of its easy access to intriguing geology, including at least two sea arches and multiple sea stacks, tide pools, pocket beaches, and coves.

Wandering the expansive tide pools of Point Grenville when the Quinault tribe allowed public access to its beaches

But the highlight of the Quinault coast is the Elephant Rock/Tunnel Island area, a curious group of rocks that features a double arch, with the front end shaped like an elephant drinking water from the sea. Adjacent Tunnel Island, at the mouth of the Raft River, is as its name implies—an island with a cave bored right through it. The nearby rock formations known as the Big and Little Hogsbacks record ancient earth history, the oldest being volcanic in origin, deposited as submarine lava flows during the Middle Eocene some 45 to 50 million years ago.

If the tribe does resume its beach-pass program, this coast is more than worth a visit. Keep abreast of developments via the Quinault Indian Nation website (see "Contacts and Resources").

the journey. But this hike provides a fabulous perch above the Lake Quinault country and a peek at Mount Olympus's multiple peaks to the north—if the weather cooperates. George A. Bauer, a highly regarded member of the Grays Harbor–based Olympians hiking club, has scaled the Colonel 201 times, reaching the top twice in 2013 at the age of seventy-five. He's a sweetheart, a veteran Olympics climber, but after hiking this trail I have to question his sanity! George would say this hike is a superb trainer for higher climbs and tougher off trail adventures, and he's right. Plus, this hike is the essential way to experience the 1961-acre Colonel Bob Wilderness, which protects the wild and wonderfully timbered Quinault Ridge.

There are two routes, a longer, more difficult one via the South Shore Road at Lake Quinault, the Colonel Bob Trail proper (14.4 miles round-trip with more than 4200 feet of gain), and a shorter but steeper route from the south that I describe here. It's far easier to day hike Bob going this way, starting on the Petes Creek Trail.

Distance: 8.4 miles round-trip
Elevation gain: 3400 feet
Difficulty: 5
Map: Custom Correct Quinault–Colonel Bob
Contact: Olympic National Forest
Notes: Northwest Forest Pass or Federal Interagency Pass required to park at trailhead. Dogs permitted on-leash. This is a seasonal route for most, with serious snow in winter. In summer, carry extra water, at least 2 liters each, or be prepared to filter from streams.

DRIVING DIRECTIONS

From US 101, 3 miles north of the tiny village of Humptulips, head east on the Donkey Creek Road (Forest Road 22, paved here) for 8 miles, to the junction with FR 2204. Go left on FR 2204 and drive 11 miles (the pavement ends in 3) to the Petes Creek trailhead.

THE HIKE

As usual, I have a couple things to get off my chest straight away. I don't appreciate place names that honor people who never came near the places. Mount Rainier? Who the hell was he, some Brit aristocrat? Don't get me wrong, I love England and I'm something of an Anglophile. But the rightful name of that mountain

OLYMPIC ELK: THE BIG BEAST OF THE RAIN FOREST

The Olympic elk is perhaps the signature mammal of the Olympic Peninsula, once hunted to dangerously low population levels. In 1909, when according to some sources the population was down to several dozen animals, President Theodore Roosevelt designated part of the existing Olympic Forest Reserve as the Mount Olympus National Monument. That's how the species became known as Roosevelt elk. Today estimates place the population in Olympic National Park at about five thousand animals. It remains prized as a game species outside the park and highly valued as food.

Bulls grow immense, multi-tined antlers, which they shed and regrow each year. They are absolutely stunning animals to see in the wild. During the "rut," bulls gather harems of cow elk and trumpet their presence to potential competitors by bugling. It's a shrill, high-pitched, multinote whistling sound, often ended with a series of lusty grunts. Spend some time outside your car in this part of the world in September or early October, and you'll likely hear the bulls—to me the sound of wilderness personified.

is Tahoma, from the Coast Salish tongue. I don't have a better name for Colonel Bob, but its current one lends nothing to the place, describes zilch. How about Mulkey Mountain, after the Lake Quinault settlers who decades past hunted and trapped here? Or Mount Quinault, for the first people here?

Or Mount Kickyerass, because that's what this hike does to most people. If you're a casual hiker, this trail is not essential to your visit to Lake Quinault country. If you're an avid hiker who wants to hike as much of the Olympics as possible, or wants a good trainer, by all means take this trail. There are big trees, pretty subalpine basins, and a summit to bag!

And that brings me to another beef, the summit. Once perched atop Colonel Bob was a fire lookout, built in 1931, torn out by the US Forest Service in 1967. This was back in the day when the primary interest of that agency was timber and logging; recreation mattered just a little, and history apparently even less. This artifact of a colorful bygone era, along with dozens around the Pacific Northwest, was demolished as a hazard and liability. The lookout alone would be a superb reason to climb this mountain. Eh, bien!

Find the trail across the road from the parking area on FR 2204 and shortly find the trailhead register. Sign in and grunt uphill, soon entering the Colonel Bob Wilderness and big trees, mostly western hemlock and red cedar. On standing snags of dead conifers, note the rampant holes of pileated woodpeckers. Along the way you'll find salmonberry thickets. Called wild raspberries by the settlers, the red ones are sweet and juicy, the orange ones not so much. Also note blue huckleberries, edible and sweet when ripe. At just less than 2 miles, find a single campsite next to a huge tree, the babbling creek close by. Busting this hike into two days by camping here would make for a much more pleasant experience.

This first portion on the Petes Creek Trail is through pleasant ancient forest, climbing in a relatively gentle way, crossing the creek, and then seriously switchbacking up to a junction at 2.4 miles with the Colonel Bob Trail proper. Along the way in places, the creek just disappears, apparently taking a subterranean route, only to reappear above and below—cool!

Go right at the junction with the Colonel Bob Trail and soon enter an open basin kept free of trees by winter avalanches coming off Gibson Peak above and to the right. Here begins a proliferation of wildflowers, not so intense as in some high meadows, but pretty nonetheless. Subalpine daisies, orange-gold tiger lilies, brilliant red columbine, paintbrush, and the white puffball blossoms of bear grass light up the trailside.

The trail now has been rocky for some time, and it only gets worse, making the tread slippery, especially on the downhill, and bending feet and ankles every which way. For the rest of the way, pretty much, you'll be gaining serious elevation. A series of switchbacks brings you to Quinault Ridge just northwest of Gibson Peak, and soon the way eases as you enter the headwaters of Fletcher Canyon and a patchwork of basalt knobs, at about 3.2 miles. Near the crossing of Fletcher Creek, find a few campsites. This is Moonshine Flat—named not for white lightning, but because this basin looks to the north and east, and in the right conditions moonbeams would be dancing in your eyes. It's a sweet place to camp.

But here is where you measure the strength of your legs and the size of your heart. You still have 1 mile and 1000 feet of elevation to gain, none of it easy. Immediately, the way climbs, contouring around several fearsome cliffs on the primary ridge between Bob and an unnamed peak just west.

The way eases briefly and then disconcertingly drops, but just a bit, and then climbs hard for the main Quinault Ridge. Gaining the ridge provides glimpses down toward Lake Quinault country and to the interior of the Olympics. The trail keeps to the narrow ridge—on your right, just west, is a beautiful subalpine basin between Bob and that unnamed associated peak, which you see now is graced by two more adjacent and marvelous spires. Climbing, you bump into the rock buttress that makes up the summit, marked by a vertical basalt blob-knob dead ahead.

Other guidebooks say that the final 100 feet or so is on steps hacked or blasted by the lookout builders. To me, this looks simply like basaltic folds, but they nonetheless provide steep footholds to the bald summit. Carefully make your way up. On a clear day you can see Lake Quinault and the multiple peaks of Mount Olympus beyond the Queets–Quinault divide on the northern skyline. Behind you, the triple crowns you've been seeing loom up and beyond, the southern flanks of the Olympic Mountains.

Soak it in, then suck it up. You've got 4+ knee-tensing downhill miles on crappy tread back to the trailhead. You'll be glad when you reach it.

QUINAULT VALLEY CRITTER WATCHING

The 30-mile drive around Lake Quinault likely affords visitors the best place to see native wildlife in its natural habitat anywhere on the Olympic Peninsula outside of remote wilderness. It's unusual NOT to see Olympic elk in the lush rain-forest bottomlands and old homestead pastures east of the lake. The Olympic, or Roosevelt, elk is the largest native land mammal on the Olympic Peninsula (it's larger than the Rocky Mountain elk), with mature bulls reaching 1000 pounds. Deer are common on this drive too, and people also regularly see black bear and occasionally even bobcat and cougar. There are pretty stops along the way as well, including two waterfalls and the July Creek picnic area, set in a small grove of giant trees right on the lake.

About 6 miles of the drive are on narrow gravel road through the bottomlands. The family car can easily handle it, but it's not a good idea to take a huge RV or pull a trailer on the backside of the Lake Quinault loop.

To drive the loop clockwise, find the North Shore Road on US 101, 1.8 miles north of Amanda Park, and head east. In 0.8 mile, note the massive Douglas

A bull elk peers through the forest of the Big Creek Bottoms along the road around Lake Quinault. (Photo by Lorna Johnston)

fir along the right side of the road; there's room to pull over here if you want to stop and give it a hug, but your arms won't reach around more than a quarter of it. Soon you'll start passing homes on the lake, and 1.9 miles from US 101, note parking on the left for the short Quinault Giant Red Cedar Trail.

Beyond July Creek the homes end, and soon, about 5 miles from US 101, you begin to enter habitat where you're likely to see elk, with the Quinault Rain Forest Ranger Station coming up on the left at 5.5 miles. The ranger station is staffed only in summer and also serves as trailhead for the Kestner Homestead and Maple Glade Trails. Elk frequent all the grassy meadows here at the ranger station, across the road, and just beyond. In the spring of 2012 I saw a cow elk with two newborn calves here.

The road turns to gravel at 7.8 miles, and at 9.7 miles you'll reach the bottoms of Big Creek—terrific spots to see elk. Notice how open the rain forest is here? Elk browse on the understory vegetation and keep it open, creating a mossy, park-like ambience under the canopy of big spruce and old maple.

Even so, elk can be difficult for the untrained eye to spot. I'd suggest looking for two things: their butts and ears. The rump of an Olympic elk is a cream-white color and often a dead giveaway, especially when the animals are moving. In addition,

JULY CREEK: SPECIAL PLACE THAT NEEDS ATTENTION

About 3.4 miles into the Lake Quinault drive, on the right (south), find the parking area for the July Creek picnic area, once a superb walk-in campground, the best on Lake Quinault, in a grove of big old conifers right on the lake. It's worth a stop, since the trees are gigantic, truly impressive, and the small grove diverse, with cedar, spruce, fir, hemlock, and maple all together. There are several dandy spots along the lakeshore as well, great for a swim on warm days and fishing for cutthroat trout and Dolly Varden when the lake is open (typically late April through October; see "Contacts and Resources" for fishing regulations). The cross-lake view to Mount Colonel Bob is noteworthy too.

It was a huge loss for campers when the Park Service converted this spot to day use only in 2002, due to concerns about campers compacting soil around the roots of the ancient trees—I'm sure maintenance costs were an issue as well. It's also disappointing to see the current condition of the place. The picnic tables are rotting and brush has seriously piled up, impeding access to the lake and picnic sites. The tall forest also cries out for interpretive signage—this is a special place!

many times I've looked through the trees and spotted the beasts motionless, but with ears up and eyes staring right at me. Drive slowly and scan the bottomlands. If a car comes up behind you, pull over and let them pass. The locals know this is great critter-watching country—they drive it too for that very reason.

At 11.8 miles, you leave the Big Creek Bottoms as the road narrows and climbs a steep hill—drive slowly! At 13 miles the pavement resumes (just for another 1.1 miles) and you enter Bunch Meadows, formerly pastures carved out of the rain forest by a pioneer family of that name. Now you're in prime territory to see elk, deer, and maybe bear, especially in spring. If you're lucky in the extreme, you might spot bobcats and cougars.

At 13.9 miles from US 101, near the end of Bunch Meadows, note the road on the left. Don't take it, but for future reference it leads 3 miles to North Fork Campground and trailheads for the North Fork Quinault Trail and the super wild and remote Skyline Ridge Trail.

Stay to the right and soon reach a bridge across the upper Quinault River at 14.1 miles. The best of your wildlife watching is done. Cross the bridge to an intersection. The left leads to Graves Creek Campground and the famous Enchanted Valley Trail—outside the scope of this book, but a truly wild and classic rain-forest backpack.

Take a right on South Shore Road to complete your loop drive. In about 0.9 mile from the bridge (15 miles overall), pull over at pretty Bunch Falls tumbling over rock and out of the rain forest on your left, to snap some pics. The road then continues to skirt the south side of the upper Quinault River, and at 19.1 miles pavement resumes. You'll pass pretty Merriman Falls on the left at 20.4 miles—you'll want a photo, though its aspect makes it a tough shoot.

Then you'll reach a residential region of the south shore area—folks here see elk, wildcats, and bear fairly often—before returning to the lake and, in order, coming to the World's Largest Sitka Spruce Trail (23.7 miles), the Rain Forest Resort Village, Gatton Creek Campground (24.1 miles), Falls Creek Campground (24.5 miles), the Quinault Ranger Station and the Lake Quinault Museum (24.7 miles), and just beyond, Lake Quinault Lodge, Willaby Campground, and the trailhead for the Rain Forest Nature Trail. At 26.9 miles you're back at US 101, 3 miles south of your starting point.

MOCLIPS TO OCEAN SHORES: NORTH BEACH AREA

IF ANY PART OF THE WASHINGTON COAST is like a fuzzy old wool sweater, tattered with thin spots at the elbows but still one of your favorites, this is it. Honestly, parts of this stretch of the coast are depressing to me, hardscrabble towns of abandoned structures that have seen better days, populated by offbeat rural characters and colorful urban castaways; intriguing sort of like the sight of an upside-down pickup in the ditch. This shoreline is so different from its wild, undeveloped cousin to the north. But I keep coming back: for the great birding, wide-open, unhindered ocean views, shiny agates, phenomenal razor clam digging, and the escape it offers from city life.

From the Quinault Reservation south past Moclips—a town perhaps on the verge of revival—to the tourist town of Ocean Shores, this coastal stretch is

Razor clam diggers pursue the tasty bivalve during a minus tide on the beach at Ocean City.

known as the North Beach area. Although to a significant degree a workingman's locale, home to loggers, shake rats, and fishermen, its main claim to fame has always been tourism. A railroad used to run from Hoquiam, along Grays Harbor and up the coast, past splendid hotels to Moclips.

The North Beach region has a long and rich tradition of razor clam digging, the best in the state. Razor clams are long, golden-shelled bivalves—up to 7+ inches long—that live in the sand right under the surf, descending deeper when alarmed. You dig them on minus tides, or close to it, and it can be a challenge. They're marvelously flavored, vaguely sweet, with an appropriate oceanic flavor. They've provided essential nutrients for centuries to the Chehalis, Copalis, and Quinault people and in the early twentieth century supported a commercial fishery that provided needed income to coastal residents. Today the harvestable clams are split between the Quinault tribe and recreational diggers.

The biggest town along the coast here is Ocean Shores, a kitschy, touristy place that I've come to appreciate. There are plenty of activities to keep you occupied, and not just clamming. Along with nearby Grays Harbor National Wildlife Refuge, the Ocean Shores area offers some of the best, most diverse bird-watching anywhere in western Washington. The list of potential sightings exceeds 260 species—pelicans, peregrines, eagles, snowy owls, albatross, gulls, guillemots, geese, ducks, loons, creepers, crossbills, waxwings, herons, and perhaps most spectacularly, shorebirds. In springtime, hundreds of thousands of sandpipers, dunlins, godwits, and dowitchers stop here on their long migration to the Arctic.

The fishing can also be fabulous here. Grays Harbor and its primary source, the Chehalis River, provide seriously good coho fishing most years, and some of these "silvers" are huge. In years of good returns, the harbor and the Humptulips River also produce fine fishing for the largest salmon, chinook (or "kings"). The "Hump" and many of its tributaries—including the Wishkah, Wynoochee, and Satsop—can offer excellent fishing for coho and steelhead, depending on a given year's run strength.

This region is not known for hiking, but there are a few very nice walks in protected areas. Griffiths-Priday State Park encompasses the entire Copalis Spit, a large sandbar that harbors the lower mile of the Copalis River and is designated a nature sanctuary—no driving on the beach. The spit makes for a fine beach hike and offers good beachcombing and excellent birding. Damon Point, now managed by the Washington Department of Natural Resources, is another ocean-built spit of sand, just inside the entrance of Grays Harbor, accessed through Ocean

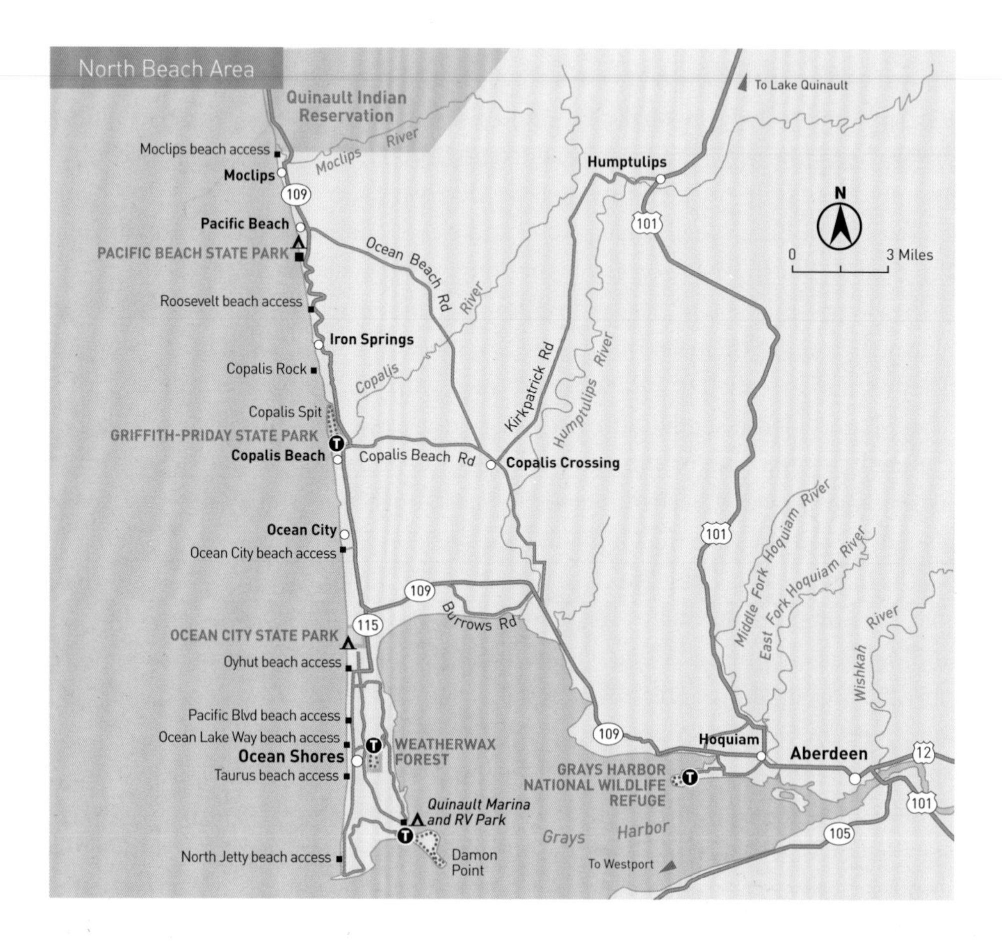

Shores. The walking and running are fine, surf perch fishing fair, windsurfing and agate hunting good, and birding excellent.

There would be far more great hiking in this region, but for most of the year and on most of the beaches, driving is allowed. These beaches have been a largely unimpeded transportation route for coastal residents for decades. Where dense forests choked off vehicle travel in the pioneer days, horses and wagons and early cars could always travel the hard-packed sand between the dunes and the surf. Beach driving is a tradition here, and for many it's still the only way to get to the razor clams. It's difficult for a person with mobility issues to walk a mile or more in sand to the clam beds. I recognize that. And beach driving is prohibited seasonally, April 15 through Labor Day, on several stretches. But still I wish beach driving was more restricted. Although all the rules that apply to public roads also apply on the beach, and the speed limit is just 25 miles per hour, many drivers can't resist spinning brodies and roaring around like NASCAR demons. More vehicle-free beach would make this coastal stretch more attractive for pure recreation: kite flying, picnicking, sand castle building, beach fires, sunset watching, and just plain walking.

GETTING THERE/STAYING THERE

From US 101 in Hoquiam, head west on State Route 109. Precisely where SR 109 veers north, at about 17 miles, turn left on SR 115 and drive 3 miles south to find Ocean Shores. Or, at that junction head north on SR 109 for Ocean City (3 miles), Copalis Beach (6 miles), Pacific Beach (15 miles), and Moclips (17 miles). All these towns offer places to stay, including two state parks (see "Camping," below). For details, visit or call Grays Harbor Tourism (see "Contacts and Resources" for all contact information).

Perched atop the windy spruce bluffs of this region are also three of what I'd call classic coastal resorts: the venerable and beloved Ocean Crest, the surf-serenaded Sandpiper, and Iron Springs. Ocean Crest, started in the 1950s by World War II navy fighter pilot Jess Curtwright and his wife, Barbara, lost its quaint, one-of-a-kind ocean-view restaurant to fire in 2011, although it is now rebuilt and reopened. Iron Springs, a collection of cabins nestled on bluffs above the ocean, has recently seen a much-needed and most welcomed renovation. I've got great memories of staying at these resorts: you can catch surf perch and dig razor clams basically right out the door of your room or cabin, and then go cook 'em up.

The upscale resort community of Seabrook is a popular newcomer. Just south of Pacific Beach, Seabrook is a self-contained beach community of Cape Cod–style cottages, spread over 300 acres, with shops, a restaurant, pool, trails, and a long stretch of ocean beach. It has been touted by newspapers and magazines nationally as a sort of Cannon Beach north. The homes range from $300,000 to $1.97 million at last check, and many of the owners participate in a vacation rental program, so the public has access to many of the cottages.

Seabrook has initiated sort of a gentrification process in the Pacific Beach/Moclips area. Other upscale houses have been sprouting on the nearby bluffs above the ocean. Is this a good thing? At first I regarded it as an uppity-yuppity intrusion on an area rich with funky character and colorful history. But if there's any place on the Washington Coast destined for renewal, it's here. The place is pretty damned nice, and the development is providing jobs in a traditionally economically depressed area.

There are two final reasons I like this part of the coast. First, any area that's got an Irish pub can't be all bad, and Ocean Shores has the Galway Bay, offering live Celtic music, an appropriately colorful and crusty owner—and Guinness on tap, of course! Second, one of my favorite coastal taverns is just up the highway in Copalis Beach, the Green Lantern, with pool tables, burgers, ales on tap, and a longtime waitress who fails to smile at all until delivering the bill. Hey, I'm OK with that—as a server she's as reliable as a good cup of coffee.

FEES AND PERMITS

Folks stopping at the area state parks for day trips are required to hang a Washington State Discover Pass in their vehicle to park (see "Contacts and Resources"). The pass is $30 a year or $10 a day and is available online, from many hunting and fishing license vendors, and at various state park locations. If you're camping at a state park, this fee is waived.

COOL BIRDS OF THE COAST

Although the Grays Harbor region arguably offers the best bird-watching on the coast, if you visit any part of the Washington Coast you'll see quite a variety—potentially up to 360 species. This is because of the coast's diverse habitats—forests, marine and freshwater shorelines, salt marshes, meadows, dunes, and tide flats. Birds will entertain you with their antics, impress you with their aerobatics, and stun you with their beauty. A great book with all the details is *A Birder's Guide to Coastal Washington*, by Bob Morse. But here are some regularly seen favorites.

Bald eagle: Our national symbol is the ubiquitous alpha predator on the entire coast—diving down to grab a small salmon from the Strait of Juan de Fuca, perched at Damon Point picking apart a hapless duck, or above a wilderness beach with talons locked, cartwheeling toward the earth (mating behavior or a fight). The sight is always a thrill.

Peregrine falcon: The fastest bird on earth, capable of 200-mile-per-hour dives, this sleek crow-sized raptor is hard to spot. They're regularly seen along the rocky north coast (Cape Flattery, La Push, and Point Grenville), where they nest on sea stacks. But your best chance of seeing them is around Grays Harbor and Willapa Bay

Pelicans glide overhead and seagulls line the beach at sunrise at Damon Point after a powerful storm churned up shoreline organisms and sparked a feeding frenzy.

in spring, where they feed on small waterfowl and shorebirds. Try Damon Point, Bowerman Basin, and Bottle Beach on Grays Harbor. On Willapa Bay, Leadbetter Point and Tokeland are good spots.

Snowy owl: Some years this large ghostly owl does not migrate south to winter in Washington, but snowies were common at Damon Point near Ocean Shores during the winters of 2011–12 and 2012–13. In 2013–14 they were spotted on Willapa Bay near Leadbetter Point.

Sanderling: This common and comical coastal shorebird is said to nest in the Arctic, but I see them year-round all along the coast near the surf. They feed on tiny invertebrates in wet sand and follow the waves in and out, running on tiny legs in a frenzied fashion. Seeing them flying in a flock can be a thing of singular beauty, flittering, fluttering, rising, and falling in uncanny unison.

Black oystercatcher: These are regular visitors to the rocky north coast—you'll know it as soon as you see one. The bill and eyes are bright red, the legs yellow, bodies black. They poke and peck at intertidal rocks for crustaceans. I almost always see them while hiking Olympic National Park's wilderness beaches.

Whimbrel: A large shorebird long of leg and bill, whimbrels are seen on mudflats with other shorebirds but also alone on the sandy shore near dunes. They walk along probing the mud and sand for invertebrates. I've seen them on the outer coast at Sand Point and Copalis Spit. Also look at Bowerman Basin and Damon Point on Grays Harbor and Leadbetter Point down Willapa way.

Loon: The red-throated, Pacific, and common loons are regular sights along the coast in saltwater bays as well as in large lakes like Ozette and Quinault. They don't often vocalize, but when they do it's a singular, yodeling wail—an iconic wilderness sound for sure. See them in Clallam Bay, Neah Bay, Lake Quinault, Grays Harbor off Ocean Shores, at Westport, and on Willapa Bay.

Brown pelican: These big, bucket-mouthed birds are regular summer sights from the Columbia River north past Point Grenville. They feed on schooling fish such as anchovies, herring, and sardines and can often be seen crashing in a clumsy fashion, headlong into the sea, to scoop them up.

Varied thrush: This beautiful bird is like a robin on acid, related and maybe 5 percent larger, with breast speckles and red and black streaks. It's a bird of the forest, and as much as their beauty I like their haunting song: a long, droning, trilled whistle. You won't see or hear them on the shore. But you will on any forest trail leading to the beach: First and Second Beach trails in Olympic National Park, all the Kalaloch beach trails, and all the forest trails around Lake Quinault.

Rufous hummingbird: You might not think of this as a coastal species, but I see the agile reddish-brown buzzers all along the ocean shore wherever appropriate flowering vegetation occurs, such as salmonberry. They were constant companions when I camped at Chilean Memorial on the wilderness beach strip, as well as at Lake Ozette. They arrive in late winter as soon as the salmonberry blooms and head south in fall. Here's a trick: wear a red bandana, since they key on the color red. They'll zing right around your head!

CAMPING

PACIFIC BEACH STATE PARK

This state park caters to the RV crowd, largely because of demand generated by the excellent razor clam digging here (surf perch fishing is often excellent too).

The 10-acre park is right on the ocean above the sand and along Joe Creek, with excellent views of the surf and 2300 feet of shoreline. The park is smack dab in the town of Pacific Beach, with its associated services. The gentrified upscale village of Seabrook is about 1 mile south, with its restaurant and shops.

The campground's big drawback is that it's wide open, with no shade and zero privacy. That's A-OK if you're in an RV but makes for poor tent camping. There are 22 tent sites, 42 RV sites with full hookups, and 2 yurts available for rent; 26 of the sites are right on the shore. Sites are reservable year-round. Cost during peak season (May 15–September 15) is $23–$26 per night; $30–$37 for hookup sites. It's a few bucks cheaper the rest of the year. The campground has potable water, an RV dump station, two restrooms, and six showers. Campfires are prohibited in this park, but you can build beach fires as long as they are 100 feet from any vegetation. Charcoal and propane barbecues are OK in the campground.

Contact: Washington State Parks. **Driving directions:** From the junction of State Routes 109 and 115 (the Ocean Shores turnoff), head north 15 miles to Pacific Beach and turn left on Main Street. In less than 0.25 mile, take another left on 2nd Street and shortly find the park.

OCEAN CITY STATE PARK

This is a huge, full-service, year-round state park, at 170 acres and 178 sites, well-wooded and within easy walking distance of the ocean and excellent razor clam digging. It isn't the best state park on Washington Coast (that would be Cape Disappointment to the south), but it's a dandy, very close to Ocean Shores and all of its services, amenities, and activities. That does bring up a question: It's called Ocean City State Park, but the town of Ocean City is almost 3 miles to the north and the city of Ocean Shores is just 1 mile south. Go figure.

The park has two short trails, one along a wetland area near the entrance (good birding) and the other from the day-use parking area through the dunes out to the ocean. Be aware that driving is allowed on the beach here for most of the year. There are four sheltered picnic tables (ten unsheltered), four restrooms, six showers, an RV dump station, and two group camps.

This park is heavily used by RV campers (up to 50 feet max), and one quibble is that when I've visited, most of the available tent sites have been in the middle of the loops, in the wide open with no privacy. That could be easily rectified if the park had a walk-in camping area. Standard sites cost $23–$26 per night; RV sites are $32–$37. Sites are reservable.

Contact: Washington State Parks. **Driving directions:** From the junction of State Routes 109 and 115, take the Ocean Shores turnoff onto SR 115. Look for the signed campground entrance in about 0.5 mile, on the right.

QUINAULT MARINA AND RV PARK

The old Ocean Shores marina is now the Quinault Marina and RV Park, owned and operated by the Quinault Indian Nation. It has boat moorage and launching available—but with access issues for boats at lower tides, due to shallow water—and an open-area campground. The year-round campground is above the beach near Damon Point and has 46 reservable sites, all with full hookups, including electricity, water, and septic. Full hookup sites cost $35; 5 sites just above the beach are $45 per night; tent sites are $20 per night, two tents allowed per site.

Contact: Quinault Marina and RV Park. **Driving directions:** From the entrance to Ocean Shores, head south on Point Brown Avenue. Go straight through the roundabout in 0.75 mile, staying on Point Brown Avenue for about 6 miles total to Marine View Drive. Turn right on Marine View Drive and shortly find the (somewhat dilapidated) marina and office on the left.

HIKING

COPALIS SPIT AND GRIFFITH-PRIDAY STATE PARK

A WHEEL-FREE SHORE FOR BIRDS AND BEACHCOMBERS

The second-best hike in the North Beach area south of the Quinault Indian Reservation, this is a 1.2-mile-long spit of sand dunes, protected as the Copalis Spit Natural Area, a designated wildlife area, and Griffith-Priday State Park. The 364-acre park is for day use only, and driving is not allowed anywhere inside the park, so it's a terrific seashore hike, with 8316 feet of saltwater shore and 9950 feet along the Copalis River. Beachcombing can be excellent after storms from late fall through midspring, and the bird-watching is often terrific.

The spit is an excellent example of how wind and waves change the seashore landscape, by piling up sand into dunes—"accretion"—and blocking the Copalis River from a direct route to the sea, shifting its flow north for more than a mile. From October through November you can also fish its mouth for migrating coho salmon. Oh yes: legend has it that silver dollars dating to the 1880s have been found here, allegedly booty from a long-ago shipwreck.

Distance: 2.5–3 miles
Elevation gain: Almost none, minor ups and downs
Difficulty: 2
Map: Griffith-Priday State Park map, www.parks.wa.gov/DocumentCenter/Home/View/1879
Contact: Washington State Parks
Notes: Discover Pass required to park. Dogs permitted on-leash.

DRIVING DIRECTIONS

From the turn to Ocean Shores on State Route 109 (the SR 109/SR 115 junction), drive north about 6 miles to the town of Copalis Beach. At the Green Lantern tavern (pool tables and brews!), go left on Benner Road and find the parking lot to the right in less than 0.25 mile.

THE HIKE

A creek that was notorious in the past for trapping cars in its soggy, sandy bed now flows roughly parallel to the Copalis River, just to the west of the parking area, and must be rounded before you can reach the ocean beach. That means about 0.5 mile of hiking north on a trail cut through the dunes from the parking area; it provides a good sample of this curious type of ecosystem, where it's not unusual to see black-tailed deer. Find the trail near the parking area restrooms, and soon note that it meanders and includes side trails to the creek, which can be waded in many places, except during high flows.

Once you reach the mouth of the creek, drop down to the beach. You'll likely immediately notice a large flock of seagulls on the edge of the sea. I think the twin mouths of the creek and the river create an ideal habitat for them, and you're also likely to see shorebirds such as sanderlings, which feed on sand-dwelling invertebrates and can be seen chasing waves and hurriedly running up and down the beach. I've also seen whimbrels here, an interesting long-legged, long-beaked shorebird, and in summer brown pelicans are common.

Follow the ocean shore north toward the mouth of the Copalis; if storms have raged in from the sea recently, follow the high-tide line looking for floats and other items washed in from near and far. Glass fishing floats from China and Japan are found here, as well as a lot of plastic floats. In the coming years you may find tsunami debris from what's now known as the Great East Japan Earthquake of 2011.

This is a great beachcombing spot for hikers, since it's one of the few areas in the North Beach area where driving is not allowed. Even so, I've seen tire tracks in the sand here, likely from locals who knew how to handle the trapping sands of Conner Creek and illegally drove the beach at night looking for flotsam.

As for silver dollars, I've never found any, but my friend has. Alan Rammer, a retired marine ecology educator for the Washington Department of Fish and Wildlife, led a field trip to Copalis Spit in the 1980s and found one. Over the next few years several more were found, and Rammer linked them to a long-ago shipwreck that lost its payroll when it sunk. That vessel was also apparently carrying gold coins, but none of them have ever been found, and I've heard of no silver dollars found in recent years.

But follow the shore north to the mouth of the Copalis and you will find sand dollars. They're plentiful near the river mouth and make fun little keepsakes, especially for kids. Across the river are several cabins and the state's only official airport right on the sandy ocean shore. It doesn't get a lot of use. If it's October or November, bring your fishing rod and some medium-sized spinners. You'll probably see anglers on the north bank of the river near the cabins, and you can catch coho salmon on the south bank as well.

If it's summertime and the weather is warm, curl around the north end of the spit and head south along the river; expect loose sand, making it harder to walk. In several hundred yards you'll find deep spots to swim. This lower end of the river is influenced by the tide. If the current is running upstream, the tide is coming in. Either way, take a refreshing dip. Look out across the river to the high bluffs beyond. Eagles can often be seen perched in the trees.

You can follow the river south and cut through the dunes back to the parking area, but the going is tough in the loose sand. So I always make my way back to the ocean shore and return the way I came.

Sanderlings reflected in a thin sheen of water at the edge of the surf

WEATHERWAX FOREST

A MELLOW STROLL IN A COASTAL FOREST

This City of Ocean Shores property is 121 acres of undeveloped coastal forest, all maturing second-growth but the last intact forest on the peninsula here. It's hiked mostly by locals and is not a major attraction for tourists, but it makes for a very nice walk. Deer frequent the forest—as they do the entire Ocean Shores peninsula—and occasionally bear are spotted here as well. For foragers, there's good berry picking (huckleberries, salmonberries) in summer and fall along a powerline that cuts through the forest.

Distance: 1-mile loop
Elevation gain: None
Difficulty: 1
Map: Forest map, www.weatherwax.info/map.html
Contact: City of Ocean Shores
Notes: Dogs on-leash welcome. Read more information from the group that fought to preserve the forest—Ocean Shores Citizens for Balanced Growth (see "Contacts and Resources").

BIG WAVES AND FOOLS

Please don't let the kids—or adults—play on beach logs in the surf. They can break legs and crush bodies. And when the surf is up, only fools play chicken with the waves.

Here is a typical warning issued by federal forecasters during an impressive blow in 2010: "GIANT WAVES ALONG THE COAST WILL CAUSE COASTAL FLOODING . . . A POWERFUL LOW PRESSURE CENTER OVER THE EASTERN PACIFIC IS GENERATING A 30 TO 35 FOOT SWELL IN THE OFFSHORE WATERS . . . FOR ANYONE VENTURING ONTO THE BEACHES . . . WAVES THIS LARGE WILL SWEEP UP THE BEACHES FASTER THAN YOU CAN RUN. THEY CAN EASILY SWEEP A PERSON OUT TO SEA. STAY FAR BACK FROM THE WATER'S EDGE. THE WAVES WILL LIKELY THROW AROUND LARGE OBJECTS AND DEBRIS SUCH AS DRIFTWOOD. DO NOT UNDERESTIMATE THE POWER OF MOVING WATER!"

Earlier that year, during a lesser storm, I saw two guys get knocked off the north jetty at Ocean Shores by a wave, one fracturing his leg. No one had any business being on the jetty at that time, yet there were at least a dozen oblivious souls gambling with the surf. Don't do it.

DRIVING DIRECTIONS

From the Ocean Shores city center, go south on Point Brown Avenue. Turn left on Ocean Lake Way and go past the Elks Club building. The road will come to a Y. Park there and walk to the right, finding the trail entrance marked with an arch.

THE HIKE

From the arched entrance, a main trail heads south for the length of the forest, with several spurs running to the west to connect with the powerline, which also runs north–south. That makes a number of short loops possible. At the arch, find a box with brochures about the forest and a decent map, or print one out online; you can't get lost here, but the map will help guide you.

Follow the main trail south through very dense forest of Sitka spruce, red cedar, western hemlock, and shore pine, with a thick understory of ferns, salal, and typical coastal forest vegetation. Stick to the main trail, ignoring for now one spur left and two right. In 0.25 mile, find a short spur left (east) leading to Duck Lake; it's not much to look at.

Back on the main trail, in another couple hundred feet, find a trail to the right. Man, the forest here gets crazy dense, with critter signs all over. This trail loops less than ⅛ mile back north to the main trail. Once there, follow the main trail south past the spur to Duck Lake and the loop trail you just took for about ⅛ mile, ignoring two more spurs to the right (west). But take a third spur right, and in a couple hundred feet reach the powerline.

The powerline swath is dead straight and fairly open, creating prime habitat for a variety of berry bushes: thimbleberry, salmonberry, red huckleberry, and evergreen huckleberry—the latter called shotberry by longtime locals. All those berries are edible, but the shotberry is best, ripening in late summer and making for excellent pies, tarts, jam, what have you. It's like a small blueberry in texture and taste. If you fancy giving it a try, bring a container here in late summer or early fall to gather your loot.

Follow the powerline almost the length of the forest before, seeing Ocean Lake Way dead ahead, taking the last spur right, back to the main trail, where you'll hang a left and return north shortly to the entrance arch.

DAMON POINT

GREAT ESCAPE TO A WILDLIFE-CRAZY SANDSPIT

A sand dune finger that pokes out into the north side of Grays Harbor, if Damon Point were a book, it would be about time, change, and how wrong first impressions can be. Once a state park and now managed as a state natural area, it can at first seem rather bland, but it fabulously rewards those who look carefully and spend some time here. This is unquestionably the best hike in the Ocean Shores area, one of the few places where driving on the beach is never allowed. It's an "accreted" landscape, created by the forces of wind and waves piling up sand and gravel. The end of Damon Point, technically called Protection Island, is open to the ocean and thus invites soulful contemplation. It's crazy with wildlife, with good surf perch fishing and agate hunting, fair beachcombing, and excellent birding. Frequently, conditions are perfect for excellent windsurfing. Get here early on a clear day and the sunrise can take your breath away.

Distance: 4 miles round-trip
Elevation gain: Minimal
Difficulty: 2–3

When the wind blows the kiteboarders ride, and it blows regularly at Damon Point.

Map: USGS Point Brown, USGS Westport

Contact: Washington Department of Natural Resources

Notes: Dogs permitted on-leash only from the parking area south for several hundred yards, perhaps 0.5 mile. Dogs prohibited on the southern 1.5 miles of Damon Point spit. In that same 1.5-mile section, vegetated uplands are closed March 1–September 15 to protect the threatened streaked horned lark and nesting snowy plovers; hikers may walk beach areas of the spit during that period. Portable toilets available at parking area. Expect to walk on loose sand in places.

DRIVING DIRECTIONS

From Ocean Shores, head south on Point Brown Avenue. Go straight through the roundabout in 0.75 mile, staying on Point Brown Avenue for about 6 miles to Marine View Drive. Turn right, passing the (dilapidated) marina run by the Quinault tribe and an associated RV campground, and find the dirt parking area on both sides of the road, just beyond a curve.

THE HIKE

From the parking area, find the short remains of an old asphalt road and walk it 100 yards or so to the beach. When you hit the sand, pretty much straight ahead and just to the left is Damon Point. Walk past a rocky area on the edge of the sea, a former jetty, with the campground on your left.

As you go, keep looking down. The point is known for its agate and petrified wood hunting. The source of those hard, translucent rocks baffles me, but every high tide shuffles the piles of gravel where they're found, and you can find them from the parking lot all the way to the end of the point, 2 miles out.

Some time ago, Damon Point was a state park day-use area, with an asphalt road all the way to the end, picnic tables, and easy access to a locally famous shipwreck, the coastal steamer SS *Catala* (long since removed). Nature changed all that, revealing the shortsightedness of state parks planners in building a road on accreted land that was once an island; storm waves breached the spit and washed away a significant stretch of the road. The road was closed and the park left for walkers only, which is as it should be. The breach is marked by a vague low point across the spit, less than 0.25 mile into the hike, and storms still breach the point here some winters, the sea flowing right across it at higher tides.

So Damon Point is a testament to the power and changing nature of the wind and waves, an excellent place to feel that power right in your face. It can be marvelously wet, windy, and wild during a storm, and you won't find many people out here then. Most of what we today call Damon Point was once Protection Island, one of many sandy shoals in Grays Harbor. The island took on enough sand and gravel over time to become linked to the mainland via a tombolo, a sand and gravel bar.

Continuing along the spit, the uplands become a bit higher, and during the nonrestricted part of the year you can walk up there and find the old road intact. Birders often follow it because it cuts through prime habitat and offers side jaunts down to the Grays Harbor side of the point. Damon Point is a bird-watching mecca. It provides critical habitat for a variety of species, including the streaked horn lark, which is listed federally as endangered and by the state as threatened. And depending on the season, you can see squadrons of brown pelicans flying low hunting for fish, majestic snowy owls perched on the point's prairie-like uplands, peregrine falcons, bald eagles, and a myriad of sandpipers and shorebirds hunting and pecking or flowing and flitting in unison. If the wind is whipping, you'll also likely see kiteboarders; some very good riders hit the waves here.

The number of people will thin out at about 0.5 mile out, and you'll often find yourself alone. That is, unless it's a winter when snowy owls are present. They were superabundant at Damon Point in the winters of 2011–12 and 2012–13, attracting hordes of birders, many with howitzer-class telephoto lenses. That led to some concern for the birds' safety. The owls winter here, a critical time in their struggle for survival, and the sheer number of people in their habitat worried birders and biologists. Some people also got too close to the birds and ended up flushing them—a violation of birding protocol.

Sometimes, however, you get close without even trying. On one trip I wandered high up on the high-tide line, not even thinking of snowy owls, to find one perched only 30 feet away. Later, the same thing occurred with a peregrine falcon; I looked up and there it was, about 20 feet away.

The very end of the point at 2 miles is a special place, the currents often swirling in eddies full of seals, with pelicans flying low overheard looking for schools of herring or anchovies to dive-bomb. You often see ships coming and going, fishing boats, and across the channel the port of Westport. Here you're standing at a historic spot. Somewhere very near here, on May 7, 1792, American captain Robert Gray in the three-masted, ten-cannon *Columbia Rediviva* became the first person of European origin, at least in recorded history, to enter the harbor that now bears his name. He noted the gutsy event in his logbook:

> *Being within six miles of the land, saw an entrance in the same, which had a very good appearance of a harbor . . . made sail on the ship; stood in for the shore. We soon saw, from our mast-head, a passage in between*

FOLLOW THE BEST AT THE SHOREBIRD FEST

The Grays Harbor Audubon Society (see "Contacts and Resources") hosts an annual Shorebird Festival, traditionally Friday through Sunday on the last weekend of April. Expert observers are posted along the Grays Harbor National Wildlife Refuge boardwalk, with spotting scopes to help visitors identify and watch the birds. The Audubon chapter also leads field trips to other areas of Grays Harbor. You'll really learn a ton about birds and birding.

the sand-bars. At half past three, bore away, and ran in north-east by east, having from four to eight fathoms, sandy bottom; and, as we drew in nearer between the bars, had from ten to thirteen fathoms, having a very strong tide of ebb to stem. Many canoes came alongside. At five p.m., came to in five fathoms [30 feet] water, sandy bottom, in a safe harbor, well sheltered from the sea by long sand-bars and spits.

Once at the end of the point, you have a few choices: You can return the way you came. You can head upland to find the old road and hasten your return (in the appropriate season). Or you can walk all the way around the point to the bay side, the most lonely spot out here, and then walk that side of the spit back to your car.

KEEP EXPLORING

The state's 683-acre Oyhut Wildlife Area is just west of the parking area and offers fine beach walking, good birding, and fair agate hunting. From the parking area, walk the obvious route south, reach the beach in several dozen yards, and take a right, strolling west.

FISHING THE NORTH BEACH AND QUINAULT AREA

Two words sum up fishing from Lake Quinault south to Grays Harbor: salmon and steelhead. Make that three words: big, salmon, and steelhead. It must be said, however, that in the opinion of most anglers, fishing for salmon and steelhead here just ain't what it used to be. Many years, not enough salmon and steelhead return to the rivers in numbers sufficient to perpetuate healthy, annual fisheries. There are a host of reasons: loss of viable spawning, rearing, and sanctuary habitat; overfishing; pollution; and in the opinion of some, the introduction of hatchery salmon and steelhead.

But most years enough fish do make it back from their epic migrations to sustain high-quality fisheries. Steelhead in the 20- to 30-pound range are taken in rivers here every year. Chinook salmon up to 40 or 50 pounds are still boated every year, in the ocean and a few rivers. Coho reaching 20 pounds are not unusual.

And there are other critters to catch as well. The best razor clam digging south of Alaska is right here on the North Beach shore. All these beaches also produce excellent fishing for red-tailed surf perch, anytime waves are gentle. Dungeness crab are taken in Grays Harbor. Cutthroat trout, both sea-run and resident, are taken in most rivers as well as Lake Quinault. The Chehalis River once supported a terrific sturgeon fishery, but that population has declined markedly, now open only on a catch-and-release basis. See "Contacts and Resources" for fishing information and regulations.

Here's a month-by-month summary of fishing opportunities in the region:

January: This is prime time for hatchery steelhead in the lower Quinault (a tribal guide is required for non-Indians) and Humptulips rivers, as well as in Chehalis River tributaries. Razor clamming is usually open at minus-tide series on the beaches between Moclips and Ocean Shores. Surf perch fishing can be good during calm periods.

February: Wild steelhead begin to move into the rivers, although they may not be killed—any with an intact adipose fin must be released. The exception is in the tribal waters of the lower Quinault. Still, anglers fish for them, as well as for the dwindling numbers of hatchery steelhead, identified by lack of an adipose fin. Perch fishing and razor clam digging are options.

March: This is the best time for wild steelhead in the lower and upper Quinault and Humptulips. Surf perch and razor clams are an option.

April: This is the best time of year for razor clam digging, with frequent morning minus tides and the clams at their fattest. Wild steelhead are an option in the Quinault, both upper and lower. Most years, the Quinault tribe opens Lake Quinault to fishing for cutthroat and Dolly Varden (a native char), and both can be very good. Many local lakes are planted with rainbows and open for trout fishing on the last Saturday of the month. Surf perch fishing is often excellent on the ocean beaches. Some folks start dropping crab pots in Grays Harbor now, typically launching boats at the Ocean Shores marina, and some crabs are taken by those wading around Damon Point, Oyhut, and the north jetty during extreme minus tides. Bottomfishing in the ocean, for black rockfish and lingcod primarily, also commences (most are fished out of Westport; see "Fishing the South Coast" in chapter 7). However, sure-footed anglers do take bottomfish from the north jetty at Ocean Shores.

May: In strong razor clam years, digging will be open at appropriate low-tide series and is typically excellent. Lake Quinault is prime now for cutthroat and Dolly Varden, and surf perch fishing can be excellent on any ocean shore.

June: Same scenario as May, except razor clamming is closed and most years chinook salmon fishing opens in the ocean. Most rivers open for fishing now, with a few summer steelhead taken in some of them, such as the Wynoochee, a Chehalis tributary.

July: Same as May and June, but the ocean definitely opens and is good for chinook salmon and coho, the latter improving toward the end of the month.

August: Same scenario as July.

September: This is a key month for salmon anglers, with the Humptulips typically opening September 1 and Grays Harbor east of Buoy 13 opening September 15. The Hump is not open every year for chinook, or "kings," but when it is it can be very good, especially after a good rain. Grays Harbor can also be excellent for kings and coho, best around the high slack tide. Sea-run cutthroat are now moving into most rivers and creeks that flow into saltwater.

October: This is another key salmon month, with more rivers opening and coho moving in along with kings. Grays Harbor can be excellent for kings and coho. The lower Quinault (tribal guide required), Humptulips, Copalis, and Chehalis tributaries (Wishkah, Wynoochee, Satsop) can all be good for coho. Fall razor clam seasons commence at evening minus tides.

November: This is the region's prime month for coho salmon in the Hump, Copalis, Quinault, and the Chehalis and its tributaries. When weather allows, razor clamming can be good on open minus-tide dates.

December: The hatchery run of steelhead moves into the lower Quinault, Humptulips, and Chehalis tributaries. Razor clamming is also an option.

GRAYS HARBOR NATIONAL WILDLIFE REFUGE

AN AERIAL BALLET: WASHINGTON'S FINEST SHOREBIRD SHOW

This place is all about mud—very important mud. The refuge protects about 1500 acres of mudflats, salt marsh, and wet uplands of Bowerman Basin on the north side of Grays Harbor, all of which serve as an essential grocery store for about a million shorebirds that migrate past here twice a year. Sandpipers, dunlins, dowitchers, plovers, and red knots stop here especially in spring to refuel during their flights between South and

A semipalmated plover and sandpipers wing in mass over the Grays Harbor shoreline.

Central America and the Arctic—some of them flying 15,000 miles. In huge living clouds they fly and flutter here, twist and turn, rise and fall like an aerial ballet, and then set down to feed in the mud for marine worms and other invertebrates. This short boardwalk trail is also a hot spot for the fastest bird on the planet, the peregrine falcon, which preys on the shorebirds and can often be seen diving on the unsuspecting birds, along with bald eagles.

Distance: 0.5 mile round-trip
Elevation gain: None
Difficulty: 1
Map: Refuge map, www.fws.gov/uploadedFiles/Refuge%20Map.pdf
Contact: US Fish and Wildlife Service, Grays Harbor National Wildlife Refuge
Notes: Open sunrise to sunset. Dogs prohibited. Pay attention to the tides—shorebirds will be closest to the boardwalk and most visible during the last two hours of an incoming tide, when the rising sea pushes them to forage at the edge of the mudflats.

DRIVING DIRECTIONS

From Hoquiam, head west on State Route 109. Turn left on Paulson Road about 0.25 mile west of Hoquiam High School at the edge of town, and then shortly turn right on Airport Way. Find parking along the final few hundred yards of the road.

THE HIKE

From the parking area, head west beyond the gate to find the wooden boardwalk, called the Sandpiper Trail and less than 0.25 mile long, shortly reaching a loop along the mudflats. The boardwalk offers several locations to stop, view, and photograph the birds. I've seen coyotes wandering the salt marshes on the eastern edge of the basin, and in fall you can see a variety of waterfowl.

But the primary attraction here are the hundreds of thousands of shorebirds that stop like clockwork in spring to feed and nourish themselves during their long migration to Arctic breeding grounds. This place is exceedingly popular during the last week of April until mid-May when the birds drop in. Bring your best camera gear—it can be quite a sight—and of course, your best binoculars.

RAZOR CLAMMING: THE GOLDEN BLADES OF THE SURF

Fifty years have not resolved the question in my mind of whether it's more enjoyable to dig razor clams or eat them. Both are bliss. Digging them is a powerful way to experience the ocean—often wet and miserably messy for sure—and back at home, the first bite brings you back out to the surf again. Cooked right, they have an almost sweet, marine flavor, not fishy at all but still reminiscent of the sea.

Digging them can be a challenge. They descend in the sand with a powerful digger and sometimes they get away. You can be reaching into the briny grit up to your armpits at the edge of the surf and—yikes!—here comes a roller. So you jump to your feet and beat a retreat. That clam will live another day. Other times, say, on a big minus tide when the surf is calm, the clams "show" like chrome hubcaps in the sun and the digging is easy. Either way, you're out there on the edge of sea and sky, a good place for the soul.

Siliqua patula makes its living by sucking in seawater through its siphon—that's what makes the telltale dimple, or show, in the sand, indicating the clam's presence—and then filtering out tiny, nutrient-rich plankton. The clam's body and shell can be more than 3 feet deep in the sand. Your mission is to excavate them, and you do that with a razor clam shovel, originally called a clam gun, or with a long, cylindrical device called a clam tube.

Most purists use a shovel, a short-handled one with a narrow, angled blade. In my experience, tubes tend to break and mutilate more clams than the shovel does. But some folks become masters with the tube and dig totally clean.

Now let me clear up a persistent misconception about the shovel and the tube. Since the tube looks more like a gun, everybody these days calls the clam tube a clam gun. Stores sell tubes as clam guns. Writers call the tube a clam gun. But it ain't, at least not originally. The original clam gun was invented in the 1940s by a Grayland man who took a regular garden shovel, cut the handle short, cut the blade into a narrow, tapered rectangle, bent it to increase the angle, and filed the end a bit sharp. In the 1950s a guy from Shelton invented the tube, calling it the Sandpiper. Over time, since it looked more like a gun, the tube took on that title. My pops, though, who first dug razor clams way before the tube was invented, always insisted on the correct terms: the shovel was a clam gun, not the tube.

Whatever your implement, take that baby out to the shore on a minus tide during an open digging date, go to the edge of the surf, and look for shows. When the surf is gentle and weather calm, they'll often be all over the place. They look like a dimple in the sand, dime to quarter sized, and sometimes will look sort of like a doughnut. If conditions are marginal and the clams are not showing, you can often make them do so by tapping the sand with the shovel handle. If you dig only the larger shows, you'll tend to get larger clams.

If you're using a shovel, insert the blade straight down into the sand a couple inches on the seaward side of the show, the top of the handle pointing toward the upland sand dunes. Wiggle the handle and blade slightly to loosen the sand, and then take out a wedge of sand above the clam by moving the blade upward and forward. Don't reef back on the handle to bend the blade—you'll likely crush the clam. Just sweep the blade forward, toward shore, so you remove a triangular wedge of sand from above the clam.

Do this one more time, but not so deep, taking a smaller wedge. Then reach down into the sand with your fingers, on the seaward side of the show; that way you'll touch the clam on its hinge side and avoid cutting your fingers on the sharper edge of the clamshell. When you feel the clam, pull out a couple more handfuls of sand so you can grasp the shell and wiggle the clam free. Sometimes those suckers are deep and it seems like you're trying to pull a tooth out of King Kong's gums. Keep after it! A determined digger rarely gives up on a clam, unless the ocean comes rolling in over it all and you have to scram.

As for using the tube, first you need to know that razor clams rest vertically in the sand, with their hinge toward the ocean and leaning slightly toward land. With the tube, you simply center the open end over the show, tilt the tube slightly shoreward, and wiggle it down into the sand. There's a hole at the top of the tube. Place your thumb over it and work the tube out of the sand. If you've done it right, you'll remove a core of sand, and the clam should be inside, intact. If not, reach your hand down into the hole and feel for the clam. It should be there and easily removed. It all sounds easy, but it takes a lot of practice!

The Washington Department of Fish and Wildlife, in conjunction with the Quinault Indian Nation in the North Beach area, sets the razor clam seasons—always fall through spring, on various dates during minus-tide series. The number of digging days is determined by the number of available clams based on population surveys and estimates. Digging areas include the Long Beach Peninsula, the Twin Harbors beaches south of Westport, and the North Beach area, designated by the state as Copalis

A limit of large, meaty razor clams and the shovel that dug them. At top, note a "show," the telltale sign in the sand of a razor clam.

Beach on the south and "Mocrocks" on the north. Kalaloch, to the north, is a traditional clamming beach but has been closed in recent years due to low clam numbers. See "Contacts and Resources" for shellfish regulations.

You can chowder, fritter, and fry razor clams, first having cleaned them by removing the guts and gills (see the Washington Department of Fish and Wildlife website, in "Contacts and Resources," under "Fishing Information and Regulations"). The traditional method is to bread the clams or dust them in flour and fry them quickly in hot butter, no more than a couple minutes on each side. Bon appétit!

RAZOR CLAMS: FRY OR FRITTER 'EM

The traditional, go-to method for preparing razor clams is to fry them fast in hot butter after shelling, cleaning, and flouring or battering them. Oh god, that's good. See the

Washington Department of Fish and Wildlife website for cleaning details, and do not overcook, no more than two minutes per side.

But there is nothing quite like a hot razor clam fritter. If you enjoy the smell of the surf and the salty flavor it can leave on your lips, the taste of a razor clam fritter will rocket you into orbit. It's sort of like a pancake straight from the sea. My mom cooked them best—I can't duplicate hers. But I can come close.

5 or 6 green onions, cut thin
½ red pepper, diced
1 clove garlic, minced
1½ cups pancake mix
1 cup chopped razor clams
1 12-ounce bottle of flat ale or pilsner
2–3 tablespoons peanut oil
Tartar sauce or aioli to serve (optional)

Mix the veggies, garlic, and pancake mix, and then add the clams with any accumulated juice. Slowly add the beer, just until the mixture is thick enough to drop from a spoon.

Heat the peanut oil in a frying pan to medium or medium-high. Drop spoonfuls of the batter into the hot oil—don't crowd (or the oil temp will drop). Drink any remaining beer.

Cook about two minutes, and then flip and cook about two more minutes. If they're not golden brown when you flip, give them a little more time.

Serve simply, with tartar sauce or aioli. Achieve lift-off!

THE SOUTH COAST

CHAPTER 7

SURF, SEA, SAND, AND INTERTIDAL MUCK—miles and miles and acres and acres of this elemental, rich, and primordial stuff—are what characterize the south coast of Washington, framed as it is by the state's two busiest coastal salmon fishing ports. Those would be Westport, anchoring the south side of Grays Harbor, and Ilwaco, just inside one of North America's greatest rivers, the mighty Columbia. Here the big, wide Columbia marks the southern boundary of Washington State.

Except for the rocky promontories of Cape Disappointment at the very southern end of the Washington Coast, the beaches from Westport to the Columbia are sandy, about 40 miles worth. This reach of coastline is interrupted only by the shoal-lined entrance to Willapa Bay—one of the most pristine estuaries on the West Coast, a major producer of oysters and clams.

The Cape Disappointment lighthouse at sunset

Recreation in this region then largely revolves around the pursuit of seafood. That's what this part of the coast means to a lot of us: salmon and bottomfish angling, along with albacore tuna fishing well offshore, surf perch fishing from the beach, and foraging for crabs, clams, and oysters.

But there is so much more to see and do here. This area's history is absolutely intriguing, pivotal even to the course of events of America as a whole, as the point where the Lewis and Clark Expedition reached the Pacific Ocean in 1805. Here the finest state park on the Washington Coast, Cape Disappointment, embraces and commemorates much of that rich history.

The environment on the south coast is so rich that wildlife watching is also superb, with much of Willapa Bay protected by the 16,000-acre Willapa National Wildlife Refuge. Birding is diverse, and it's not unusual to see deer, elk, and bear. Kayak and canoe paddling in Willapa Bay and its rivers is a great way to get to know this intriguing environment—a greatly underappreciated activity here. You can paddle into lonesome areas that feel pretty darned wild.

And if you love to use your feet, you've got not only miles of ocean beach to wander but also miles of surprisingly unique trails, including walks to an ancient cedar forest on an isolated island and through old-growth spruce forests to historic lighthouses and military ruins.

Another fascinating aspect for me are the seaports. I just love kicking around working docks where nets are spooled, crab pots stacked, and oyster shells piled. The little backwater ports are my favorites, places like Nahcotta and Bay Center. But I like the more active ones as well. Westport and Ilwaco are important and famous ports among fishermen in Washington, both hubs of interesting maritime activity and always busy in summer.

Willapa Bay splits the south coast: the so-called Twin Harbors of Westport and Tokeland to the north, Long Beach Peninsula to the south. Also to the south, the Willapa National Wildlife Refuge and Long Island within are standouts, as is Cape Disappointment State Park. These two places are so special I'm treating them as distinct regions, even though they are very much part of the region embraced by the Long Beach Peninsula.

The towns of note along this part of the coast, north to south, are Westport, Grayland, Tokeland, Raymond, South Bend, Ocean Park, Long Beach, and Ilwaco. The conjoined municipalities of Aberdeen and Hoquiam are the largest cities in this region. They're not on the coast per se, being several miles inland on Grays

Harbor and the Chehalis River. But they do offer most any kind of service you could need: restaurants, motels, groceries, gas, car repairs (visit Greater Grays Harbor Inc. online; see "Contacts and Resources"). However, the smaller towns on the coast will give you that true ocean ambience.

By the way, in case you're wondering, you are most definitely mispronouncing the place name Willapa. It's not will-LAP-ah, as many a local TV newsperson has mangled. It's WILL-a-paw.

THAT BIG RIVER ON THE BORDER

A huge entity unto itself, the Columbia River pours turbulently into the ocean at the Washington–Oregon border, its bar wrecking so many ships that it's been called the Graveyard of the Pacific. It delivers to the sea the fourth-greatest volume of freshwater of any river in America and for centuries has fueled epic salmon fisheries.

Although its fish runs and habitat have been diminished by dams—Grand Coulee Dam was built with no fish passage whatsoever and destroyed an early run of giant chinook (the "June hogs")—the Columbia still produces more than one million salmon and steelhead each year. In fact, the Columbia's run of big chinook alone—"king" salmon as fishermen call them—surpassed one million fish in both 2013 and 2014. So sportfishing at the mouth of the river—the so-called Buoy 10 fishery—and just offshore continues to be excellent most years. The mouth of the river also produces excellent recreational catches of Dungeness crabs.

The big river also flushes into the sea such a massive amount of sediment that it affects the landscape for dozens of miles north and south—most tangibly, creating over eons the 28-mile sandy finger known as the Long Beach Peninsula.

WESTPORT TO TOKELAND: THE TWIN HARBORS

PERCHED AT THE SOUTH ENTRANCE TO Grays Harbor, Westport is a colorful town, the busiest commercial fishing port on the Washington Coast and best known recreationally as a shoving-off point for traditional and superb ocean sport fisheries for salmon, bottomfish, and tuna. Over the last thirty years it's also become the epicenter for surfing in Washington, the locus being Westhaven State Park along the harbor's south jetty. From here south, it's pretty much a straight shot of sandy shoreline, providing good razor clam digging, for 16 miles to the funky fishing village of Tokeland.

This so-called Twin Harbors region, also called South Beach by some, is famous locally for its approximately 1000 acres of cranberry bogs. The October harvest is a curious and colorful spectacle, giving the area yet another nickname: the Cranberry Coast.

Chasing ocean waves on the edge of sea and sky

What I find fascinating about this coastline between the two major bays of the south coast is what the ocean gives and what it takes, geologically. On the north end, at the Grays Harbor mouth, the ocean has added significant acreage in sand that it sent ashore after construction of the south jetty. Land just south of the jetty extends about half a mile beyond what it did before the jetty was built. Two worthwhile state parks—Westhaven and Westport Light—now protect much of this new land. On the south end, at the north entrance to Willapa Bay, the persistent currents of the sea have done just the opposite, removing significant acreage—along with roads, homes, a graveyard, and a lighthouse. The Pacific continues to gnaw away. You can take in this bizarre scene yourself at the appropriately named Washaway Beach. For sure, humans have played a huge role in this give

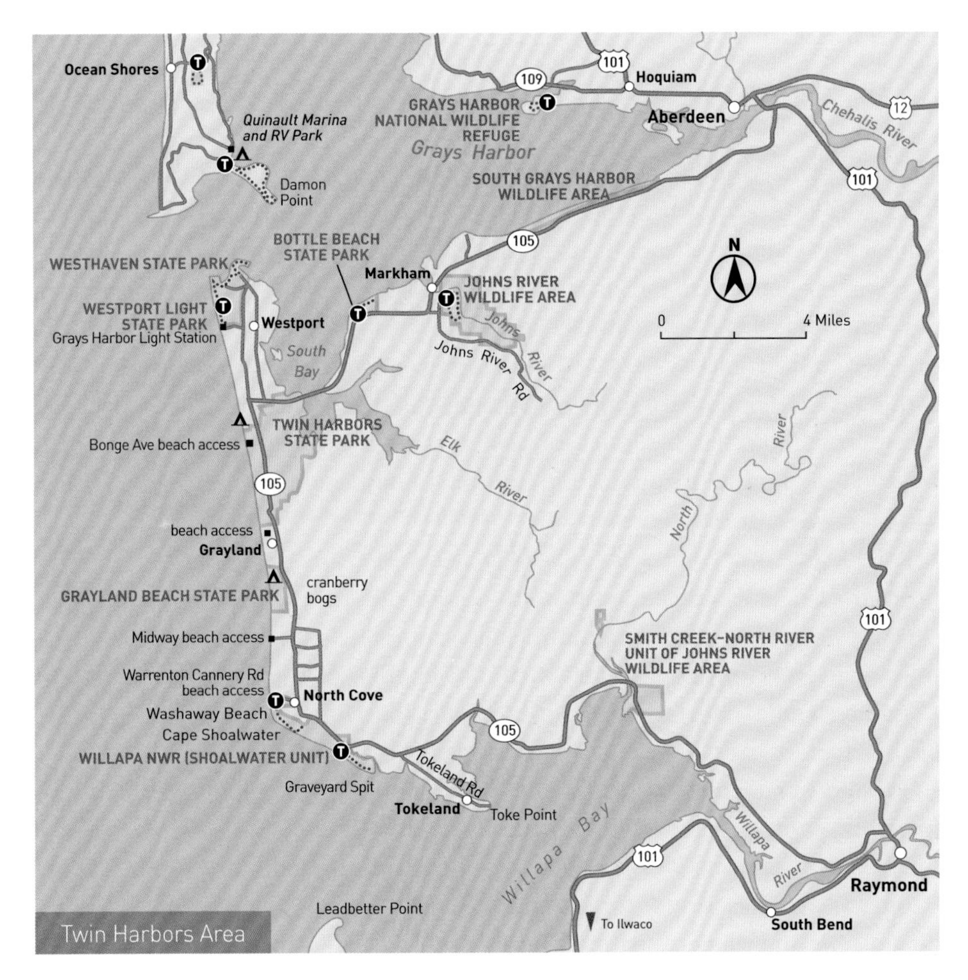

Fishing and tender boats, including a commercial crabber loaded with pots at left, at the Westport Marina

and take by altering the natural flows in both Grays Harbor and the Columbia River with protective jetties. But that big, wide Pacific Ocean has done the work, supplied by sediments from the Columbia.

Hiking is not superb in this region, or at least the hiking is not wilderness in any sense. But there are definitely some fun jaunts. Camping is decent, mostly oriented to the trailer/RV set, at Twin Harbors and Grayland Beach state parks. Birding is excellent. I have some personal history here, since my dad co-owned a Westport salmon charter service for several years, and what I enjoy is just knocking about, exploring. It's interesting country, honest country.

GETTING THERE/STAYING THERE

From US 101 in Aberdeen, head south on State Route 105 for 17.7 miles to the "Westport Y." Turn right on South Montesano Street to reach Westport in 2.2 miles. For points south, stay on SR 105 for another 0.25 mile to the "Westport T" and turn left (south). Grayland is in 4 miles. For Tokeland, continue 8.1 miles farther, turn right on Tokeland Road, and reach the town in another 1.7 miles.

Westport and Grayland offer plenty of motels/hotels and other places to stay, including Twin Harbors State Park and Grayland Beach State Park, as well as a full range of services (visit the Westport-Grayland Chamber of Commerce; see "Contacts and Resources" for all contact information). That includes charter-boat fishing and whale-watching trips (in spring), a large marina with gas docks, and full marine services. Tokeland offers a small, colorful commercial and sportfishing port and is home of the historic Tokeland Hotel, which also operates a fine restaurant (tell Scott and Katherine that Greg says "Hey!").

FEES AND PERMITS

You'll need a Washington State Discover Pass for day-use parking at the five state parks here and for state wildlife lands such as Johns River ($30/year, $10/day; fee is waived if you're camping). The vehicle access pass that comes with your fishing or hunting license will also work for state wildlife lands.

CAMPING

TWIN HARBORS STATE PARK

Twin Harbors is a big camping state park with 265 campsites, but I'm not a big fan because most sites lack privacy. To cram that many sites into about a third of the park's 172 acres necessitates that the sites be close together. But this is a popular park, with about 3700 feet of ocean shore. It's used heavily by fishermen who come to Westport to chase salmon, by razor clam diggers, and by retired folk pulling trailers or small RVs. A bummer for me is that beach driving is allowed right out front of the park all year, and drivers can access the beach via Bonge Avenue along the park's south boundary. (Be advised: this access to the beach is notoriously sandy and cars get stuck all the time; if you don't have four-wheel-drive, forget it.)

One nice thing here is the trails: a couple miles wind through the beach dunes, mostly connecting the park's camping areas and the ocean. There are also two horseshoe pits and a day-use picnic area.

The park straddles the road, with many of the tent sites on the west (ocean) side and most of the hookup sites on the east. There are 219 tent sites, 42 hookup sites (max rig length is 35 feet), 4 walk-in hiker/biker sites, and 2 yurts. All can be reserved. Peak-season cost ranges from $12 a night for primitive spots to $20–$31 for standard spots and $32–$42 for full hookup sites.

Contact: Washington State Parks. **Driving directions:** From US 101 in Aberdeen, head south on State Route 105 for 17.7 miles, passing the "Westport Y" and soon seeing signs for the park and the entrance on the left.

Dunes and beach grass at Grayland Beach State Park

GRAYLAND BEACH STATE PARK

Another huge and popular state park at 412 acres, with 7444 feet of splendid ocean coast, Grayland Beach offers trailer/RV sites with full hookups to water, power, and sewer and can take rigs to 60 feet. That's not my kind of camping, although I have enjoyed a stay here in one of the primitive walk-in sites. Our tent was surrounded by evergreen huckleberry bushes, with ripe berries, and one evening a black-tailed deer, a doe, wandered right past us. It was an enjoyable stay.

This park is popular during fall-through-spring razor clam seasons, since you can walk onto the beach and dig right there. The long stretch of ocean beach is also great for picnicking and especially kite flying. The beach is open to vehicles year-round, though, so keep an eye on the little ones.

OK, that's the wow. Now here's the whammy: campsite prices are what I'd call exorbitant. Washington State Parks bases rates on a park's popularity, and because this one takes on big RVs with full hookups, it's damned popular, and pricey. Don't blame State Parks. Blame rigid state legislators who can't seem to grasp that recreation is an economic engine; for decades they've refused to adequately fund Washington's priceless heritage of fabulous state parks. Did I mention that Washington is about the only state in the western United States without an official tourism agency?

Peak-season prices range from $12 a night for primitive spots to $20–$31 for standard spots and $32–$42 for full hookup sites. Yurts? On a weekday $86 a night, $97 on weekends—seriously!

The campground includes 58 full hookup sites (2 ADA accessible), 38 sites with water and electricity (2 accessible), 16 yurts (10 accessible), 4 standard sites (1 accessible), and 4 primitive walk-in sites. Reservations are available. There are four restroom facilities with eight showers. Some sites offer paved driveways that accommodate larger RVs. There's also an RV dump station.

Contact: Washington State Parks. **Driving directions:** From US 101 in Aberdeen, head south on State Route 105 for 17.7 miles, passing the "Westport Y" (the right goes to downtown Westport) and soon reaching the "Westport T." Turn left (south) to continue on SR 105 for about 4 miles into Grayland, taking a right at the park sign on Cranberry Beach Road. You'll soon see the marked park entrance on your left.

HIKING

THE ESSENTIAL WESTPORT LOOP

A BUSY COASTAL PORT IN ONE SUPER LOOP

This definitive Westport hike (of my own invention) takes in everything cool about the busiest fishing port on the Washington Coast. It includes the historic Grays Harbor Light Station and two state parks—Westport Light and Westhaven—the Westport Maritime Museum, the town's bustling boat basin, the popular surfing spot at Jetty Beach, and ocean agate beaches just south, all stitched together by the paved Westport Dunes Trail. Almost everything you need to experience at Westport can be taken in by hiking this route. It's not a single defined trail, but a looping jaunt that hits the town's highlights. There are just two other activities necessary for the avid recreation-minded person's Westport portfolio: take a charter-boat fishing trip for salmon and go surfing.

The 107-foot-tall Grays Harbor Light Station is the third-tallest lighthouse on the West Coast and the tallest in Washington.

Distance: 5.5-mile loop
Elevation gain: About 150 feet, including the climb of 135 spiraling steps of the Grays Harbor Light Station (recommended) and the observation tower on the edge of Westport Marina
Difficulty: 2
Map: South Beach visitors' guide, available at most any retail store in town
Contact: Washington State Parks
Notes: Discover Pass required to park at Westport Light. Dogs are A-OK on-leash. Bicycles allowed on the Dunes Trail and it makes for a nice ride. It's also a terrific jogging route. Restrooms available. Worthwhile tours of the lighthouse are given February–November.

DRIVING DIRECTIONS

From US 101 in Aberdeen, head south on State Route 105 for 17.7 miles, passing the "Westport Y" (the right goes to downtown Westport) and shortly coming to a stop sign at the "Westport T." SR 105 heads south, but a spur goes north; take it right. In about 2 miles, go left on Ocean Avenue, shortly finding a large parking area at Westport Light State Park.

THE HIKE

It's so appropriate to begin and end this jaunt at the Grays Harbor Light Station, a beacon guiding mariners since 1898 and at 107 feet, the third-highest lighthouse on the West Coast and the tallest in Washington. Let it guide you as well.

You'll see the lighthouse as you approach the park. When it was built all those 115 years ago, the ocean was just 300 feet away. Now it's about 3000 feet away, due to accretion of sand sediments that built up after the construction of the

Grays Harbor south jetty in the early 1900s. The serendipitous consequence is that today there is a very cool dune trail through this new land and, in parallel, a fabulous ocean beach to walk.

As you know by now, the ocean soothes the soul, so start on that side of the loop. From the parking lot, take the obvious asphalt trail to the west—this is the south end of the Westport Dunes Trail. Where it turns north, go straight to the beach; you'll hit the Dunes Trail on the return.

As soon as you see the surf you'll also likely see families flying kites, picnicking, or building sand castles. Plus, due to the jetty and the beach gradient, the surf tends to be large here most of the time, and any gravel pile you see on the beach here is likely to contain agates. One summer day, my wife the Agate Queen found two translucent dandies even though the beach was busy. All told, this is prime real estate for ocean hiking.

The only bummer is that driving is allowed on the ocean beach between Labor Day and April 15, on the southern half-mile or so of this route. So the best season for this hike is April 16 through Labor Day.

Head north on the beach, watching the brown pelicans fly low like prehistoric bucket mouths, and let the sea breeze brush your temples and ease your mind. You can see the jetty about 1 mile up north, and as you proceed you'll see wetsuit-clad people on boards in the surf. This beach is the single most popular surfing spot in Washington State, happily and appropriately protected by 79-acre Westhaven State Park.

As you near the jetty, you'll want to stop and watch the surfers. The surf is not international caliber here, but they get some very nice breaks, especially during storms fall through spring. Nonetheless, it's most popular among surfers in the sweet summertime, when the state park parking lot is typically jammed.

Approaching the jetty at 1.3 miles, see the well-beaten path out of the dunes down to the beach on the right? Take it, climbing the short sandy hill and finding the Dunes Trail intersecting. Follow the Dunes Trail around the parking area toward town. Where you can, climb up to the left and look over the water. That's Half Moon Bay. The surf can get decent here during a good blow out of the northwest.

Continue on through the most boring part of the hike, holding your nose when you smell the city wastewater treatment plant and entering town at about 2 miles. Soon you'll see the docks and reach Westhaven Drive, the main road along the marina, and a cool observation tower. It overlooks several "finger jetties," the two main jetties north and south and in between, at the entrance to Grays

Harbor—discovered and entered by Captain Robert Gray aboard the *Columbia Rediviva* on May 7, 1792.

From there, follow Neddie Rose Drive out along the rock-lined finger that encloses the Westport boat basin, passing the circular Fisherman's Monument and finding Float 20 near Harbor Charters. Walk the float out, past charter boats, working boats, and more, and at the end climb the catwalk that ends in 100 yards or so at the entrance to the boat basin.

Here you're at the route's halfway point, about 2.2 miles, looking out over the finest fishing port on the Washington Coast, a workingman's port most definitely, full of trawlers, trollers, crabbers, long-liners, seiners, charter boats, and sport boats. This is the epicenter of the coast's commercial fisheries. Salmon are landed here, as are albacore tuna, halibut, rockfish and cods, whiting, Dungeness crab, shrimp, anchovies, and sardines. It's ranked as the eleventh-largest port in America for edible landed catch.

Walk back along Neddie Rose Drive to its intersection with Westhaven Drive, the main drag along the docks, and head uptown. You'll walk by charter-boat offices, doughnut shops, and gift shops across from the docks and by all manner of colorful craft out on the floats. You can actually toss baited crab traps off the dock here and catch legal-sized Dungeness crabs.

Just past Dock Street, between Floats 5 and 7, find the Maritime Museum, housed in a former Coast Guard station, a quaint Cape Cod building built in 1942. A surf rescue boat is displayed in the yard, and inside one building there's a complete vintage Fresnel lens, circa 1880, once housed in the Destruction Island Lighthouse up the coast—very cool. Adjacent structures house whale skeletons. The Coast Guard vacated the station in 1972, when a modern one was built a few blocks away. If the museum is open, it's worth the $5 admission.

You can break up this hike by stopping at any of several restaurants in town. The Half Moon Bay Bar at the Islander Hotel (near the tower) is a personal favorite. It's something of a watering hole for stinky/crusty commercial fishermen—my kind of folks.

Backtrack to the Dunes Trail at the end of Westhaven Drive, and start heading back. At Westhaven State Park (about 4.5 miles), however, instead of dropping down to the beach from whence you came, stay on the Dunes Trail. Immediately enter the interesting dunes environment, tall beach grasses waving in the breeze, the path gently rising and falling here and there, with benches and interpretive signs nicely scattered along the way. You've got about 1 mile back to your car, and if you tire of the dunes, several paths along the way cut through the grasses and to the great wide ocean, where the view ends at the curvature of the planet.

JOHNS RIVER WILDLIFE AREA

WATCHING BIRDS AND BEASTS ALONG A COASTAL ESTUARY

The Johns River flows through a broad estuary before spilling into Grays Harbor, making this a decent area to stroll quietly with your binoculars looking for elk, deer, and wetland/tideland-type birds. Wildlife watching is the main draw in this 1500-acre wildlife area. A short, paved wheelchair-accessible path leads to a wildlife-viewing blind, and a grassy path continues beyond. There's also a boat launch here used by salmon fishermen (who typically fish Grays Harbor), and some anglers fish the Johns River itself in late summer/fall for sea-run cutthroat. You can also wander the old dirt road on the north side of the wildlife area; locals who know the way say there's a pioneer cemetery in the forest here.

Distance: 2 miles round-trip
Elevation gain: None
Difficulty: 1
Map: Wildlife area map, http://wdfw.wa.gov/lands/wildlife_areas/johns_river /Johns%20River (click link at "How to Get Here")
Contact: Washington Department of Fish and Wildlife
Notes: Discover Pass required to park, or the Fish and Wildlife vehicle access pass that comes with your fishing/hunting license. Dogs permitted. Vault toilet available in the parking area. Hunting allowed during the fall deer and elk seasons and well into the winter during waterfowl seasons, although most duck and goose hunters head into Grays Harbor from the boat launch.

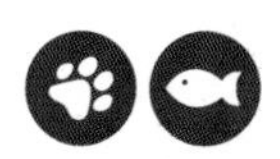

DRIVING DIRECTIONS

From Aberdeen, drive south and west on State Route 105 about 11 miles. Turn left on Johns River Road and then left again on Game Farm Road, and follow it about 0.1 mile to the parking area/boat launch.

THE HIKE

From the parking area, head down the obvious asphalt path and immediately enter classic coastal marsh and tidelands, the haunts of blue herons, terns, grebes, songbirds, ducks, geese, and in spring, shorebirds.

Years ago I stopped here to check out the boat launch and found a bank angler wiling away his time. We got to talking and soon a fish struck, and he reeled in a beautiful sea-run cutthroat of about 16 inches. Since that time, the Washington Department of Fish and Wildlife has developed the site a bit, putting in the paved path and blind.

The path turns with the twists of the Johns River estuary, full of salt marsh rushes, sedges, grasses, and such, dank and pungent. You'll reach the blind in 0.5 mile, a good place to stop, snack, and sit quietly watching for creatures. When I was here once in December, two groups of six or seven trumpeter swans flew low overhead. The paved path ends at the blind, but a grassy route continues atop an old dike into the best area for seeing elk (mornings and evenings are best). At 1 mile the trail climbs into forest, a good turnaround point since it soon reaches Johns River Road.

KEEP EXPLORING

At least another mile of old road follows dikes on the other (north) side of the river. Back when I was a cub reporter for Aberdeen's *Daily World*, locals told of an old pioneer cemetery in the woods above the estuary, as well as the rusting

Wildlife viewing is the draw at Johns River Wildlife Area. See the white dots against the trees? They're trumpeter swans.

hulk of an old steam donkey. Steam donkey? It was an early steam engine/winch system used to yard logs up to landings, where they could be loaded on trains. I'm pretty sure the donkey and cemetery are on private lands, if they exist, and I never searched them out. But the walking on the north side of the river is swell all by itself. Find a rough parking area on the east side of SR 105, just north of the Johns River Bridge and across from the Ocean Spray cranberry plant.

BOTTLE BEACH STATE PARK

FLITTER AND FLUTTER: A GREAT SPOT TO SEE SHOREBIRDS IN SPRING

Best known as a birding location during the spring shorebird migration, Bottle Beach is a 75-acre day-use state park with 6500 feet of beach on the south shore of Grays Harbor, reached by a short boardwalk trail. Grays Harbor is one of the most important feeding areas along the West Coast during the spring and fall shorebird migrations between Central and South America and the Arctic breeding grounds. About a million sandpipers, dunlins, dowitchers, red knots, and other shorebirds stop here each spring, and a good percentage use Bottle Beach. This area is also used by waterfowl hunters November through February. Many other birds can be seen as well—the peregrine falcon hunts shorebirds here—with a species list of more than 130.

Distance: 1.4 miles round-trip
Elevation gain: Almost none
Difficulty: 1
Map: Grays Harbor Audubon Society map, www.ghas.org/bottle.php
Contact: Washington State Parks
Notes: Discover Pass required to park. Dogs permitted only during waterfowl hunting seasons. Boardwalk is accessible to those with limited mobility. Restrooms available at the trailhead.

DRIVING DIRECTIONS

From US 101 in Aberdeen, head south on State Route 105 about 14 miles, finding the state park sign and parking area on the right. It's about 2.5 miles west of the Johns River Bridge.

THE HIKE

From the parking area, follow the boardwalk trail as it winds 0.7 mile through meadows and wetlands to the beach. Stop at the three wildlife-viewing platforms/blinds along the way. The best time to see the shorebirds—and it can be quite a spectacle when thousands are gathered—is the last ten days of April and the first ten days of May. The best viewing time is the three hours before high tide. Some of these birds migrate 15,000 miles twice a year. For more information about birding at Bottle Beach, contact the Grays Harbor Audubon Society.

You can get down to the beach and wander in either direction for more than 1 mile total, but please don't during the shorebird migration when birders are using the viewing platforms. It's A-OK during other times of the year, but this is not the most scenic stretch of shore.

WASHAWAY BEACH

A SHORE BEING SWALLOWED BY THE SEA

This strange hike begins on the ocean and follows the receding shoreline south to the north shore of Willapa Bay. The scenery is pleasant, like any saltwater shore, but not outstanding. What makes Washaway Beach interesting is the curiosity factor: the tangible evidence, wreckage really, of the ocean's relentless power to shape the land. Washaway Beach is the most rapidly eroding area of the entire West Coast, the shore losing an average of 100 feet annually for the last hundred years. Here you find houses on the brink—most abandoned—the debris of homes already devoured, roads that end suddenly on the edge, and most curiously, dozens of pipes sticking up out of the sand. They're best seen at low tide and formerly served homes that have long since disappeared—water pipes mostly, it would appear. One trip I found one still spouting water into the surf.

Distance: About 4 miles round-trip
Elevation gain: None
Difficulty: 2–3
Map: Washington Department of Ecology, Coastal Atlas, Warrenton Cannery Road Beach Access, https://fortress.wa.gov/ecy/coastalatlas/tools/PublicAccessReport.aspx?beach=WS09190
Contact: Washington Department of Ecology

A small house and outbuildings near Washaway Beach, presumably moved inland before they could be swallowed by the ocean.

Notes: Dogs are A-OK on-leash or off. This is a great running route when the tide is low enough to expose firm sand. One note of caution: This is not a place you want to be at high tide, particularly during the bigger highs of winter and especially when the wind is blowing out of the west. Those conditions have ravaged this shore for a hundred years, and they can trap you against the high bank.

DRIVING DIRECTIONS

From US 101 in Aberdeen, head south on State Route 105 for 17.7 miles, passing the "Westport Y" (the right goes to downtown Westport) and soon reaching the "Westport T." From there, drive south on SR 105 about 8 miles, taking a right at the small grocery onto Warrenton Cannery Road, the southernmost beach-access road in the Twin Harbors area. I suggest that you park along the access road before reaching the beach and walk south, especially if you don't have four-wheel-drive. Twin Harbors beaches are notorious for car-trapping loose sands, and the Warrenton Cannery Road approach was closed for a couple years due to coastal erosion, reopening just in 2013. You can also access Washaway Beach at several road ends south of the Warrenton Cannery Road, including Old Highway 105, its broken terminus teetering on a 10-foot-high bluff above a shore piled with driftwood.

THE HIKE

Walk south from Warrenton Cannery Road along typical ocean shore. In about 0.5 mile, the shore gradually turns a corner and heads southeasterly into the uncertain maw of Willapa Bay.

Those of us drawn to the dynamic edge where water meets land know that the interaction between those forces changes things. The Washington Coast is constantly eroding, rebuilding, piling rocks, removing them, adding sand or taking it away. River mouths by their very nature change shape and form. That's precisely what's happening at Washaway Beach, on a dramatic scale. The channel of Willapa Bay, where it meets the ocean, for a century has been deepening and moving north—shifting sand into shoals on its south side, eating away at the land on the north. Cape Shoalwater, as it used to be called, lost 12,303 feet from 1965 to 1980, and the process continues. The cape was once a huge spit, with roads, houses, a lighthouse, a cemetery. Most of it is gone. The Washington Department of Ecology website (see "Contacts and Resources") includes an interesting map showing how the shore has changed.

On the upland side, the shore begins appearing chaotic, with jumbles of driftwood and fallen trees, tarps, wrecked hot tubs, pieces of former homes, and you begin to see the vacant houses perched right on the edge. Ahead in the distance is one resolute home, surrounded by "riprap," or piles of large, jagged rocks and pieces of concrete, placed there as a bulwark against the sea.

In about 1 mile, if the tide is down a bit, look out at the surf, typically gentle here except when the winter storm winds blow. See the pipes sticking up vertically? A lot of them. Uncanny!

Somewhere in this area in late 2009 and early 2010, storms tore out a major section of the shore and revealed the ribs and decking of an old shipwreck, more than 100 feet long, iron spikes protruding from its heavy timbers. It became quite an attraction and was believed to be the remains of the freighter *Canadian Exporter*, which grounded here in the fog in August of 1921. There was nothing left when I visited in 2013.

If the tide is low, and it should be for this hike, go around the riprap of the armored home (at 1.5 miles), almost an island. Just south is where Old Highway 105 ends precipitously, at the edge of a lagoon. You can continue about another 0.5 mile—look for that spouting pipe in the surf—until reaching the rock groin known as Jacobsens Jetty, built to protect the relocated SR 105. Turn about and head back.

GRAVEYARD SPIT

AN EASY STROLL ALONG THE MAW OF WILLAPA BAY

This sandy beach is a great place to walk the dog and, quite often, to just be alone with the wind and the waves. Maps call it Graveyard Spit, but locals I've asked aren't familiar with the name. It's not far from the North Cove Pioneer Cemetery, located on the west side of State Route 105 and built decades ago, after the sea washed away portions of an older graveyard, allegedly floating coffins. Records show that Graveyard Spit was once less of a spit and more of a contiguous piece of land off today's Washaway Beach, extending well out into the sea. So I'll leap to the conclusion that somewhere off this spit is the original location of the cemetery. I've never seen any ghosts or spookiness here, though.

Distance: Less than 2 miles round-trip
Elevation gain: None
Difficulty: 1
Map: Washington Department of Ecology, Coastal Atlas, North Cove Beach Access, https://fortress.wa.gov/ecy/coastalatlas/tools/PublicAccessReport .aspx?beach=WS09200
Contact: Washington Department of Ecology
Notes: Dogs permitted on-leash or off

DRIVING DIRECTIONS

From US 101 in Aberdeen, head south on State Route 105 for 17.8 miles, passing the "Westport Y" (the right goes to downtown Westport) and soon reaching the "Westport T." From there, drive south on SR 105 about 10 miles, beyond the blink of a village called North Cove. Where the highway nears the shore, look for a rock jetty extending into the sea. Just past that, find a large pullout on the west side of the highway.

THE HIKE

Drop down from the pullout on a short road/path to the beach and note immediately a curious burnt-orange rock edging into the ocean, with a small cave. Apparently it's a piece of bedrock uncovered by the voracious sea here, which

The rock outcrop and small sea cave here mark the beginning of the walk along Graveyard Spit.

for decades has insistently been inching eastward, consuming land, roads, and houses. That's why SR 105 is heavily armored with large rock.

Hit the beach and head south along the shore. If it's fall you might see fishing boats seeking salmon; and mostly in spring but also fall, look for migrating shorebirds such as sandpiper and dunlins, which stop here to feed. The beach is wide open with occasional driftwood, the uplands basically a sand dune backed by a lagoon. The scenery is not outstanding, but there's plenty of space to walk or run and let the dog get some exercise. You can walk the spit about 1 mile south until you reach the lagoon entrance, your turnaround point.

BEACH ACCESS

 WESTHAVEN STATE PARK

If you want to ride ocean waves in Washington, this is the place to start, the most popular surfing spot in the state, 79-acre Westhaven State Park. The Grays Harbor south jetty extends into the sea here and separates the two main parts of this day-use-only park, a beautiful stretch of ocean beach on one side and Half

Moon Bay on the other—both places can get decent breaks, such as they are here in the Northwest, depending on the weather. The shoreline is sweet on both sides of the jetty too, totaling 1215 feet, with the ocean side being the more popular area for picnicking, kite flying, walking, and agate hunting. No driving is allowed on the beach at Westhaven anytime of year, providing a welcome respite for soul-searching ocean walkers.

Anglers wander out on the jetty to fish for salmon, rockfish, and perch, and Dungeness crab are taken in Half Moon Bay. Surf perch can be taken from shore too, but be advised to go well south of the surfers, who find the best breaks within a few hundred yards of the jetty. The park is also about midway along the asphalt Westport Dunes Trail, with Westport Light State Park 1.3 miles south and the Westport boat basin about 1 mile east.

Did I mention popular? Westhaven's got a large parking lot that in summer nonetheless overflows. Incidentally, you'll need a state Discover Pass to park here. A restroom facility includes showers/wash-off facilities so surfers can de-brine themselves and their wetsuits.

Contact: Washington State Parks. **Driving directions:** From US 101 in Aberdeen, drive State Route 105 south and west toward Westport, watching for signs. In 17.7 miles, take a right at the "Westport Y" onto South Montesano Street. Follow that 2.2 miles into Westport, going through downtown toward the marina, and finding the marked park entrance on the left.

WESTPORT LIGHT STATE PARK

With 3500 feet of ocean shore, 212 acres of sand dunes, and the tallest lighthouse in Washington State (on adjacent Coast Guard land), this is an awesome day-use-only state park. It's terrific for ocean strolling, especially from April 15 through Labor Day weekend, when driving on the beach is not allowed. Personally, I wish driving on the beach were never allowed here, since there's plenty of open beach to the south and the razor clam digging is not very good here anyway, an activity best reached by vehicle.

Agate hunting is good on this beach, surf perch fishing can be good, and you've got that spectacular mariner's beacon, at 107 feet high the third tallest on the West Coast, built in 1898. Volunteers with the Westport Maritime Museum conduct tours of the lighthouse February through November ($5). It's worth it.

Officially called the Grays Harbor Light Station, 135 steps spiral to the top, where you can see up close the light's original third-order Fresnel lens. It's no longer used but was built in Paris more than a hundred years ago, with a frame of brass holding concentric rings of glass prisms.

The spacious parking area also serves as the south trailhead for the paved 2.3-mile Westport Dunes Trail to Westport and includes a restroom facility. There are also 15 unsheltered picnic tables with flip-top braziers for barbecuing. You need a state Discover Pass to park here.

Contact: Washington State Parks. **Driving directions:** From US 101 in Aberdeen, drive State Route 105 south and west toward Westport, passing the "Westport Y" in 17.7 miles (the right goes to downtown Westport) and shortly coming to a stop sign at the "Westport T." Here SR 105 heads south, but a spur goes north; take it right. In about 2 miles, go left on Ocean Avenue, shortly finding a large parking area and restrooms at Westport Light State Park.

WILLAPA BAY AND LONG BEACH PENINSULA

ONLY TWO MAJOR INDUSTRIES FUEL this fascinating corner of Washington State: fishing/shellfish production and tourism. Sure, there's logging and timber production in the forests just to the east. But along the coast, the mainstays are producing things from the sea and having fun—the two often happily intertwined.

This is a region with an exquisitely dynamic environment. On the south, the huge Columbia River rushes insistently to the ocean, over centuries delivering sediment that created the Long Beach Peninsula, which in turn embraces and protects the rich, shallow tidelands of Willapa Bay. Since the peninsula stretches 28 miles from remote shoals at the bay's entrance south to Cape Disappointment and the Columbia, the tourism folks like to call it the longest beach in America. Whether or not that's true, it's a long, thin finger of accreted sand, 1.5 miles thick at its widest.

The rich and pungent Willapa Bay shore at Leadbetter Point State Park as the tide recedes.

The Columbia, of course, although much diminished in capacity since the arrival of white people, remains one of the world's biggest producers of salmon. Salmon fishing at the mouth and on the ocean can be excellent. Willapa Bay in turn is one of the biggest oyster- and clam-producing regions in the country, while the oceanside shores of the peninsula represent one of Washington's five major razor clam beaches. Add to that the priceless Willapa National Wildlife Refuge, and there are a lot of fun things to do here.

The hiking in this area is surprising in its quality. Most is not wilderness, but there are forests of gnarly big spruce and cedar; old, spooky, windswept lighthouses and military ruins; and wildlife-rich coastal jungles and tidelands to explore. A worthwhile 8.2-mile biking and hiking trail through forest and sand dunes links the towns of Ilwaco and Long Beach.

The place is not without its creature comforts. The peninsula has developed a reputation for fine dining that features locally produced food at spots such as the Shelburne Inn pub (Seaview), The Depot (a former railroad station, Seaview), the 42nd Street Café & Bistro (Seaview), and Jimella & Nanci's Market Café (Ocean Park). My advice: order the oysters fall through spring, salmon summer through fall (preferably chinook), and Dungeness crab just about anytime.

GETTING THERE/STAYING THERE

This is another far-flung corner of Washington State, the southwestern yin to the northwestern yang of Cape Flattery, and likewise a good four-hour road-trip from the Seattle area—170 miles to Ilwaco at the mouth of the mighty Columbia. Portland is actually closer, 109 miles away, which accounts for a definite Oregonian influence on the Long Beach Peninsula. From the Washington side, head south from Aberdeen on US 101, reaching Raymond in 25 miles. Continuing southwesterly on US 101 to Ilwaco in another 46 miles.

The towns of note, north to south, are Raymond, South Bend, and Bay Center on the mainland side; Nahcotta, Ocean Park, and Long Beach on the Long Beach Peninsula; and at the mouth of the mighty Columbia, the fishing port of Ilwaco. Raymond and South Bend are working towns tucked along the Willapa River upstream of Willapa Bay. They don't offer a lot in terms of tourism or recreation, but they have a full range of services (visit the Willapa Harbor Chamber of Commerce; see "Contacts and Resources" for all contact information).

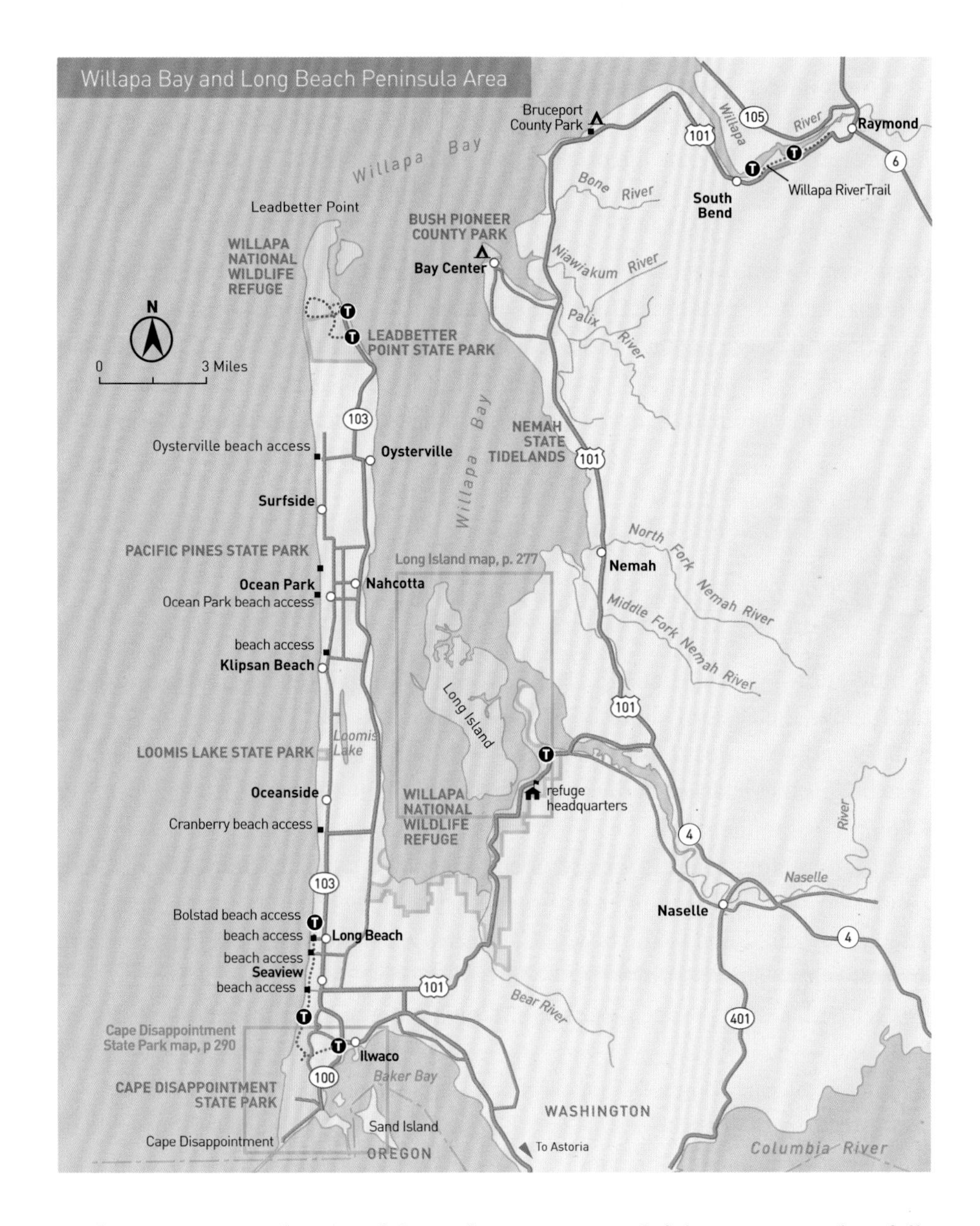

Ilwaco is more of a sportfishing than commercial fishing port, with a full-service marina and several charter fishing services. It offers a few places to eat and stay and is also home to US Coast Guard Station Cape Disappointment, the largest search and rescue station on the Northwest Coast.

A variety of private tent/RV campgrounds are scattered along Long Beach Peninsula, as well as motels and resorts (visit the Long Beach Peninsula Visitors Bureau), anchored by the historic Shelburne Inn established in 1896.

FEES AND PERMITS

Surprisingly, you don't need a federal recreation pass to park anywhere on the Willapa National Wildlife Refuge. You do need a Washington State Discover Pass to park for day-use at state parks (campers don't need one) (see "Contacts and Resources"). The pass is $30 a year or $10 a day and is available online, from many hunting and fishing license vendors, and at various state park locations.

CAMPING

BRUCEPORT COUNTY PARK

A little-known gem operated by Pacific County, this park is perched atop a high bluff above the eastern shore of Willapa Bay, with great views of that massive estuary and 40 campsites spread across its 42 acres in tall spruce forest. Its only drawback is that it lacks nearby attractions—although the little port village of Bay Center is just to the south.

The campground and park are open seasonally, typically mid-May through Labor Day weekend, and offer bathrooms with showers, a day-use area, and an interesting trail down to the beach. Campsites are first come, first served. There are 8 primitive sites ($10/night), 23 standard sites ($15/night), and 8 hookup sites (power, water, and sewage disposal; $21/night) that can handle trailers/RVs up to 30 feet.

Contact: Pacific County. **Driving directions:** From the public boat launch on the west end of South Bend, drive west and then south on US 101 for 5 miles, finding the marked park entrance on the right.

BUSH PIONEER COUNTY PARK

Tucked out of the way on the end of a little peninsula that hosts the funky fishing village of Bay Center, this park and campground are small but quiet and cool,

A short trail from the Bush Pioneer County Park campground leads to this quiet cove on Willapa Bay—best explored at low tide.

perched on a bluff above Willapa Bay. The park is managed by Pacific County but run day to day by the Chinook Indian Nation, which maintains a small office at the park entrance. The park offers restrooms with showers, a baseball field, basketball hoops, play area, and access to the mudflat shores of the bay via a brushy trail. A short walk away is the interesting tidewater marina of Bay Center, full of fishing boats, oyster dredges, and colorful old salts, served by the Dock of the Bay, a comfy café that serves honest food.

The campground is open seasonally, typically May 15 through Labor Day weekend. The 10 standard campsites (no hookups) are first come, first served, and cost $15 per night, $10 if you arrive by bicycle or on foot.

Contact: Chinook Indian Nation. **Driving directions:** From the public boat launch at the west end of South Bend, follow US 101 west and then south about 11 miles to Bay Center Dike Road and turn right (west). In 3 miles, turn right at Dock of the Bay Café on 2nd Street, cross over a tidal lagoon that hosts the marina, and find the park entrance in 0.5 mile (from the café).

WILLAPA NATIONAL WILDLIFE REFUGE

Protecting 15,000 acres of critical habitat and hugely productive tidelands of Willapa Bay—at 260 square miles, one of the largest and most intact estuaries in the nation—this federal refuge is absolutely essential in maintaining the character of the south coast of Washington. It was established by FDR in 1937 to protect migratory and wintering populations of geese, ducks, shorebirds, and wading birds, which can number in the hundreds of thousands. The refuge also preserves salt marshes, dune habitat, coastal forests, and vast beds of eel grass, which provide essential habitat for a myriad of marine species, including salmon, crabs, clams, oysters, and invertebrates.

A major percentage of all the oysters eaten in the United States comes from Willapa Bay, and the refuge includes leased tidelands for shellfish culture. Problems remain, for sure, including a persistent infestation of introduced and invasive spartina grass that converts mudflats to marshes and crowds out habitat for shellfish, birds, fish, and other wildlife. Many are concerned about the use of pesticides by oyster growers to eliminate burrowing sand shrimp, a native species that smothers the beds growers use to culture Pacific oysters, an introduced species. The bay's native Olympia oysters survive in pockets after being grossly overharvested late in the nineteenth century and replaced by oysters from Japan.

The bay's native salmon runs have also been devastated over time, primarily by intensive logging as well as overharvesting. It's estimated that for every square mile of land in the surrounding hills, about 5 miles of logging roads have been built, overloading streambed spawning gravel with sediment. Logging practices are far less damaging today, but restoration work remains and, of concern to many, wild salmon runs to a significant degree have been replaced by hatchery-produced salmon.

Without the refuge, however, the bay's natural resources would be in far, far worse shape. The federal refuge designation provides priceless protection for an incredible diversity of species.

Hunting, primarily for waterfowl, is allowed in season (fall into winter) and can be extremely good. Bowhunting is also allowed for deer, elk, and bear on Long Island in September.

Bird-watching is excellent as well, especially in winter due to northern migratory species that spend the cold months here—as do the predators that seek them—and in spring during the shorebird migration. More than two hundred species have been recorded, including swans, geese, ducks, loons, pelicans, shorebirds, egrets, rails, jaegers, woodpeckers, owls, falcons, hawks, eagles, larks, finches, waxwings, tanagers, swallows, sparrows, and many other songbirds. Hiking and paddling are two great ways to experience the refuge.

Driving directions: The refuge has sections in several areas of Willapa Bay, from Leadbetter Point at the tip of the Long Beach Peninsula to the southernmost reaches of the bay. The refuge headquarters is along US 101 near Long Island, about 13 miles north of Ilwaco and about 34 miles south of Raymond.

HIKING

WILLAPA RIVER TRAIL

A SMOOTH PATH ALONG A LAZY RIVER

Following the bed of a former Northern Pacific Railroad line for 56 miles between the towns of Chehalis and South Bend, the Willapa Hills Trail will one day be a marvelous cross-country route through a relatively little-known pastoral reach of western Washington. For now, it's paved at either end, mighty lonesome and sketchy in the middle, and for our purposes relevant only on its far west side, where an interesting blacktop stretch follows the sleepy lower Willapa River between the towns of Raymond and South Bend, across and along tidal channels busy with blue herons. This part of the route is known locally as the Willapa River Trail, nicely accented by metal art sculptures of things like eagles, ducks, and a fisherman. It's a nice bike ride too. You'll not want to travel great lengths to take this hike—it's used mostly by locals for exercise, and lightly at that. But it provides an interesting look at a little-traveled workingman's reach of the coast.

Distance: 7 miles round-trip
Elevation gain: None

Difficulty: 2
Map: Rails-to-Trails Conservancy map, www.traillink.com/trail/willapa-hills-trail-.aspx
Contact: Washington State Parks and Pacific County
Notes: Dogs permitted on-leash

DRIVING DIRECTIONS

Find the north trailhead for this section at Riverfront Park in Raymond (home of the city's Northwest Carriage Museum and Seaport Museum). From US 101 in Raymond, drive west on Heath Street about 0.2 mile to 3rd Street, finding the park entrance on the left. The south trailhead is along Summit Avenue off US 101, near the north end of the town of South Bend.

THE HIKE

Starting at the north trailhead in Raymond, the river scenes begin immediately, after you leave a public pier and then bridge the meandering south fork of the Willapa River. Then you'll transit a shopping area on the outskirts of town and return to the south fork at one of its oxbow bends, at about 0.75 mile. Look across the river here at Weyerhaeuser's gritty Raymond lumber mill, the town's major employer, where trees are barked and then scanned by computers to be efficiently cut into boards.

At 1 mile, pass an industrial park and shortly pick up the tidally influenced main stem of the Willapa River. Here you can look north over the water to clear-cut hills—perhaps where some of those trees at the mill came from.

Continuing on, pass marshes, tidal flats, docks, ruined buildings, and old piers, the latter dreams of a once-bustling logging and fishing community, before passing over Skidmore Slough and arriving at the trail's end on the north side of South Bend, at 3.5 miles.

LEADBETTER POINT

HIKING THE WILDEST REACH OF THE SOUTH COAST

A surprisingly wild network of trails and ocean beach on the uninhabited north tip of the Long Beach Peninsula, at both Leadbetter Point State Park and adjacent lands of the

Willapa National Wildlife Refuge, provides miles of wandering where you can count on seeing critters. On my first trip here I almost immediately spooked a red-tailed hawk out of the low branches of a spruce tree, clutching its unidentified breakfast in its talons. I hadn't hiked much farther when I spotted a trail of bear tracks in the mud along Willapa Bay. On another visit I spotted river otters frolicking in a tidal channel exposed at low tide and then a seal hauled out on the ocean shore. If you're strong of leg, you can day hike this entire network of trails and beach in a day. But I'd suggest you pack your binoculars and lunch, take your time, and follow the recommended route. It traverses an interesting mix of dunes and shore pine/spruce/shrub forest, with ocean on one side and bay on the other—the best example of this mix of habitat, and the wildest, on the Washington Coast.

Distance: 4-mile loop (described), options up to 10 miles round-trip
Elevation gain: Minimal, minor ups and downs
Difficulty: 2–3
Map: Leadbetter Point State Park map, www.parks.wa.gov/documentcenter/home/view/1899
Contact: Washington State Parks and US Fish and Wildlife Service, Willapa National Wildlife Refuge
Notes: Day use only, no camping. Dogs permitted in the open tideland areas of the refuge during waterfowl hunting seasons but not on refuge trails. This hike is best done late spring through midfall; the two trails to the ocean beach typically flood knee-deep in the wetter months. Marked dunes habitat on the ocean side is closed seasonally to protect nesting snowy plovers.

DRIVING DIRECTIONS

From US 101 in Seaview, drive north on State Route 103 for approximately 19 miles. SR 103 (here also called Stackpole Road) ends at a refuge parking area, but the recommended route begins at the state park parking area, the first you come to at 0.5 mile before the road ends.

THE HIKE

From the south trailhead, walk east down a short dirt road to the primal tidelands of Willapa Bay. This route is a big loop that combines the 2.9-mile Dune

On the bay side of Leadbetter Point, the waves washed ashore this weathered spruce log that resembles some strange creature—a spruceosaurus, perhaps?

Forest Loop in the state park with two refuge trails, Weather Beach and Bearberry, out to the ocean. That gives you a long walk on the bird-rich tidelands of Willapa Bay, through shrub-intense dunes to the ocean beach and back, with a return through thick spruce forest. It's not for everybody. This is not a wide-open, stunning mountain landscape. It's far more closed in and subtle, except for the shoreline sections, and for some perhaps monotonous.

You'll have a decent chance of encountering black bears, which are abundant here and throughout the Long Beach Peninsula. Bring bear spray and bells if you desire, but you won't need them; these bears are not known to be aggressive.

As soon as you reach the bay in a few hundred yards, pull out your binoculars. Depending on the season, look for teal, wigeon, pintails, ring-necked, long-tailed, and other ducks, geese, sometimes swans, pelicans, grebes, cormorants, and loons. Even snowy owls are spotted here during some winters.

Head north along the bay on the obvious footpath through the salt marsh. Low tide reveals the bay's vast acreage of pungent, rich, muddy tidelands; in terms of biomass production, these are some of the richest lands on Earth. In about 0.6 mile you'll leave the state park and enter refuge lands. A path to the left (west) leads to the refuge parking lot and just beyond, to a wooden viewing platform. But continue northerly, following signs for the Bearberry Trail and soon veering away from the bay.

At 1 mile into the hike you'll reach a junction, the left path looping back to the refuge parking lot. Stay right and soon transition from marsh grasses to dense coastal shore pine/shrub habitat, with evergreen huckleberry prominent (ripe with berries usually in late summer). That's why it's called the Bearberry Trail. The way gets dense, but you'll soon note a transition from shrub to a sedge/grass dune sort of habitat. Listen for the surf. Climb a short hill, and at 1.75 miles the ocean is in sight.

Usually this is a pretty lonesome ocean beach. As I discovered one spring day, however, beach driving is allowed here during razor clam seasons, and it wasn't lonesome at all. Your route heads south from here, but along the way find a drift log and stop for lunch. Take your shoes off and splash your toes in the surf. Watch for shorebirds like sanderlings, usually in a small flock, or the curious whimbrels, which are larger, long of leg and beak, and usually alone.

Continue south along the ocean and at about 2.2 miles look for a pole and sign on the uplands that marks another trail heading back toward the bay, the Weather Beach Trail. Follow it east and inland, through more thick pine/shrub habitat.

At 2.8 miles find an intersection and go right, southbound now, back on the Dune Forest Loop in the state park. Soon the habitat transitions into a thick, spooky coastal spruce forest. At 3.5 miles the trail turns east, passing a marshy area and ending at the state park lot and your vehicle at 4 miles.

KEEP EXPLORING

If you do reach the end of the Bearberry Trail and find the ocean beach quiet—typical except during clamming seasons—head north along the shore to the seldom-visited north tip of the Long Beach Peninsula, about 2 miles away. This sandy tongue is really remote, the tip of the Long Beach Peninsula, where Willapa Bay spills into the ocean. You probably won't see a soul up there—you can run naked with the waves if you want, let the sea breeze tickle your titties. At your inclination, turn around and head back from whence you came. If you tack this on to the recommended route, it adds 4 miles, for a total hike of 8 miles. The variety of loop possibilities here can net you up to 10 miles of exploring.

The Discovery Trail wanders through the dunes of the Long Beach Peninsula, offering plenty of side trails to the ocean like this one near Beards Hollow.

DISCOVERY TRAIL

PATH THROUGH DUNES PROVIDES HISTORICAL PERSPECTIVE

Mostly paved with some boardwalk, this popular trail snakes through second-growth forest from the fishing village of Ilwaco on Baker Bay to join Cape Disappointment State Park near Beards Hollow. It then heads north through ocean dunes to the town of Long Beach. It was built just before the Lewis and Clark bicentennial years (2005–6) and includes interesting interpretive panels and sculptures about that journey and seashore ecology, along with other interesting displays—like a complete skeleton of a juvenile gray whale. There are multiple access points, the most popular in the Seaview–Long Beach area—accessible to hotels there and offering ocean views for that entire length. It's a terrific walk, run, or bike ride.

Distance: 6.2 miles one-way from Long Beach to Beards Hollow; 8.2 miles one-way if you continue to Ilwaco
Elevation gain: Minimal; if you continue to Ilwaco, about 270 feet on the way back to Cape Disappointment State Park

Difficulty: 1–3, depending on how far you go

Map: From the Long Beach Peninsula Visitors Bureau, http://funbeach.com/other-businesses/peninsula-discovery-trail-maps

Contact: Washington State Parks and City of Long Beach

Notes: Discover Pass required to park. Hounds on-leash are A-OK.

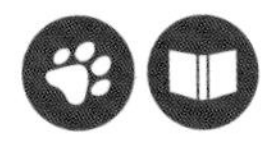

DRIVING DIRECTIONS

For the north trailhead in the town of Long Beach, drive north from Ilwaco on US 101 for 1.8 miles and continue north on State Route 103. Turn left (west) on 26th Street North in 4.5 miles, and drive a short distance to the trailhead.

There are several other trailheads: in Ilwaco along the SR 100 loop; in Cape Disappointment State Park at Beards Hollow (Discover Pass required); and along the Long Beach Peninsula, west off of SR 103 at 30th Street South, 38th Place, 17th Street South, Sid Snyder Drive, Bolstad Street, and 16th Street North. Leave a car at Beards Hollow to hike the recommended route one-way.

THE HIKE

From the north trailhead, walk, run, or bike south on the obvious asphalt trail in the grassy dunes, the ocean beating a steady rhythm just west. This is the most popular stretch of the Discovery Trail, here in the tourist-laden town of Long Beach, but it also features some very cool interpretive displays. You'll come to the first one almost immediately, a bronze sculpture called Clark's Tree, commemorating and replicating a carving that Captain William Clark left in a tree presumably nearby, on November 19, 1805.

My favorite comes after 1.8 miles on asphalt and boardwalk, another bronze sculpture, this one of Clark and a 10-foot sturgeon he found on the ocean shore, along with a basalt monolith. The latter marks the farthest point north that Clark reached on his exploration of the area in 1805, the tree and sturgeon commemorating events he noted in his journals: "I proceeded on the Sandy Coast 4 miles, and marked my name on a Small pine, the Day of the month & year, and returned to the foot of the hill, from which place I intended to Strike across to The Bay, I saw a Sturgeon which had been thrown on Shore and left by the tide 10 feet in length and several joints of the back bone of a whale which must have foundered on this part of the Coast."

At 2.4 miles is another curiosity, the skeleton of a 38-foot gray whale that washed ashore several years ago. By 3 miles you're leaving the busy Long Beach area, and the trail takes on a more natural character, weaving through dunes and big beach grass, never far from the surf.

At 6.2 miles you'll reach a neat nook of Cape Disappointment State Park, rocky Beards Hollow, the north tip of the assemblage of stone on the southernmost Washington Coast, topped by the cape itself. This is a lovely little pocket beach for a picnic, and if you left a car here, you're done. If not, eat and run—it's 6.2 miles back the way you came.

BEACH ACCESS

LOOMIS LAKE STATE PARK

This small day-use park (13.5 acres) on the Long Beach Peninsula provides foot access to the Pacific Ocean and includes 425 feet of shoreline, but it's not heavily used because driving is allowed on this beach year-round. Razor clam diggers who lack four-wheel-drive or prefer not to drive on the beach (cars with low traction can get stuck in the sand) do use it during clamming dates, though. A trail leads from the parking area through dunes to the ocean, about ⅛ mile. The park includes a paved parking area, 24 picnic sites (some with wind screens), and restrooms. You'll need a state Discover Pass to park here.

Just north of the park on the other (east) side of State Route 103 is a Washington Department Fish and Wildlife access site to actual Loomis Lake, with a rough boat launch. You'll need a Discover Pass or Fish and Wildlife Access Pass to park. Fishing is open from the last Saturday in April through October 31. Loomis Lake is 2.9 miles long, is planted with rainbow trout, and provides critical habitat for some interesting species, including trumpeter swans in winter, native cranberries, and the carnivorous sundew plant. It would make an interesting canoe or kayak paddle.

Contact: Washington State Parks. **Driving directions:** From the intersection of US 101 and State Route 103 in Seaview, drive north on SR 103 about 11 miles, finding the signed park entrance on the left (west). For the Fish and Wildlife access site on Loomis Lake, continue north about 0.5 mile and take a right on the signed dirt road.

PACIFIC PINES STATE PARK

Another small day-use park that provides foot access to the ocean on the Long Beach Peninsula, Pacific Pines encompasses almost 11 acres and includes 590 feet of shoreline. It's a good place to park during razor clam seasons if your car is not suitable for driving on the sandy beach. The northern third of the peninsula provides the best razor clamming in the area, and this park is just about that far up. A trail leads about ⅛ mile from the parking area through pretty sand dune meadows to the beach. The park also offers restrooms and picnic areas. Discover Pass required to park.

Contact: Washington State Parks. **Driving directions:** From the intersection of US 101 and State Route 103 in Seaview, drive north on SR 103 a little more than 14 miles to the town of Ocean Park. Continue north on Vernon Avenue (where SR 103 veers right) for less than 1 mile, taking a left on 274th Place into the park.

PADDLING

WILLAPA BAY TIDEWATERS

PRIMAL TIDAL CHANNELS

Seven rivers spill into the massive, relatively undeveloped estuary of Willapa Bay—an intricate network of tidelands that is a major producer of oysters in America—and several of the waterways offer unusual kayak or canoe paddles into isolated channels rich in wildlife. Typically, you'll be paddling high tides upstream through salt marsh meadows where elk are common and into deep, spooky coastal forests, following narrow sloughs as they wind upstream and at times paddling under fallen logs. Bone River will give you a taste. You can also paddle out into the bay, which is usually rampant with waterfowl in winter and rich with shorebirds in spring.

Distance: 3–4 miles round-trip to explore the Bone River
Difficulty: 2–3
Map: State-designated water trail map for Willapa Bay, http://wwta.org/water-trails/willapa-bay-trail; or Washington Department of Ecology, Coastal Atlas, https://fortress.wa.gov/ecy/coastalatlas/tools/Map.aspx

Contact: Washington Department of Ecology, Washington Department of Fish and Wildlife
Notes: At low tide the bay and lower rivers are largely deep, gooey mud where you can easily get stuck. So paddle during the higher tides, with the general plan to launch near the middle of an incoming tide and follow the flood upstream. When the tide turns and begins ebbing, turn around so you can make it back to the launch site before low tide. NOAA has tide charts, http://tidesandcurrents.noaa.gov. Carry all necessary safety gear, especially a Coast Guard–approved personal flotation device.

DRIVING DIRECTIONS

From South Bend, drive US 101 south for 8 miles. Find a dirt road on the east side of the highway, just north of a bridge. Follow it to a rough boat launch on the north bank of the Bone River.

THE PADDLE

The Bone is a sluggish but pretty stream that snakes through the jungles of the Willapa Hills, with multiple tendrils in its tidal areas. It makes for an otherworldly paddle through elk-rich salt marsh meadows.

It has something of a sorrowful history. The land at the mouth, the launch site, and just upstream was claimed as a homestead in 1853 by James Swan, who later wrote a popular book, *The Northwest Coast; or, Three Years' Residence in Washington Territory.* The land at the launch site at that time was an overgrown meadow, formerly a village of a band of the Chinook tribe, abandoned and burned after all of its members succumbed to an epidemic. The disease was likely smallpox, which decimated Northwest Coast tribes repeatedly in 1775, 1801, 1836–38, 1853, and yet again in 1862. These and other diseases introduced by Europeans are believed to have eliminated up to 90 percent of the Native population on the coast, most of them well before Swan arrived.

In Swan's day it was known as the Querquelin or Mouse River. Today there's no hint of a tragic past, and you can paddle for miles. I paddled here several years ago with friends on a calm winter day, launching an hour or two before high tide, first paddling downstream briefly into the bay past the big-moon eyes of a harbor seal and then among large flocks of wigeon and teal. When we paddled back upstream, a duck hunter with his dog was launching a rowboat full of decoys.

Heavy shooting commenced, for an hour or less, and when we returned the hunter was gone, no doubt with his limit of ducks.

The lower few miles of the Bone meander through open salt marsh meadows, and sure enough we saw a herd of elk before paddling narrow channels deep into dark woods, a place where certainly elves and ents and other mythical creatures wreak mischief in the absence of human eyes. We paddled perhaps 2 miles upstream before heading back to the launch site.

 OTHER WILLAPA BAY RIVERS TO PADDLE

Niawiakum and Palix rivers: The two join just before spilling into Willapa Bay and both flow through some of the most pristine salt marsh habitat on the coast. The three forks of the Palix River offer miles of tidewater paddling. Both rivers can be paddled from a launch at the village of Bay Center, but there's also a Washington Department of Fish and Wildlife concrete boat ramp on the main Palix, along US 101.

Contact: Washington Department of Fish and Wildlife. **Driving directions:** For the Bay Center launch, drive US 101 for 11 miles south of South Bend to Bay Center. Turn right (west) on Bay Center Dike Road. At the marina, turn right on 2nd Street, crossing a bridge, and take an immediate right. The Fish and Wildlife launch site is on US 101, just south of the Palix River bridge, about 11.5 miles south of South Bend. A state Discover Pass or a Fish and Wildlife vehicle access pass is required to park here.

Smith Creek and North River: A state boat ramp at the mouth of Smith Creek provides access to a huge network of channels and sloughs on that stream and the North River, which join where they both spill into the north side of Willapa Bay. Curiously, strings of houseboats line places on the main channel and major sloughs of the North River, a throwback to a hardy, isolated lifestyle that began decades ago. Almost 650 acres here comprise the Smith Creek–North River Unit of the state's Johns River Wildlife Area, providing habitat for deer, elk, raptors, waterfowl, shorebirds, songbirds, and other creatures.

Contact: Washington Department of Fish and Wildlife, Johns River Wildlife Area. **Driving directions:** From Raymond, drive north 10.4 miles on State Route 105 and turn right at the public fishing sign just across the Smith River bridge. A state Discover Pass or a Fish and Wildlife vehicle access pass is required to park here.

WILLAPA NATIONAL WILDLIFE REFUGE: LONG ISLAND

TUCKED INTO OUR SLEEPING BAGS LATE one moonlit night at Long Island's Pinnacle Rock Campground, my wife and I were stirred by footsteps and a mysterious humming. We'd seen only one other person since kayaking to the island two days before and were the only campers for miles. "What the . . . ?" I thought, "Someone's walking into our campsite after midnight?" The humming sounded like it was a woman's; as the sound neared our tent, the pace of the footsteps slowed and the humming stopped. The footsteps went slowly past our tent, turned around, and then went back the way they'd come. Finally, I unzipped the tent flap and hollered, "Who are you?"

There was no reply, but the footsteps sped up and went into the woods, snapping twigs as they disappeared. We turned on our headlamps, got out, and looked over the campsite—nothing touched, the food stowed safely inside a

Two kayakers take a break on the shore of Long Island at Pinnacle Rock Campground.

bear canister. We turned back in but didn't sleep much, with every little nighttime noise perking up our heartbeats.

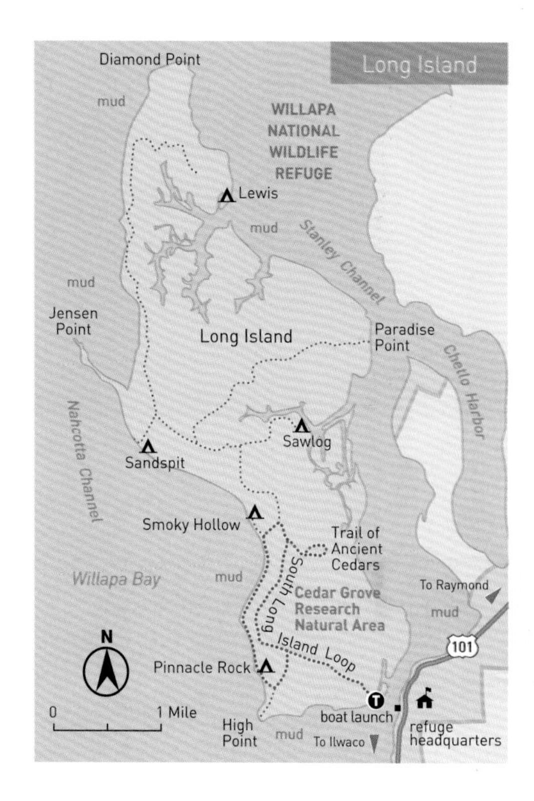

In the morning, there were no footprints in the surrounding grass. This being part of the Willapa National Wildlife Refuge, I thought perhaps a researcher was staying on the island and took a stroll to gauge nighttime wildlife activity—raccoons, deer, otters, bears—along the shore? Later, I emailed then refuge manager Charlie Stenvall. No, he replied, there had been no researchers on the island.

I can only conclude it was a bear wandering the beach. We'd seen bear scat when we arrived. Several years ago, I interviewed a grad student who was researching the island's bear population. He told me it was one of the densest populations of black bears in the United States. But I can't explain the spooky humming noise. I swear it sounded just like a woman humming softly, even sweetly. If it wasn't a woman, wasn't a bear, perhaps a spirit of the Chinook people who'd once lived on the island? Tribal lore maintains that members isolated themselves on the island to escape a smallpox epidemic in the 1850s.

My takeaway is that Long Island is a very wild and special place, where you can often experience solitude, just you, the critters—and whatever!

The biggest estuarine island on the West Coast, at 5460 acres and 7 miles long, Long Island is an uninhabited, forested gem inside the Willapa National Wildlife Refuge. It has five small boat-in campgrounds and is heavily visited only during the September bowhunting season and late spring/summer weekends. At any given time, there are far more bears and elk on this island than people. The oldest things here are red cedar trees, some of them behemoths more than nine hundred

The namesake of Pinnacle Rock Campground during a low tide on Willapa Bay, viewed across tidelands strewn with oysters

years old in a 243-acre grove spared the logger's ax, one of the last truly coastal groves of ancient cedar in America.

When skies are clear on a full-moon night, you might find it almost too loud to sleep. Captain William Clark of the famous Lewis and Clark Expedition noted in his journal a noisy night in 1805 not too far away, along the lower Columbia River near present-day Ridgefield: "I could not Sleep for the noise kept by the Swans, Geese, white & black brant, Ducks &c. on a opposit base, & Sand hill Crane, they were emensely numerous and their noise horrid." I know exactly what he meant. Camping one April night, I heard the constant screech of gulls, apparently feeding on the mudflats in the moonlight; a honking cacophony of geese; and the plaintive wail of loons. At one point, a barred owl belted out its throaty "oo-oo-ah-ooooah" hoot repeatedly, very close to the campsite.

Long Island is simply crazy with wildlife, unlike just about any other hiking/paddling destination in Washington. Please be careful though. The wind and waves can get serious here.

GETTING THERE/STAYING THERE

The refuge headquarters is on the mainland across from the southeast corner of the island, on US 101 about 13 miles north of Ilwaco and 34 miles south of Raymond (see "Contacts and Resources"). Five small boat-in campgrounds with a total of 20 campsites are scattered along the shellfish-rich shores of Long Island, making it an ideal venue for sea kayak and canoe paddling.

The hitch is that there are no bridges to Long Island; you must access it by private boat. But it's a short crossing from the boat launch at refuge headquarters to a landing on the south end of the island, which is connected to the gravel road/trail system. Boaters must heed the tides, because at lower tides shallow Willapa Bay is largely mudflats. Also watch the weather, since the wind can definitely blow here. Bears are known to wander the campgrounds, so definitely hang your food and garbage or store it in a bear-proof canister, and practice Leave No Trace camping techniques. Please note: dogs are not allowed on Long Island.

FEES AND PERMITS

You don't need a federal recreation pass to park anywhere in the Willapa National Wildlife Refuge. The only permit requirement is in September, when the island is open to bowhunting for elk, deer, and bear; you must get a permit to camp on the island during that time (available at refuge headquarters).

CAMPING

Long Island's five campgrounds are scattered at varying distances from the boat launch site at refuge headquarters. They are all available first come, first served. All the sites feature picnic tables and steel fire rings with grates. Each campground has a vault toilet. They are, north to south:

LEWIS CAMPGROUND, on the northeast corner of the island, some 7.5 miles from the launch at refuge headquarters, with just 2 sites.

SAWLOG CAMPGROUND, on a slough on the east side of the island, about 3.7 miles from the refuge launch, with 6 sites.

SANDSPIT CAMPGROUND, 5.6 miles from the refuge launch on the western shore of the island, with 3 sites tucked into the forest just above the beach. There is a public steamer clam bed open for digging just north on the spit; but watch for signs marking private tidelands, and steer clear of those (see "Contacts and Resources" for shellfishing regulations). Some paddlers and motorboaters access this campground from Nahcotta, across the bay on the inside of the Long Beach Peninsula, about 4.5 miles away.

SMOKY HOLLOW CAMPGROUND, on a beautiful gravel beach about 2 miles south of Sandspit Campground, about 3.6 miles from the refuge launch, with 4 sites. A wetland here attracts birds but also generates a lot of bugs. I met a somewhat freaked-out young couple here in 2014 who reported a bear prowling the campground in the middle of the night.

PINNACLE ROCK CAMPGROUND, on the island's southwest shore, marked by a mini-monolith just offshore, is about 2 miles from the refuge launch, with 5 campsites. The best is on the grass directly above the shore—the scene of our late-night mystery. A public shellfish bed here is open to steamer clam digging and oyster shucking.

HIKING

SOUTH LONG ISLAND LOOP

ALONG THE ISLAND SHORE AND THROUGH THE ANCIENT FOREST

Savor the sweet spots of the island on this loop—its interesting timbered beaches and the ancient cedar forest. The hike is recommended especially for those camping at Pinnacle Rock or Smoky Hollow campgrounds but is also feasible for day hikers who boat across from the refuge launch to the landing on the south end of the island. About 10 miles of former logging roads weave along the island and, along with actual paths to the campgrounds, provide a fun-for-wandering trail network, with plenty of loop options. The main north–south route is called Center Road and still sees vehicle use for maintenance work by refuge staff.

Distance: 4.8 miles round-trip from Pinnacle Rock or Smoky Hollow; 7.9 miles round-trip from the boat landing at the island's south end
Elevation gain: About 300 feet
Difficulty: 3
Map: Refuge map, www.fws.gov/uploadedFiles/Region_1/NWRS/Zone_2/Willapa_Complex/Willapa/Documents/WLP_long_island_trail_map_2013.pdf

Contact: US Fish and Wildlife Service, Willapa National Wildlife Refuge
Notes: Not hikable at high tide, so check tide tables to time your hike accordingly for an outgoing tide.

DRIVING DIRECTIONS

To reach the boat launch at refuge headquarters, drive US 101 about 13 miles north of Ilwaco or 34 miles south of Raymond. The boat ramp is directly across the highway from the headquarters; you can launch directly on the concrete ramp or on the shore on either side.

THE HIKE

I devised this route while camping at Pinnacle Rock but will begin describing it where day hikers start, at the landing on the south end of the island. Head generally north on Center Road, winding up a hill that offers decent views of the island's south shore before entering second-growth forest. At 1.6 miles, note a sign for Pinnacle Rock and take the left path, climbing briefly and then at 2 miles reaching a Y.

The left fork drops to High Point, a rocky bench with extensive meadows; for future reference, deer and elk are often seen there, sometimes bear. But take the right fork, dropping toward the shore. At 2.1 miles reach Pinnacle Rock Campground, the beach here grassy, the scene most pleasant. Look offshore just some 100 yards—Pinnacle Rock.

Head north on the beach, passing a sweet campsite, the campground's vault toilet, and a path to other sites. Here begins a 1.6-mile stretch of curious shore with a high, forested bank on the upland side. The beach alternates between fist-sized cobbles, gravel, and reeds, the rocks heavy with jasper and other hard stones. Refuge rules prohibit collecting anything, but you can wonder all you like about why this island has so much rock that no doubt was fashioned by Native people into tools—choppers, knives, arrowheads.

Here and there you'll have to skirt fallen trees by walking the edge of the tide flats. If the tide is low enough, you'll likely see barges at water's edge, with crew working cultured oyster beds.

About 1.5 miles north of Pinnacle Rock, 3.6 miles from the landing, note an open path in the shoreline timber, heading uphill. You're going to take it, but first wander several hundred yards north and check out Smoky Hollow Campground.

Sunlight filters through the tangled limbs of an ancient red cedar in the old-growth grove on Long Island.

Like Pinnacle Rock, this is a sweet spot—on clear evenings the sunsets at both spots will blow your boots off.

Head back south to that uphill path and follow it easterly, through dense green forest, reaching Center Road at 3.9 miles. Go right (south), and shortly find a sign on the left for the "Don Bonker Cedar Grove Trail" (named for the former congressman who fought for its preservation). A short spur leads to a loop where the big-tree show begins.

I've seen more magnificent cedar groves, but this one is special—and curious, being in such a lowland, maritime setting. Although the island has a history of logging that began in the early 1900s, including hosting a floating logging camp, the loggers never reached 240-some acres of the cedar grove. Today the gnarled, aged beasts twist from thick bases into candelabra-like crowns in a dense, wet grove.

Follow the grove trail out, returning to Center Road at 4.8 miles. Head south, in 1.6 miles closing the loop at the sign for Pinnacle Rock. If you're day hiking, return south the way you came, 1.6 miles to the landing, for a total of 7.9 miles. If you're camped at Pinnacle Rock, turn right and return to camp for a total of 4.8 miles.

TEAL SLOUGH CEDAR TRAIL

SAMPLING THE LAST OF THE GIANT TEAL SLOUGH RED CEDARS

A short trail near Long Island and the Willapa National Wildlife Refuge headquarters dips into a remnant grove of very old coastal red cedar, dutifully attended by massive Sitka spruce but ignobly surrounded by clear-cuts. A sliver it is, this piece of ancient forest, but wild enough to still host old growth–dependent and federally protected spotted owls and marbled murrelets, plus big shaggy beasts like elk.

Distance: 0.9 mile round-trip
Elevation gain: About 140 feet
Difficulty: 2
Map: Teal Slough brochure, www.fws.gov/uploadedFiles/Region_1/NWRS/Zone_2/Willapa_Complex/Willapa/Documents/teal%20slough%20brochure.pdf
Contact: US Fish and Wildlife Service, Willapa National Wildlife Refuge
Notes: Dogs allowed on-leash

DRIVING DIRECTIONS

From Raymond, drive south on US 101 about 32.2 miles, finding a gated gravel road on the left (east) side of the road. Park here, but do not block the gate; there is room for perhaps three vehicles. A trail signboard marks the spot, which is not super obvious; it's about 1.6 miles north on US 101 from the Willapa National Wildlife Refuge headquarters.

THE HIKE

Cinch your belt because you might lose your pants on this trail, as short as it is; at least I almost jumped out of mine when I spooked an elk, which suddenly crashed noisily but unseen through the dense forest. Startled at first, I knew exactly what it was and caught a glimpse of it on my way out.

From the parking area, walk around the gate, marked by a trail sign, and walk uphill on the gravel road. Soon you'll start seeing large, snaggy-topped old red cedars on the left, then right, along with many spruces thick of girth and mostly lacking tops, victims of the coastal wind.

At 0.25 mile, a sign on the left marks an actual trail departing the road. Follow it and soon pass at least four giant cedars on both sides of the trail, characteristically candelabra shaped on top with many spiky trunks, almost always with a smaller spruce or hemlock sprouting from the sides. The trail ends in less than 0.5 mile overall at one particularly impressive cedar, likely some eight hundred years old, leaning markedly with its weight, the terrain, and time.

Circle it and imagine that once, one or two hundred years ago, all the forest here was populated by similar gargantuan specimens. Now, hereabouts, this is all that's left, along with the larger grove of old red cedar nearby on Long Island, maybe just 0.5 mile away as the raven flies.

Return the way you came.

PADDLING

LONG ISLAND

A CURIOUS AND UNINHABITED COASTAL ISLAND

With five cozy campgrounds, public shellfish beds, big trees, rich wildlife, and interesting shoreline, Long Island makes for a mighty fine multiday canoe or kayak paddle—or day paddle. Some paddlers will circumnavigate the island on a long day trip. But you can make it as easy or difficult as you desire. The closest campground, Pinnacle Rock, is not far from the refuge launch, with virtually no open water to cross. The premier way to experience the island is on a two- or three-day trip. Many reach the island by motor boat as well. You don't have to paddle to get here.

Distance: 17 miles to circumnavigate the island, 20 miles if you explore the intricate sloughs on the eastern shore; 4.4 miles round-trip from refuge launch to Pinnacle Rock Campground; 7.6 miles round-trip from refuge launch to Smoky Hollow Campground; 9.6 miles round-trip from refuge launch to Sandspit Campground
Difficulty: 3, due to tides and frequent wind
Map: Refuge map, www.fws.gov/uploadedFiles/Region_1/NWRS/Zone_2/Willapa_Complex/Willapa/Documents/WLP_long_island_trail_map_2013.pdf; or for more detail, NOAA's Willapa Bay nautical chart 18504, www.charts.noaa.gov/OnLineViewer/18504.shtml
Contact: US Fish and Wildlife Service, Willapa National Wildlife Refuge
Notes: Exercise caution paddling here. This is the southern coast of Washington, where the wind can really blow. Check the weather forecast and especially the tides. You can't reach any of the campgrounds by boat during lower tides, since the island is surrounded by mudflats then. If you get stuck in the mud at low tide, you'll have a dreary, several-hour wait. I know of at least one kayaking fatality here, an inexperienced paddler who got caught in rough water rounding a point in winter while paddling with an experienced friend. It is advisable to bring a weather radio on extended trips, and sit tight ashore if things blow up. Bring a cell phone to alert family and friends; you'll have coverage. Wear a Coast Guard–approved personal flotation device and carry all necessary safety gear: pump, extra paddle, spray skirt, and the like. And leave a trip plan with someone at home.

DRIVING DIRECTIONS

To reach the boat launch at refuge headquarters, drive US 101 about 13 miles north of Ilwaco or 34 miles south of Raymond. The boat ramp is directly across the highway from the headquarters; you can launch directly on the concrete ramp or on the shore on either side.

THE PADDLE

Personally, I've only paddled as far north as Sandspit Campground, about midway up the west shore of the island, so that's what I'll describe. From the refuge launch,

A kayaker packs up while waiting for high tide.

paddle straight across to the island shore, just several hundred yards, and then follow the shore southerly, in 0.3 mile passing the landing near the island's south end. The shore is pleasant here, mostly meadow (look for deer and elk), and beyond becomes heavily timbered. At about 1 mile you'll reach a crescent-shaped bay.

Just beyond the shoreline there's a low bluff backed by extensive meadows; this is the east side of High Point. High Point is reached at 1.6 miles; here the current can curl and push a bit during extreme tides, and be prepared for north wind as you round the rocky point, since you are now open to a long north–south fetch.

Paddle north just outside a curving bay, and at 2.2 miles look for a small building on the island's western shore. That's the vault toilet of Pinnacle Rock Campground, and if that's your destination, land anywhere; just north of the can is a sign marking the campground and a path to sites in the forested uplands.

In just 1.6 miles north along beautifully timbered shores—some of the trees dead and spiky/spooky, some fallen over onto the beach—you'll reach Smoky Hollow Campground, 3.8 total miles from the refuge launch, perched just above a gorgeous gravel beach. Smoky Hollow is also easily spotted, given its vault toilet and a sign.

The shore now curves northwesterly. In 2 more miles of paddling forested shore, reach Sandspit Campground at 4.8 miles.

CAPE DISAPPOINTMENT STATE PARK

FRET NOT ABOUT THE NAME: Cape Disappointment State Park does not disappoint. From the rugged bluffs marking the massive Columbia River mouth, to the oceanside campground, to 8 miles of spruce forest trails, to tandem historic lighthouses, this is without question the finest state park on the Washington Coast. In fact, it is one of the finest state parks in the entire Northwest, enormous at 1882 acres, with 2 miles of superb ocean beaches and hallowed with history significant for not only the state but the country.

Right here some 210 years ago, in 1805, the principals of the epic Lewis and Clark Expedition sighted their steadfast goal up close when they felt the briny spray of the Pacific Ocean. Just upriver, they'd mistaken the expansive mouth of the Columbia for the ocean: "Great joy in camp," Clark wrote in his journal from Chinook Point.

A wind-sculpted Sitka spruce tree frames the North Head Lighthouse.

"We are in View of the Ocian, this great Pacific Ocean which we [have] been So long anxious to See."

Members of the party twice hiked into what is now Cape Disappointment State Park, visiting spots known today as Waikiki Beach and Beards Hollow, climbing McKenzie Head and camping just beyond. Today the park's informative Lewis and Clark Interpretive Center memorializes the journey and other local history, perched appropriately on a bluff near the top of 287-foot Cape Disappointment. In light of its history, Cape Disappointment is a designated National Historic District, added to the National Register of Historic Places in 1975.

But this history includes more than just Lewis and Clark. The cape itself was named by British sea captain John Meares in 1788, who had been unable to locate a river (the huge Columbia) reported three years prior by Spanish explorer Bruno de Hezeta.

And there's even more. For decades these lands served as the coastal artillery site of Fort Canby, which from 1863 to 1947 guarded the entrance to the Columbia; a lot of ruins remain. The Cape Disappointment Lighthouse is one of the oldest on the West Coast. You can hike to it and look out over where in 1792 American fur trader Captain Robert Gray became the first person of European origin to sail into the mighty Columbia. The park's other lighthouse, North Head, is a classic as well.

The trails here are remarkably diverse and full of surprises, traversing old-growth spruce forests, wandering to the weathered lighthouses on windy bluffs, and passing old gun emplacements, observation posts, and pocket ocean beaches. For good measure, toss in surf fishing, jetty fishing, and crabbing.

Next to it all is the relentless urgency of the largest body of water on planet Earth, the Pacific Ocean, offering any beach activity: strolling, picnicking, sand castle making, kite flying, and simply gazing. The views here over the sea are stupendous, the sunsets magnificent. You owe it to yourself to visit this place.

GETTING THERE/STAYING THERE

From Interstate 5 in Olympia, head west on State Route 8 to Montesano and then south on State Route 107 to US 101. Follow US 101 south to the Long Beach Peninsula, taking a left on SR 103 to Ilwaco. From US 101 in Ilwaco, follow signs to the park, heading northwest on State Route 100 (SR 100 is a loop, and this is the north side of it) to the park entrance in 3.6 miles.

Cape Disappointment State Park

The park features a big, year-round campground with multiple loops, as well as cabins and yurts for rent—you can even rent the North Head Lighthouse keeper's quarters (see "Camping/Cabins" below). The park also includes a small store, with firewood, food, and refreshments. The park's day-use area offers 20 unsheltered picnic tables.

FEES AND PERMITS

You need a Washington State Discover Pass to park. The pass is $30 a year or $10 a day and is available online, from many hunting and fishing license vendors, and at various state park locations. There are also separate charges for the interpretive center ($5 for adults, $2.50 for kids) and tours of North Head Lighthouse ($2.50 for adults, free for those seventeen and younger).

LEWIS AND CLARK INTERPRETIVE CENTER

Its setting atop the windy bluffs of Cape Disappointment is as fabulous as the center itself, directly above the pounding surf and Waikiki Beach, a long stone's throw from a 150-year-old lighthouse marking the treacherous Columbia River bar. Next to the emplacement for gun battery Harvey Allen, of the former Fort Canby, this spot provides one of the two most stupendous viewscapes of the south Washington Coast (see Bell's View Trail for the other). From here you can see the scenic Cape Disappointment Lighthouse just south, and directly west extending out into the seemingly endless sea, the north jetty of the Columbia River bar.

This is the precise area where US merchant sea captain Robert Gray became the first person of European descent to enter the mighty Columbia. Having observed a strong outflow of muddy water while earlier sailing north along the coast, on his return in May of 1792 Gray steered his 83.5-foot, three-masted, ten-cannon *Columbia Rediviva* through the shifting sands of the river's mouth. Gray had correctly theorized that this was the "Great River of the West." He spent nine days here, traveling some 12 to 15 miles up the river trading with the powerful Chinook Nation. Thirteen years later, Lewis and Clark arrived here overland, and the center's exhibits and displays portray this history.

The center is open year-round (but closed Mondays and Tuesdays, October–March) and is a good place to ask about Cape Disappointment State Park in general (see "Contacts and Resources"). Admission is $5 for adults, $2.50 for kids.

Driving directions: From US 101 in Ilwaco, head northwest on State Route 100 to the park entrance in 3.6 miles, taking a right and in a few hundred feet passing the fee station. Drive straight past the main park entrance and up a short hill to the center's parking area. The center itself is reached via a short trail, about 1/8 mile that gains about 200 feet of elevation. Disabled parking is available next to the center; turn right at the sign just before the main parking lot. Like all areas of the park, you'll need a state Discover Pass to park.

The Lewis and Clark Interpretive Center is perched on the rocky prominence of Cape Disappointment, next to Battery Harvey Allen of the former Fort Canby.

The park's boat ramp on Baker Bay includes a 135-foot dock and is very popular during the "Buoy 10" salmon season (August–September), inside the mouth of the Columbia River. The launch fee is $7 (an annual pass is available).

CAMPING/CABINS

Camping is available year-round, with 137 standard campsites, 60 with full hookups, 18 with water and electricity only, and 5 primitive sites. Most of the campsites are in loops very near the Pacific Ocean, just south of scenic North Head. Although the campground is fairly open, some sites offer a level of privacy, with the premium ones on the westerly side of several loops very near the surf. Another group of sites are located away from the main campground near the park entrance, many on the shores of O'Neil Lake. The park has an RV dump station and eight restrooms with fourteen showers. Maximum RV length is 45 feet. Cost ranges in peak season from $12 a night (primitive sites) to $42 a night (full hookups).

Also available are 14 yurts and 3 cabins ($69/night peak season, $59/night other times), all near O'Neil Lake. The cost in my opinion is preposterously high, especially given the minimal amenities—bunk beds and futons and that's about it.

You can also rent the North Head Lighthouse keeper's quarters and two assistant keepers' houses ($154–$437/night, depending on the season, with a two-night minimum). Pricey, but they are well appointed, spacious, and offer all the comforts of home (no cable TV or Wi-Fi though).

Contact: Washington State Parks

HIKING

WESTWIND TRAIL

LAST CALL FOR A JAUNT THROUGH OLD SPRUCE FOREST

The Westwind is an easy up-and-down trail that bounces through a mossy-damp forest of crazy-shaped Sitka spruce and connects the top of North Head and its lighthouse with the ocean cove to the north known as Beards Hollow. But you'd better hike it soon: it's no longer being maintained by the park and will be allowed to revert to forest. That's too bad, since the forest is big, some of the trees old-growth and huge. There are parking areas on both ends of the trail, and I'd suggest combining this hike with the 0.2-mile Bells View Trail and the 0.3-mile loop down to the North Head Lighthouse—they all meet at the lighthouse parking area.

Distance: 1.6 miles round-trip
Elevation gain: About 250 feet, most of it climbing from Beards Hollow
Difficulty: 2
Map: Cape Disappointment State Park map, www.parks.wa.gov/DocumentCenter/Home/View/1850
Contact: Washington State Parks
Notes: Discover Pass required to park. Dogs permitted on-leash.

DRIVING DIRECTIONS

From US 101 in Ilwaco, head northwest for 2.2 miles on State Route 100. Turn right on the North Head Road to reach the lighthouse parking area.

THE HIKE

On the north side of the lighthouse parking area, find the trailhead and a Y. Take the right fork; the left is the Bells View Trail. The Westwind Trail winds to the right, through a deep-green forest of mostly mature Sitka spruce and western hemlock, critical nesting habitat for the marbled murrelet, an old growth–dependent seabird listed as threatened since 1992.

Washington State Parks decided to let this trail revert to forest with the 2014–15 construction of a new 2000-foot-long path linking the nearby Discovery Trail to North Head. Signs will be removed, but no deconstruction is planned. That means you'll be able to hike the Westwind Trail for a few years before it becomes overgrown.

The path is lined with moss, ferns, and salal and presents a puzzle: at about 0.5 mile, note how some of the spruce are ramrod straight and tall, while the branches of others sweep out in all sorts of weird shapes from the butt, sometimes absolutely candelabra-like and other times with massive lopsided branches. I'll leave it to the botanists to explain why, but it gives the trail a welcome, weird ambience. In moist months you'll find a proliferation of fungi too.

Some spruce and hemlock here have wide, spread-out butts, the result of having sprouted on rotting nurse logs decades ago, sending roots down around their hosts. Captain William Clark noted this phenomenon while traveling the area in 1805: "I observed in maney places pine of 3 or 4 feet through growing on the bodies of large trees which had fallen down, and covered with moss and yet part Sound."

The trail bounces over roots and rills through the forest, at about 0.5 mile descending into a gully with a dead-end branch that leads to a bench and a marginal view of the sea. Then it drops through the woods to the Beards Hollow parking area. Unless you want to visit Beards Hollow, which is worth a visit but you can also drive nearly to it, turn around here at 0.8 mile.

When the Westwind Trail is no longer, I'll hike its neighbors and then repair to the Shelburne Inn pub at Seaview to mourn its passing with a martini. Dry, just a drop of vermouth, and three olives please!

BELLS VIEW TRAIL

QUICK TRIP THROUGH THE WINDS OF NORTH HEAD HISTORY

This short, paved, and wheelchair-accessible trail starts at the North Head Lighthouse parking area and leads high above the churning ocean, whipped by not only the sea breeze but also the winds of history. This trail offers the best view anywhere of the 28-mile reach of the Long Beach Peninsula. The history is minor, for sure, a footnote in

American coastal defenses, but the concrete artifacts left are intriguing, and what isn't left is just as fascinating.

Distance: 0.4 mile round-trip
Elevation gain: Almost none, maybe 20 feet
Difficulty: 1
Map: Brochure available from entrance station, or Cape Disappointment State Park map, www.parks.wa.gov/DocumentCenter/Home/View/1850
Contact: Washington State Parks
Notes: Discover Pass required to park. Dogs permitted on-leash.

DRIVING DIRECTIONS

From US 101 in Ilwaco, head northwest then south for 2.2 miles on State Route 100. Turn right on the North Head Road to reach the lighthouse parking area.

THE HIKE

From the parking area, don't head west to the lighthouse, but rather find the trailhead on the north side of the lot. There are two paths. Take the paved one on the left. The dirt one on the right is the Westwind Trail (it's sweet too!).

The smooth trail climbs almost imperceptibly, soon passes a wooden water tower, and offers views on the left of the North Head Lighthouse and the sea. Lickety-split you'll find interpretive panels that explain how at one time North Head was a busy place, with not only the lighthouse and keeper's quarters but also nearby observation posts, searchlights, a weather station, and a radio transmitter/receiver facility that set records decades ago for wireless communication. Most are artifacts of the park's former incarnation as Fort Canby.

Much of the west side of North Head was open decades ago, the forest cut down to accommodate the facilities and improve the seaward view. The forest has regrown, as you soon see from the robust Sitka spruce on the east side of the trail, with huge, sweeping lower branches. Some of the spruce atop North Head take on uncanny shapes, no doubt due to the influence of strong ocean winds. To say this place can be breezy is like saying it's a little damp in the coastal rain forest. North Head, in fact, is one of the foggiest and windiest spots on either coast of the United States.

An observation platform at the end of the Bells View Trail provides a superb look north along the tide-washed Long Beach Peninsula.

A bit beyond, at about 0.3 mile, you'll arrive at a puzzling, multilevel pill-box-like structure on the left, concrete and rectangular, with horizontal slits that obviously allowed observation. Very cool, but what the heck is it? It's a lookout station built in 1943, designed to provide the coordinates of potential enemy ships to the multiple batteries of big, 6-inch cannons at nearby McKenzie Head and Cape Disappointment. This structure was known as a Triple Base End Station. Once there was a tower at the top, long since removed. During World War II, servicemen with binoculars, telescopes, and range and position finders staffed this facility. The fort's guns (you can see two examples at Fort Columbia State Park, 10 miles to the east) could hurl an explosive projectile 15 miles. But they were never fired in hostility.

Explore the end station—you can go inside and climb on top—then follow the trail out to a nice new viewing platform. The peninsula stretches as far as you can see, on a clear day, that is, the surf curling into its sandy shore for mile after mile. Below is rocky Beards Hollow. On a very clear day, it's said, you can see the Olympic Mountains from this spot. This trail was rebuilt, paved, and enhanced with a wooden viewing platform in 2012, funded by a state Wildlife and Recreation Program grant.

Nothing visible is left of the weather station, which operated into the 1950s, or the radio station, which in 1909 set a record for wireless transmission by communicating with a ship at sea 3500 miles away. The trail is named for Pacific County commissioner Tom Bell, who helped establish the area north of the lighthouse as a public park in the 1930s.

KEEP EXPLORING

Intrepid hikers will find a rough path through high beach grass and thick salal leading from the base of the viewing platform west a couple hundred yards to an increasingly narrow spine on North Head. Do not take the kids down there! It leads out to an airy edge, with views south to the lighthouse, soon reaching a small concrete structure that housed the big searchlights, on a precipice some 150 feet above the sea.

NORTH HEAD TRAIL AND LIGHTHOUSE

FOLLOW CAPTAIN CLARK'S FOOTSTEPS TO A HILLTOP BEACON

Hike the former ocean shoreline to the second major headland of the Cape Disappointment region and its beacon atop, largely along a big spruce bluff with a base left high and dry by sediments that accumulated after the construction of the Columbia River jetties some one hundred years ago. Your goal, the high point—geographically and aesthetically—is North Head and its picturesque lighthouse, built circa 1898, where the sea still bashes against the rocks below. You'll pass the approximate location of the 1805 campsite of Captain William Clark's Corps of Discovery, who paused here while surveying the ocean coast from the Columbia to the present town of Long Beach. This trail offers nice ocean views and the forest is mature Sitka spruce with large, sweeping lower branches. You can leave a car at the North Head parking area (an optional starting point) to reduce the mileage.

Distance: 4.1 miles round-trip
Elevation gain: About 300 feet
Difficulty: 3
Map: Cape Disappointment State Park map, www.parks.wa.gov/DocumentCenter/Home/View/1850
Contact: Washington State Parks
Notes: Discover Pass required to park. Dogs permitted on-leash. Expect some mud on the tread, especially during the wetter months.

The North Head Lighthouse was built in 1898 on a dramatic perch above the sea that's considered one of the windiest spots on the West Coast.

DRIVING DIRECTIONS

From US 101 in Ilwaco, head northwest then south on State Route 100 to the park entrance in 3.6 miles, taking a right and in a few hundred feet passing the entrance station. Then turn right again at the first intersection. In about 0.4 mile, find the small trailhead parking area on the left, marked by a monument to Lewis and Clark. To leave a car at North Head, from US 101 in Ilwaco drive northwest then south on SR 100 for 2.2 miles, and turn right on North Head Road to reach the lighthouse parking area.

THE HIKE

From the southern trailhead parking area, cross the road and find the trail beginning along swampy low ground in deciduous forest, on what once must have

CAPE DISAPPOINTMENT AND NORTH HEAD: CLASSIC LIGHTHOUSES OF THE WINDSWEPT BLUFFS

A lot of us "collect" lighthouses as eagerly as we do peaks or agates, and here at Cape Disappointment State Park are two for easy bagging, including the oldest in Washington State.

According to Washington State Parks, the Cape Disappointment Lighthouse is the oldest functioning lighthouse on the West Coast. Automated in 1973, it was first lit in October of 1856, and its beacon shines 220 feet above the sea, atop a modest 53-foot tower. The grounds of the lighthouse are open, but the tower closed. Reach the lighthouse via the 0.6-mile Cape Disappointment Trail, which leaves from the Lewis and Clark Interpretive Center parking area.

The North Head Lighthouse, built circa 1898, is perched in a dramatic location, the light 194 feet above the sea atop a 65-foot tower. Often foggy, rainy, and dreary, this place is one of the windiest spots on the West Coast. A short trail leaves the parking area on North Head Road, dipping by the quaint Victorian-style keeper's quarters. Tours are offered May through September by State Parks volunteers ($2.50 for adults, free for those seventeen and younger).

been a short isthmus between the north end of O'Neil Lake (the one you saw on arriving at the park) and the ocean. The big sea is now almost a mile away!

In a few hundred yards, you'll find a sign and a circle of rocks marking the approximate location of Clark's camp on the night of November 18, 1805. It's probably not the exact spot, since Clark left no specific indication. But judging from his journals, he and his men camped somewhere near here. That day the Clark party had finally reached the Pacific (Lewis and three others had reached it a few days earlier). Clark noted in his journal the mood of his men: "much Satisfied with their trip beholding with estonishment the high waves dashing against the rocks & this emence ocean."

At about 0.6 mile, the trail begins to climb the south end of the complex of headlands known as North Head, rounding a knob and climbing to a lovely, wind-swept bluff with views out over the park campground to the sea. Some of the Sitka spruce here are thick-butted beasts.

You'll reach the North Head parking lot at 1.8 miles. Most people tour the North Head Lighthouse the easy way by parking here. But if you're an active person, it's better to combine it with the longer hike. Either way, the lighthouse is perched on a stunning spot, and its history is intriguing.

Go left at the lot and follow the paved road past the two restored red-roofed structures that were the quarters of the head keeper and assistant keeper, which now can be rented for overnight stays. The path drops gently to awesome views of the sea and Cape Disappointment to the south and then curls to the lighthouse, about 0.25 mile from the lighthouse parking area, a tad more than 2 miles overall, your halfway point. The lighthouse is a pretty white tower with two support buildings, 65 feet high and 194 feet above the sea. It was built to correct something of an oversight, so to speak, just 2 miles north of the Cape Disappointment Lighthouse, which by 1898 had already logged a few decades of serving mariners. But that lighthouse had been built to guide mariners into the Columbia River after dozens of wrecks there, many fatal. It could not be seen well by ships coming from the north, since North Head blocked the view. So another light was built.

Circle the structure and look down at the sea crashing into the rocks below. Every time I come here the scene is so special it knocks me out. If the weather is grand, sit on a bench and enjoy a picnic. Watch the sunset. Realize, however, that over the course of a year, the weather at this spot can get intense. First, many days are split-pea-soup foggy. Second, it rains buckets and the wind really blows. In 1926 gusts here were measured at 126 miles per hour—until the measuring instrument blew away.

Perhaps then the fate of one lightkeeper's wife is not surprising. The couple had lived here for more than twenty years when in 1923 she was diagnosed with "melancholia." Soon thereafter she went for a walk with her dog and never returned. Her coat was found on the ground at the edge of a cliff. Slide marks were discovered, her body lifeless below at the edge of the sea. Mary Pesonen was buried in Ilwaco; two years later Finnish-born lightkeeper Alexander Pesonen died and joined her there.

Behind the detached support building, a paved path heads uphill through thick beach grass, ferns, and salal to the keeper's quarters, passing them and returning to the parking area. Retrace your steps through the forest to the trailhead below and your car.

FISHING THE SOUTH COAST

The south coast of Washington is the epicenter of ocean sport fisheries in the state, primarily for chinook and coho salmon but also for albacore tuna and bottomfish, such as rockfish, lingcod, and even halibut. The two primary ports are Westport, on the south side of Grays Harbor, and Ilwaco, just inside the Columbia River. Both offer a variety of charter fishing services.

But there is a lot more. The Buoy 10 fishery at the mouth of the Columbia can be phenomenal in strong run years for big chinook and coho—"kings" and "silvers" in the angler's parlance. Grays Harbor and Willapa Bay can both be excellent for chinook and coho, as can a few rivers.

Dungeness crabbing can also be superb in the big river's estuary, with a bonus limit of twelve. The sandy shores of the Long Beach Peninsula offer excellent razor clam digging and surf perch fishing. A very good sturgeon fishery once occurred here, but as this population has dipped, the fishery is now open on a catch-and-release basis only. This region is not known for steelhead fishing, but a handful of rivers do produce some fish mostly for locals, including the Willapa, Johns, North, Nemah, and Naselle. All of those, plus virtually every other tidal stream in the region, can produce good fishing for sea-run cutthroat. In both cases, only marked hatchery fish (those lacking an adipose fin) may be kept.

There are also at least three locations for good steamer clam digging (mostly Manila clams) or oyster shucking on Willapa Bay: the Nemah state tidelands along US 101 on the east side of the bay; the Long Island state tidelands, accessible by boat only; and public tidelands at the state shellfish lab at Nahcotta on the west side of the bay, good for oysters only. See "Contacts and Resources" for all fishing and shellfishing regulations.

Here's a month by-month synopsis of south coast fishing:

January: The main game is surf perch fishing during (usually infrequent) calm periods and razor clam digging on open minus-tide dates. If I lived here, no doubt I'd regularly hit the Willapa, Nemah, North, and/or Naselle rivers for hatchery steelhead.

February: Exactly the same as January.

March: Razor clamming, surf perch fishing, and steelheading in the Willapa and Naselle are your options.

April: This is the best month for razor clam digging, with the tasty bivalves at their annual fattest and the month loaded with morning minus tides. You start seeing a lot of surf perch anglers as well; they'll often dig clams during the morning low tide and then fish perch on the incoming to high tide. Westport and Ilwaco charter boats begin fishing for bottomfish now, mostly lingcod and rockfish, and both are usually very good. A few anglers start heading out into the Columbia River above the Astoria Bridge to troll for spring chinook—these fish are known as the highest quality of any type of salmon, rich and oily.

May: In some years, razor clam digging is open early in the month, before closing until fall. But the main focus is bottomfish in both the ocean and along the jetties (south Grays Harbor and north Columbia River), as well as surf perch.

June: Bottomfish and surf perch are options, but most years a fishery for marked hatchery chinook only opens in the ocean off Ilwaco and Westport (Marine Areas 1 and 2), and it can be very good. Both 2013 and 2014 were strong chinook years, and many anglers did very well.

July: The ocean salmon fisheries are full-on now off Westport and Ilwaco, for both chinook and coho. Bottomfish and surf perch are also options.

August: The ocean salmon fisheries are typically still underway and good, with coho by now gaining respectable size. But a lot of angler effort shifts into the very lower Columbia River with the opening of the Buoy 10 fishery (August 1), so named for the buoy that marks the downstream boundary. Most of this fishery occurs around the Astoria Bridge and just upstream near Tongue Point, and it can be extremely good for chinook—some of them beasts in the 30- to 50-pound range. Later it comes on for coho, some of them 12 to 16 pounds. Willapa Bay also opens August 1 and can be very good early for chinook, fished mostly from the Washaway Beach area to the east of Tokeland. Charter boats out of Ilwaco and Westport begin heading offshore (from 40 to 100 miles) for albacore tuna, and that fishery can be extremely good, the fish very strong fighters (not to mention very tasty).

September: Ocean fisheries, limited by catch quotas, are usually over by Labor Day at the latest. The Buoy 10 fishery can be very good now for coho, and Willapa Bay typically remains good early in the month for chinook. At midmonth, Grays Harbor and the lower Chehalis River open for salmon fishing, most years including chinook (sometimes marked hatchery fish only), and can be very good in strong run years from the Buoy 13 boundary east past Hoquiam. This is also the prime month for albacore tuna out on the big blue. Salmon fishing is also an option in the North, Willapa, Nemah, and Naselle rivers. Surf perch fishing can be excellent.

October: There is still some activity in Willapa Bay and Grays Harbor for salmon, but by now most anglers are fishing the rivers: the Chehalis, North, Smith Creek, Willapa, Nemah, and Naselle. Fall razor clam seasons commence on the Long Beach Peninsula and Twin Harbors ocean beaches on minus-tide dates. Surf perch fishing can be good. So can crabbing, in the lower Columbia River. The crabs seem to move into the estuary in the fall, and another factor improving your odds is that commercial crab seasons are typically closed until December.

November: River fisheries now focus mainly on coho, runs of which peak later than chinook. Crabbing in the Columbia and razor clamming and perch fishing are also options.

December: Winter steelhead fishing is now a good option in the North River, Smith Creek, and in the Willapa, Nemah, and Naselle rivers. Razor clamming and perch fishing are other options.

SMOKY BARBECUED SALMON

I've steaked and fried salmon, filleted and fried it, poached it, baked it, caked it (a great way to use leftovers), grilled it, and broiled it, but my fallback preparation for this quintessential Washington seafood is the tried-and-true kettle barbecue. Unless it's pouring outside, invariably I'll fillet the salmon and cook it in the barbie, adding a few chunks of alder or apple wood to give it that authentic Northwest flavor.

Let's start with a few unassailable salmon and cooking facts: All salmon are not equal. The richest, oiliest salmon work best, in this order: chinook (king), sockeye, coho (silver), and pink (humpy). I've never cooked chum salmon; it's the lowest quality, unless it's a few specific early races. Spring-run chinook are the best, super dense with healthy omega-3 fatty oils, with a rich, oceanic flavor and super satiny texture.

A gas grill might be convenient, but it ain't a barbecue. I use a real kettle barbecue with a lid and charcoal briquettes. To my taste buds, this simply provides the best flavor.

2–4 cloves garlic
2–4 tablespoons extra virgin olive oil
1 fillet chinook or sockeye salmon, 1–5 pounds

1 teaspoon to 1 tablespoon salt, or similar amount of shoyu (soy sauce)
1 teaspoon to 1 tablespoon fresh ground pepper
1–5 chunks alder or apple wood, 1 inch or so wide and 2–3 inches long
2 tablespoons chopped Italian parsley
½ to 1 lime or lemon

If you have a folding steel-mesh device with handle for cooking things on a barbecue, it works really well. But they're a cleanup hassle, so I usually simply put the salmon fillet in an open foil boat to fit, skin-side down.

Chop the garlic and heat it in the olive oil until it's just simmering; then remove it from the heat and let cool. One hour before barbecuing, even two, pour the olive oil/garlic mixture over the salmon and season with the salt or shoyu and pepper. I use more than you might expect. Seasoning the fish early will semibrine it and is most important for a thick fillet, say a king of 1.5 to 2 inches.

Fire up the barbie, and never use a gas starter. I use a simple electric starter with a heating element. Spread the coals evenly and thinly, and just before putting the salmon on, add two or three of the wood chunks. Then put the grate on.

Put the salmon on the grate, either skin-side down on a steel-mesh device or in a foil boat (don't close the foil). Put the lid on the barbecue, all vents open. Watch the smoke pour out, and go sit down with your preferred beverage.

You can check the progress now and then, but put the barbecue lid back on after checking. If you're using a steel-mesh barbecue device, cook the fish most of the way through before flipping it and cooking for a few minutes more. If you're using foil, let the fish cook through without flipping—but don't overcook!

Cooking time depends on fillet thickness and how many briquettes you use. A thin piece of sockeye might take ten minutes. A fat piece of chinook might take twenty-five minutes (add more wood chunks when the smoke thins out). Recognizing the fine line between done and overdone comes with experience.

To check doneness, slice the thickest part of the fillet with a knife and look inside—if it's just pink and a hint uncooked in the middle, get that fish off of there and cover it with foil. By the time you've plated the rest of your meal, garnished the fish with parsley and a slice of lime or lemon, and poured the viognier, it will be ready. Bon appétit!

MCKENZIE HEAD TRAIL

RUINS OF A COASTAL ARTILLERY BATTERY

What is not here anymore—along with a nice ocean view—is what makes the short-but-sweet trail to McKenzie Head so worthwhile. More than two hundred years ago, Captain Clark and eleven men climbed to the top of the 90-foot round knob and then camped just north of its base. What else is no longer here? The two 6-inch cannons that comprised Fort Canby's Battery 247 during World War II. The guns are gone, but the fortifications and other military ruins remain on this hill of spruce forest and tall beach grass. The history feels alive.

Distance: 0.5 mile round-trip
Elevation gain: 90 feet
Difficulty: 1–2
Map: Cape Disappointment State Park map, www.parks.wa.gov/DocumentCenter/Home/View/1850
Contact: Washington State Parks
Notes: Discover Pass required to park. Dogs permitted on-leash.

DRIVING DIRECTIONS

From US 101 in Ilwaco, head northwest then south on State Route 100 to the park entrance in 3.6 miles, taking a right and in a few hundred feet passing the entrance station. Then turn right again at the first intersection. In about 0.4 mile, find the small trailhead parking area on the left, marked by a monument to Lewis and Clark.

THE HIKE

Pause to read the trailhead plaque commemorating the Corps of Discovery and then head uphill. The wide path, an old road, climbs immediately in open forest. In about ⅛ mile on the right, you'll see a mossy-roofed concrete structure, reached through a meadow of beach grass and ferns. Now lacking windows and doors, it's no doubt a building that once supported the battery. The coastal jungle seems well on its way to consuming the structure.

The forest appears well on its way to reclaiming this old military structure that no doubt supported the Battery 247 guns during the Fort Canby years.

The path then curls up and around to ocean views and the batteries at 0.25 mile, their dark and spooky shell magazines below and rusting, circular swivel carriages above. All the land west of this head is new land, accreted after the construction of the north jetty in the late 1800s. When Clark was here, the ocean combers beat against the base of this hill.

This is not the best ocean view in Cape Disappointment State Park, not by far, and was probably better two hundred years ago. The Corps of Discovery's Sergeant John Ordway noted in his journal for November 18, 1805: "Went over a bald hill where we had a handsome view of the ocean. we went a Short distance on the coast and Camped for the night." But the breeze atop McKenzie Head feels good, and the relics are intriguing. Plus, the short walk in the footsteps of Clark and crew feels poignant, despite the distance of two centuries.

COASTAL FOREST LOOP

SHORT LOOPS TO BIG TREES AND RIVER VIEWS

This lopsided figure-eight of a trail loops through big coastal spruce forest, with views out over Baker Bay and the Columbia River. It's nice enough, some of the Sitka spruce are big, but if your time here is limited, put this hike on your second tier of options.

Distance: 1.5 miles in two loops
Elevation gain: About 130 feet
Difficulty: 2
Map: Cape Disappointment State Park map, www.parks.wa.gov/DocumentCenter/Home/View/1850
Contact: Washington State Parks
Notes: Discover Pass required to park. A leashed Rover is A-OK.

DRIVING DIRECTIONS

From US 101 in Ilwaco, head northwest then south on State Route 100 to the park entrance on the right in 3.6 miles; but don't turn right. Instead, take a left just before the park store, toward the park boat ramp, and then an immediate left into a gravel parking lot. Find the trailhead in the northwest corner of the lot, marked by a small sign.

THE HIKE

The trail climbs immediately on the hill above the park's boat launch into a pretty forest of spruce and hemlock, with a classic coastal understory of ferns, salal, and other shrubbery. Soon reach an intersection. Go right, the trail dropping a bit before beginning to climb. There are some big Sitka spruce trees here, some 10 feet thick at the butt.

At about 0.75 mile, a side path leads left to an overlook of Baker Bay and the fishing port of Ilwaco. Back on the main loop, the route continues in similar fashion, turning 180 degrees and following the ridge that parallels the main park access road back to the small loop and then the parking lot.

CAPE DISAPPOINTMENT TRAIL

SCENIC MUST-DO HIKE TAKES IN BOATLOAD OF HISTORY

Pack some snacks and prepare to take in a freighter load of fascinating American history, the single best view in Washington of the turbulent Columbia River mouth—the "Graveyard of the Pacific"—and the breezy heights of 287-foot Cape Disappointment. You can shorten this hike by half by parking at the Lewis and Clark Interpretive Center lot. But I recommend you hike the full trail from the park entrance area, because it's the premier way to fully experience the basaltic headland that marks the south end of the Washington Coast—a rampart noted by a succession of explorers hundreds of years ago. The route is not that long anyway and includes one of the longest continually operating lighthouses on the West Coast, the marvelous interpretive center, an old artillery battery, the pocket cove of Dead Mans Hollow, and some big spruce trees. You'll be following some important footsteps as well.

Evening light illuminates Cape Disappointment and its quaint lighthouse above the often-turbulent Columbia River Bar—sometimes called the Graveyard of the Pacific.

Distance: 2.4 miles round-trip
Elevation gain: About 300 feet
Difficulty: 2–3
Map: Cape Disappointment State Park map, www.parks.wa.gov/DocumentCenter/Home/View/1850
Contact: Washington State Parks
Notes: Discover Pass required to park. Dogs allowed on-leash.

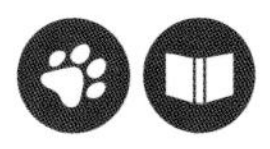

DRIVING DIRECTIONS

From US 101 in Ilwaco, head northwest then south on State Route 100 to the park entrance on the right in 3.6 miles; but don't turn right. Instead, take a left just before the park store, toward the park boat ramp, and then an immediate left into a gravel parking lot. The trailhead is across SR 100, at the foot of the high bluff just south of the park entrance fee station.

THE HIKE

At the trailhead, you'll be starting on the path Captain William Clark took when he first reached the Pacific Ocean in 1805. At your destination, you'll be looking out over where Captain Robert Gray became the first person of European origin to enter the Columbia River in 1792.

The trail climbs immediately into big spruce forest, winding up the cape and soon topping out on a windy bluff in more-open forest, blanketed by meadows of tall beach grass. Deer are often seen here. You're basically right above and just east of Waikiki Beach, where Clark saw close up the goal of the Corps of Discovery: the biggest ocean on Earth, the Pacific.

At 0.5 mile reach the interpretive center atop the cape, well worth the admission price ($5 for adults, $2.50 for kids). But first, wander around the adjacent Battery Harvey Allen to the left, which once housed three 6-inch cannons, each with a range of 15 miles. It's all just concrete today, no guns remain. Officers no longer bark orders here. But stick your head into one of the magazines of this battery and imagine: for decades this place was busy with soldiers training, maintaining, observing, recording, detailing, lifting, no doubt at times cursing, and carrying on. These batteries were first in place during the Civil War, served by horse-drawn carriages!

A nearby battery hosted two 6-inchers. Later a battery of four 12-inch mortars was added not far away. The remains of those two installations are intact but not open to the public, being part of the Coast Guard station. Occasionally they test-fired those guns—the roar must have been tremendous. It's a lot quieter today. You'll hear the wind, waves, seagulls, and occasionally the loudspeaker of the Coast Guard station, tucked into Baker Bay at the foot of the cape's east flank.

Visit the interpretive center, or save it for another day, and then follow the trail just south of the battery, which leads shortly through forest to a junction with a short stretch of the Cape Disappointment Trail that begins at the interpretive center parking area. Stay to the right and keep going. Soon note the Coast Guard station below to the left.

And soon to the right, see the interesting pocket cove? That's Dead Mans Hollow, at about 1 mile, named after the body of a sailor who washed up from a shipwreck on the Columbia River bar. You can't go down to the cove, as inviting as it appears, since it's part of the Coast Guard station and posted "No Trespassing." You might also be wondering how nearby Waikiki Beach was named. A body washed up there too, that of a sailor from Hawaii.

Soon the trail picks up a paved road coming from the station and winding up the hill past an old concrete structure. The Coast Guard maintains the automated lighthouse as well as an adjoining observation station. Soon the road tops out and just below, there it is, the oldest continually operating lighthouse on the West Cost, first casting a beam in 1856. The Cape Disappointment Lighthouse looks old too, but quaint! The black and white, metal-domed tower stands 53 feet, its light 220 feet above the sea.

Walk down and take it all in: the ocean and north jetty on the west, the great wide mouth of the Columbia to the south. Look north too: there's the interpretive center atop an adjacent bluff of the cape and beyond, Waikiki Beach.

Now imagine crewing aboard an eighteenth-century three-masted sailing ship along an utterly wild ocean shore, buffeted by a stiff current flowing through shallow surf from the south side of a tree-topped, rocky headland: "At four, a.m., saw the entrance of our desired port bearing east-south-east, distance six leagues; in steering sails, and hauled our wind in shore. At eight, a.m., being a little to wind-ward of the entrance of the Harbor, bore away, and run in east-north-east between the breakers, having from five to seven fathoms of water. When we were

SEEING THE FOREST FOR THE TREES

This is the short list of trees you should familiarize yourself with if you really want to know the Washington Coast:

Western red cedar, the incredibly useful "tree of life" to the Native tribes, who made house planks, dugout canoes, boxes, skirts, and even diapers from it. It burns readily and is the go-to driftwood for beach fires.

Sitka spruce, so common on the sea bluffs, often burl-ridden and shaped crazily in bonsai or krummholz fashion by prevailing ocean winds.

Western hemlock, which thrives in low light conditions and often sprouts atop decaying cedar "nurse logs" in the rain forest.

Douglas fir, which grows to immense proportions; very common and makes great firewood—and houses.

Big-leaf maple, the broad-spreading, hauntingly beautiful deciduous tree of the rain forest that is often draped by veils of pale green club moss.

Red alder, a very common hardwood often found in pretty groves along river bottoms.

over the bar, we found this to be a large river of fresh water, up which we steered. Many canoes came along-side."

This was the "discovery" of the mighty Columbia River on May 11, 1792, by the bold American mariner and fur trader Robert Gray, who wrote this in his log. Although other seafaring explorers had suspected a big river here, none had been able or daring enough to risk their ships by crashing through the combers. Gray named the river after his ship, the *Columbia Rediviva.* Although the Columbia River bar remains at times rough and difficult, it's now protected by jetties north and south. It's a lot different than when Gray was here.

One final thing to say: sunsets can be delightfully dramatic from this spot. It's 1.2 miles back to your car, but if you have a headlamp it's no problem. Optionally, park at the interpretive center lot, just 0.6 mile away. You'll have plenty of light left to make it back the short distance after the vastness of the sea swallows that giant flame ball.

CONTACTS AND RESOURCES

GENERAL INFORMATION

Federal Interagency Pass (America the Beautiful Pass), www.nps.gov/findapark/passes.htm, 888-275-8747

Northwest Forest Pass, www.fs.usda.gov/main/olympic/passes-permits/recreation, 800-270-7504

Olympic National Park, 3002 Mount Angeles Road, Port Angeles, www.nps.gov/olym, 360-565-3130 (general visitor information), 360-565-3100 (Wilderness Information Center)

Olympic Peninsula Visitors Bureau, www.olympicpeninsula.org, 800-942-4042

Washington Department of Natural Resources, www.dnr.wa.gov/RecreationEducation/Recreation, 360-902-1000 (Olympia HQ), 360-374-2800 (Olympic region), recreation@dnr.wa.gov

Washington State Discover Pass, www.discoverpass.wa.gov, 866-320-9933

Washington State Parks, www.parks.wa.gov, 360-902-8844 (general information), https://washington.goingtocamp.com, 888-226-7688 (campground and lodging reservations)

FISHING INFORMATION AND REGULATIONS

Clallam Bay–Sekiu Chamber of Commerce, www.clallambay.com, 360-963-233

Makah Indian Nation, http://makah.com, 360-645-3015 (Makah marina), 360-645-2374 (Big Salmon Fishing Resort)

Olympic National Park, www.nps.gov/olym/fishregs.htm (fishing rules)

Quinault Indian Nation, www.quinaultindiannation.com, 888-616-8211

US Geological Survey, Washington stream-gauging stations, http://waterdata.usgs.gov/wa/nwis/current/?type=flow

Washington Department of Fish and Wildlife, http://wdfw.wa.gov/fishing (fishing, sport fishing, shellfishing rules), 360-902-2500 (fishing hotline), 866-880-5431 (shellfishing hotline), http://wdfw.wa.gov/fishing/salmon/sockeye/ozette_lake.html ("Ozette Lake Sockeye Salmon" information sheet), http://wdfw.wa.gov/fishing/shellfish/razorclams ("Razor Clams" information sheet), http://wdfw.wa.gov/fishing/shellfish/razorclams/clean_prepare.html (cleaning razor clams)

THE NORTHWEST CORNER: SEKIU/CLALLAM BAY, NEAH BAY, LAKE OZETTE

Big Salmon Fishing Resort, Neah Bay, www.bigsalmonresort.net, 866-787-1900

Clallam Bay–Sekiu Chamber of Commerce, www.clallambay.com, 360-963-2339

Clallam County, www.clallam.net/Parks, 360-417-2291

Friends of Hoko River State Park, 360-963-2442, able@olypen.com

Makah Indian Nation, http://makah.com, 360-645-2201

Olympic Coast National Marine Sanctuary, http://olympiccoast.noaa.gov, 360-457-6622

THE NORTH COAST: LA PUSH, HOH RIVER, KALALOCH, QUEETS RIVER

Bogachiel State Park, www.parks.wa.gov/478/Bogachiel, 360-374-6356

Forks Chamber of Commerce, 1411 S Forks Avenue, Forks, http://forkswa.com, 800-443-6757

Kalaloch Lodge, 157151 US 101, www.thekalalochlodge.com, 866-662-9928

Olympic National Park, Hoh Rain Forest Visitor Center, 360-374-6925
Olympic National Park, Kalaloch Campground reservations, www.recreation.gov
Olympic National Park, Mora Ranger Station, 360-374-5460 (open intermittently in summer only)
Quileute Indian Nation, www.quileutenation.org, 360-374-6163

THE CENTRAL COAST: LAKE QUINAULT, GRAYS HARBOR, MOCLIPS, OCEAN SHORES

City of Ocean Shores, www.osgov.com, 360-289-3099
Grays Harbor Audubon Society, http://ghas.org
Grays Harbor Tourism, http://visitgraysharbor.com, 800-621-9625
Lake Quinault area website, www.quinaultrainforest.com
Lake Quinault Lodge, 345 South Shore Road, Quinault, www.olympicnationalparks.com/accommodations/lake-quinault-lodge.aspx, 800-562-6672
Lake Quinault Museum, 354 South Shore Road, Quinault, www.lakequinaultmuseum.org
Ocean Shores Citizens for Balanced Growth, Weatherwax Forest information, www.weatherwax.info
Ocean Shores Interpretive Center, 1033 Catala Avenue SE, Ocean Shores, www.osgov.com/interpcenter.html, 360-289-4617
Olympic National Forest/Olympic National Park, Quinault Ranger Station, 353 South Shore Road, www.fs.usda.gov/recarea/olympic/recreation/recarea/?recid=47695, 360-288-2525
Quinault Indian Nation, http://quinaultindiannation.com, 888-616-8211
Quinault Marina and RV Park, 1098 Discovery Ave SE, Ocean Shores, 360-289-4789, or visit the marina's Facebook page
US Fish and Wildlife Service, Grays Harbor National Wildlife Refuge, www.fws.gov/refuge/grays_harbor, 360-753-9467 (Olympia HQ)

THE SOUTH COAST: WESTPORT, TOKELAND, WILLAPA BAY, LONG BEACH PENINSULA, CAPE DISAPPOINTMENT

Chinook Indian Nation, www.chinooktribe.org/bush-county-park.html, 360-875-6670
City of Long Beach, www.longbeach.gov, 562-570-3100 (parks department)
Greater Grays Harbor Inc., www.graysharbor.org, 800-321-1924
Lewis and Clark Interpretive Center, Cape Disappointment State Park, www.parks.wa.gov/187/Lewis-Clark-Interpretive-Center, 360-642-3029
Long Beach Peninsula Visitors Bureau, http://funbeach.com, 800-451-2542
Pacific County, www.co.pacific.wa.us, 360-875-9334
US Fish and Wildlife Service, Willapa National Wildlife Refuge Headquarters, 3888 US 101, www.fws.gov/refuge/willapa, 360-484-3482
Washington Department of Ecology, www.ecy.wa.gov/ecyhome.html (general information), www.ecy.wa.gov/programs/sea/coast/erosion/washaway.html (Washaway Beach erosion)
Washington Department of Fish and Wildlife, http://wdfw.wa.gov/, 360 902-2200 (general information), Johns River Wildlife Area, http://wdfw.wa.gov/lands/wildlife_areas/johns_river
Westport–Grayland Chamber of Commerce, www.westportgrayland-chamber.org, 800-345-6223
Willapa Harbor Chamber of Commerce, http://willapaharbor.org, 360-942-5419

BIBLIOGRAPHY

Boyd, Robert T., Kenneth M. Ames, and Tony A. Johnson. *Chinookan Peoples of the Lower Columbia.* Seattle: University of Washington Press, 2013.

Capoeman, Pauline K., ed. *Land of the Quinault.* Taholah, WA: Quinault Indian Nation, 1990.

Eells, the Rev. Myron. *The Indians of Puget Sound. From Nine 1887 Notebooks.* Seattle: University of Washington Press, 1985.

Gunther, Erna. *Indian Life of the Northwest Coast of North America: As Seen by the Early Explorers and Fur Traders during the Last Decades of the Eighteenth Century.* Chicago: University of Chicago Press, 1972.

Hezeta, Bruno de. *For Honor and Country: The Diary of Bruno de Hezeta.* Portland, OR: Western Imprints, 1985.

HistoryLink.org. "British Explorer Captain James Cook Names Cape Flattery on March 22, 1778." www.historylink.org/index.cfm?DisplayPage=output.cfm&file_id=5035.

Journals of the Lewis and Clark Expedition. http://lewisandclarkjournals.unl.edu/index.html.

Kirk, Ruth. *The Olympic Seashore.* Port Angeles, WA: Olympic Natural History Association, 1962.

Kirk, Ruth, and Richard D. Daugherty. *Archaeology in Washington.* Seattle: University of Washington Press, 2007.

McDonald, Lucile. *Swan among the Indians: The Life of James G. Swan, 1818–1900.* Portland, OR: Binford & Mort, 1972.

McNulty, Tim. *Olympic National Park: A Natural History Guide.* New York: Houghton Mifflin, 1996.

Molvar, Erik. *Hiking Olympic National Park.* Helena, MT: Falcon, 1999.

Morse, Bob. *A Birder's Guide to Coastal Washington.* Olympia, WA: R.W. Morse Company, 2001.

Nokes, Richard J. *Almost a Hero: The Voyages of John Meares, R.N., to China, Hawaii and the Northwest Coast.* Pullman: Washington State University Press, 1998.

———. *Columbia's River: The Voyages of Robert Gray, 1787–1793.* Tacoma: Washington State Historical Society, 1991.

Pojar, Jim, and Andy MacKinnon. *Plants of the Pacific Northwest Coast: Washington, Oregon, British Columbia and Alaska.* Vancouver, BC: Lone Pine Publishing, 1994.

Rau, Weldon W. *Geology of the Washington Coast between Point Grenville and the Hoh River.* Bulletin no. 66. Olympia: Washington Department of Natural Resources, Geology and Earth Resources Division, 1975.

———. *Geology of the Washington Coast between the Hoh and Quillayute Rivers.* Bulletin no. 72. Olympia: Washington Department of Natural Resources, Geology and Earth Resources Division, 1980.

Romano, Craig. *Day Hiking: Olympic Peninsula.* Seattle: Mountaineers Books, 2007.

Schultz, Stewart T. *The Northwest Coast: A Natural History.* Portland, OR: Timber Press, 1990.

Spring, Ira, and Harvey Manning. *100 Hikes in Washington's South Cascades and Olympics.* Seattle: Mountaineers Book, 1998.

Swan, James Gilchrist. *The Northwest Coast; or, Three Years' Residence in Washington Territory.* New York: Harper and Brothers, 1857; reprint, Charleston, SC: BiblioLife, 2009.

Vancouver, George. *A Voyage of Discovery to the North Pacific Ocean and Round the World, 1791–1795.* London: Hakluyt Society, 1984.

Wood, Amos L. *Beachcombing the Pacific.* Chicago: Henry Regnery Company, 1975.

INDEX

ACKNOWLEDGMENTS

My heartfelt thanks go to my constant companion along the shore, on the trail, and in life, my wife, Lorna Johnston; to Tom Northup and the late Barbara Northup, for sharing their depth of coastal knowledge, hospitality, and friendship; to my colleague Angelo Bruscas for his hospitality, friendship, and updates on coastal news; to my longtime friend and hiking bodhisattva Bryn Beorse, for his companionship on ocean backpacks and advice; to artist Bridget Beorse for her enthusiasm and help in getting this project published; to Joe Hymer, for his friendship and sharing his knowledge of coastal fisheries; to Lloyd "Buzz" Wisecup, for his friendship and unstinting hospitality and for sharing his considerable knowledge of king salmon fishing; to Mountaineers Books editor in chief Kate Rogers, for taking on a project that perhaps doesn't quite fit the guidebook mold; to Kirsten Colton, for her wise supervision of the project; and to Julie Van Pelt, for her somewhat exasperating but essential, keen copyediting.

ABOUT THE AUTHOR

Greg Johnston is a Seattle-area native, lifelong outdoors nut, and journalist who has worked as a reporter for the *Associated Press*, the *Daily World*, and *Seattle Post-Intelligencer* newspapers and AOL's Patch Media Corp. He has been captivated by the Washington Coast since vacationing along the ocean annually as a child with his family, and for several years his father co-owned a salmon fishing charter business in Westport. As an environmental and outdoors reporter for the *Daily World* and *Seattle P-I*, he covered dozens of stories on the coast. These included Indian fishing rights issues in the 1970s, pollution and environmental degradation in coastal rivers, declining native salmon runs, the loss of wetlands habitat, the impact of harbor dredging on marine life, and activities such as hiking, backpacking, beachcombing, sea kayaking, fishing, and clam digging. He lives in Kirkland, Washington, with his wife and has three grown children—a tattoo artist, a teamster, and a sergeant in the US Army infantry—as well as two grandchildren.

MOUNTAINEERS BOOKS is a leading publisher of mountaineering literature and guides—including our flagship title, *Mountaineering: The Freedom of the Hills*—as well as adventure narratives, natural history, and general outdoor recreation. Through our two imprints, Skipstone and Braided River, we also publish titles on sustainability and conservation. We are committed to supporting the environmental and educational goals of our organization by providing expert information on human-powered adventure, sustainable practices at home and on the trail, and preservation of wilderness.

The Mountaineers, founded in 1906, is a 501(c)(3) nonprofit outdoor activity and conservation organization whose mission is "to explore, study, preserve, and enjoy the natural beauty of the outdoors." One of the largest such organizations in the United States, it sponsors classes and year-round outdoor activities throughout the Pacific Northwest, including climbing, hiking, backcountry skiing, snowshoeing, bicycling, camping, paddling, and more. The Mountaineers also supports its mission through its publishing division, Mountaineers Books, and promotes environmental education and citizen engagement. For more information, visit The Mountaineers Program Center, 7700 Sand Point Way NE, Seattle, WA 98115-3996; phone 206-521-6001; www.mountaineers.org; or email info@mountaineers.org.

Our publications are made possible through the generosity of donors and through sales of more than 600 titles on outdoor recreation, sustainable lifestyle, and conservation. To donate, purchase books, or learn more, visit us online:

MOUNTAINEERS BOOKS
1001 SW Klickitat Way, Suite 201 • Seattle, WA 98134
800-553-4453 • mbooks@mountaineersbooks.org • www.mountaineersbooks.org

Mountaineers Books is proud to be a corporate sponsor of The Leave No Trace Center for Outdoor Ethics, whose mission is to promote and inspire responsible outdoor recreation through education, research, and partnerships • The Leave No Trace program is focused specifically on human-powered (nonmotorized) recreation • Leave No Trace strives to educate visitors about the nature of their recreational impacts and offers techniques to prevent and minimize such impacts • Leave No Trace is best understood as an educational and ethical program, not as a set of rules and regulations • For more information, visit www.lnt.org, or call 800-332-4100.